CW01654429

CRUCIBLE 2

1ST SEPTEMBER - 31ST OCTOBER 2014

GLOUCESTER CATHEDRAL

Gloucester Cathedral is very grateful to the following funders and sponsors whose generous contributions helped to make this exhibition possible:

Lead sponsor Willans LLP | solicitors

Margaret Sheather Ltd
The Austin and Hope Pilkington Trust

Heartfelt thanks go to the numerous people who have been involved in bringing Crucible2 to Gloucester Cathedral.

Published by
the Chapter of Gloucester Cathedral
12 College Green,
Gloucester,
GL1 2LX
01452 528095
www.gloucestercathedral.org.uk

Photography - Steve Russell Studios
© Chapter of Gloucester Cathedral, 2014

All rights reserved. No part of this publication may be reproduced, stored in a retrieval system, or transmitted in any form, or by any means, electronic, mechanical, photocopying, recording or otherwise, without the prior permission of the publisher and copyright holder.

ISBN 978-0-903770-10-1

ST PAUL IN ATHENS

The Dean of Gloucester reflects on why it is important that exhibitions like Crucible2 are in a Cathedral, with a little help from St. Paul.

Acts of the Apostles Chapter 17

While Paul was waiting for them in Athens, he was deeply distressed to see that the city was full of idols. So he argued in the synagogue with the Jews and the devout persons, and also in the marketplace every day with those who happened to be there. Also some Epicurean and Stoic philosophers debated with him. Some said, "What does this babbler want to say?" Others said, "He seems to be a proclaimer of foreign divinities." (This was because he was telling the good news about Jesus and the resurrection.) So they took him and brought him to the Areopagus and asked him, "May we know what this new teaching is that you are presenting? It sounds rather strange to us, so we would like to know what it means." Now all the Athenians and the foreigners living there would spend their time in nothing but telling or hearing something new.

Then Paul stood in front of the Areopagus and said, "Athenians, I see how extremely religious you are in every way. For as I went through the city and looked carefully at the objects of your worship, I found among them an altar with the inscription, 'To an unknown god.' What therefore you worship as unknown, this I proclaim to you.

St Paul was a rare combination as a radical conservative. He knew the context of his time and yet he also needed to proclaim to that context something new in the hope of Jesus Christ. Crucible2 also offers something new in a familiar context and some who visit will wonder at these modern 'idols' in the context of this great Cathedral dedicated to the Holy and Indivisible Trinity. Why here? Crucible2 is here because all life is to be found here. Its varied images will speak to us all in different ways about the world and ourselves.

The Cathedral is both sacred space and common ground, and it is literally in the crucible of this meeting that we can find truth and grace. The church does not hide from the world, it is in the world for its salvation. At its worst, the church succumbs to the demands and desires of the world around it. At its best, the church points to a greater calling and the fact that, even though many may not know what they worship, there is something more, something which connects with the soul.

For nearly a thousand years this Cathedral has stood to speak to the soul through worship and hospitality, through teaching and engagement. This is a place where heaven and earth touch if just for a moment, and if we look beyond our human designs, then we can glimpse the work of God, here and in our lives.

I hope you enjoy your visit to the Cathedral and Crucible2. But there is more here than this, there is the salvation of your soul, if you will but seek it.

The Very Revd Stephen Lake,
Dean of Gloucester

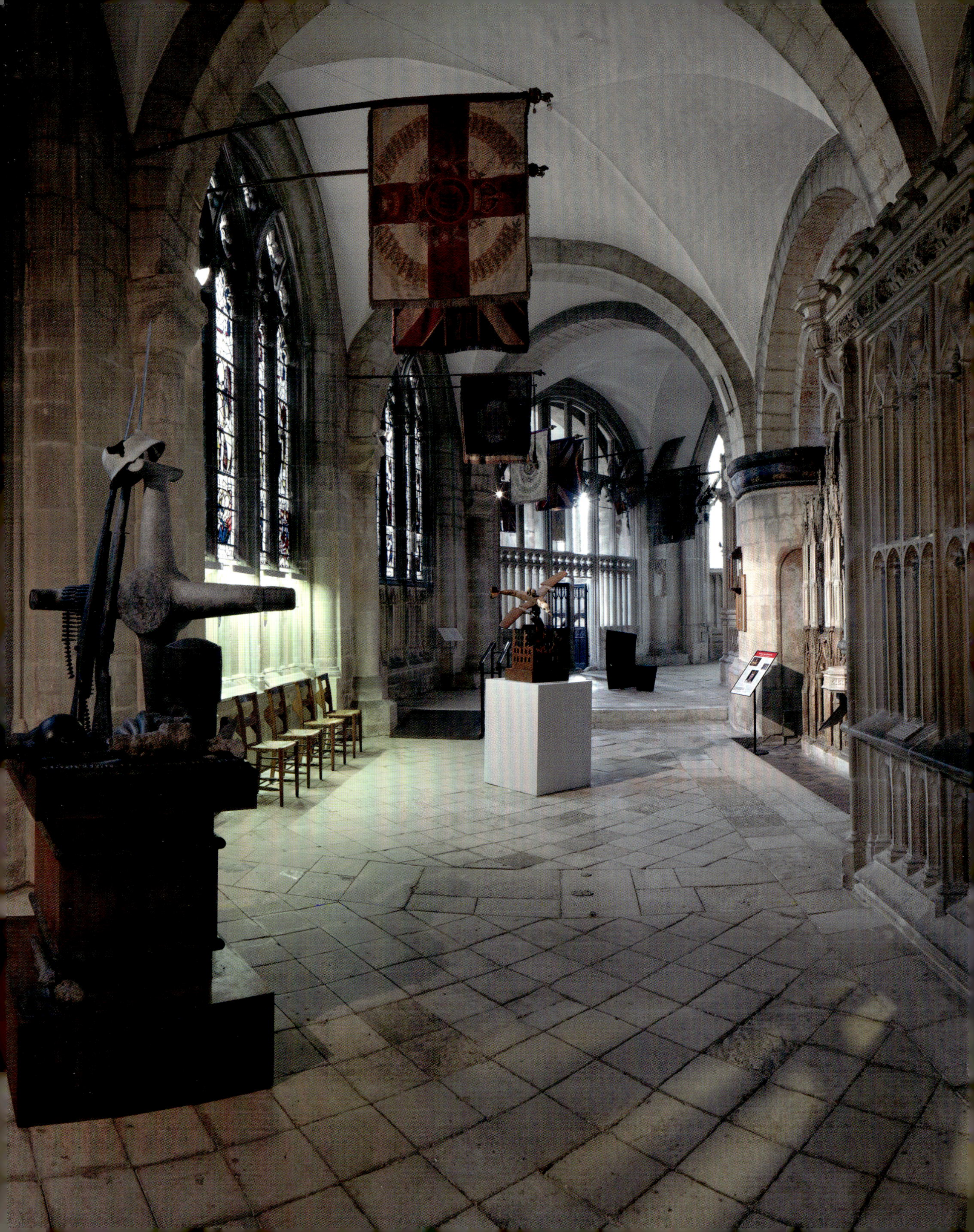

Lead sponsor

willans

Willans LLP | solicitors

Gloucester Cathedral is probably the most important building in Gloucestershire and is a major work of art in itself. The first Crucible exhibition was amazing in the way it used the spaces in the Cathedral, some of which are over 900 years old, to offset a wide variety of modern sculpture. The mellow stone was a perfect foil to the patina of modern bronze.

Sculpture seems to feel at home in the Cathedral, even if it is very modern and abstract. There is already so much sculpture within the fabric of the Cathedral, created over many centuries, in the ornamentation of the building itself and the wonderful carving in the medieval and Tudor tombs. The current generation has added to this with its own very talented team of masons led by Master Mason Pascal Mychalysin. As well as restoration work, they have created the splendid new gargolyes on the south aisle and the graceful statue of the Abbess Kyneburga.

The lost wax process used by the highly skilled craftspeople at Pangolin Editions is over 6,000 years old. They create the bronzes at the foundry near Stroud from maquettes delivered to them by the artists – and these models come in all manner of materials and sizes. Gallery Pangolin curated the last Crucible exhibition with an artist's eye for the juxtaposition of form and space, placing the sculptures within the Cathedral to show them to maximum effect.

Willans is a mere 67 years old and we have very different skills from the countless artists who have contributed to this wonderful exhibition. As a local firm of solicitors known for giving sound private and commercial legal advice rather than for craftsmanship, we feel very privileged to be involved in bringing Crucible2 to the county. I am sure it will be another great feast of the arts in Gloucestershire.

Gloucester Cathedral and Gallery Pangolin have done a splendid job in bringing such an outstanding exhibition of national importance to our iconic, historical setting in Gloucester.

I hope you find the exhibition intriguing and that you enjoy every aspect of it.

Margaret Austen
Managing partner of Cheltenham law firm Willans LLP

CONTENTS

ANTHONY ABRAHAMS b.1926

'The two pieces I have in this exhibition share at least one characteristic: tension, hopefully in balance.

The man is poised between assertiveness and vulnerability, confident but alert to the dangers of a world that so often seems haphazard.

The woman is determined, moving forward but hindered, perhaps willingly on occasion, by strictures and echoes from Eden.'

West of Eden
Anthony Abrahams
Bronze
Edition of 9
103cm high

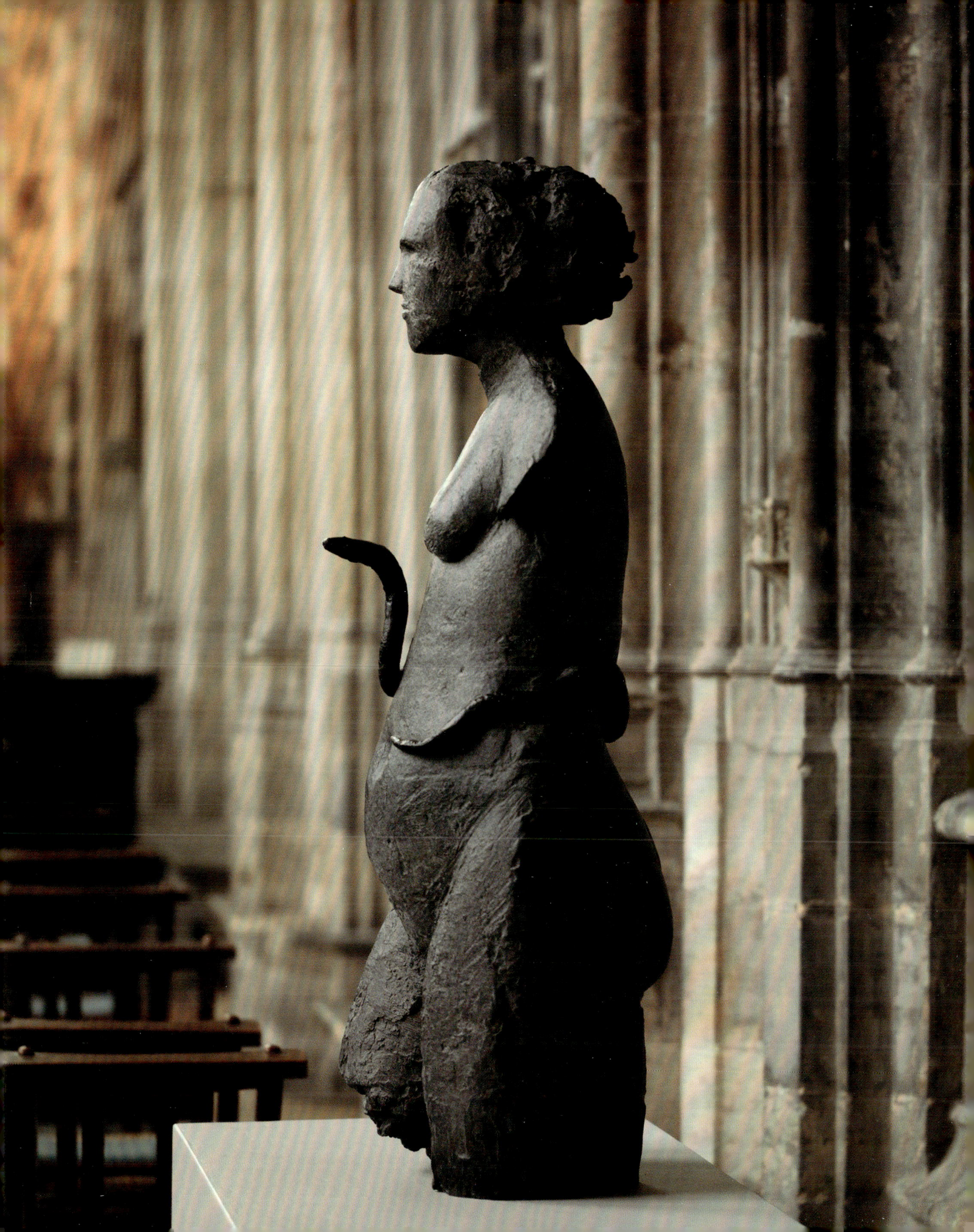

Man with Raised Arm

Anthony Abrahams

Marble

Unique

135cm high

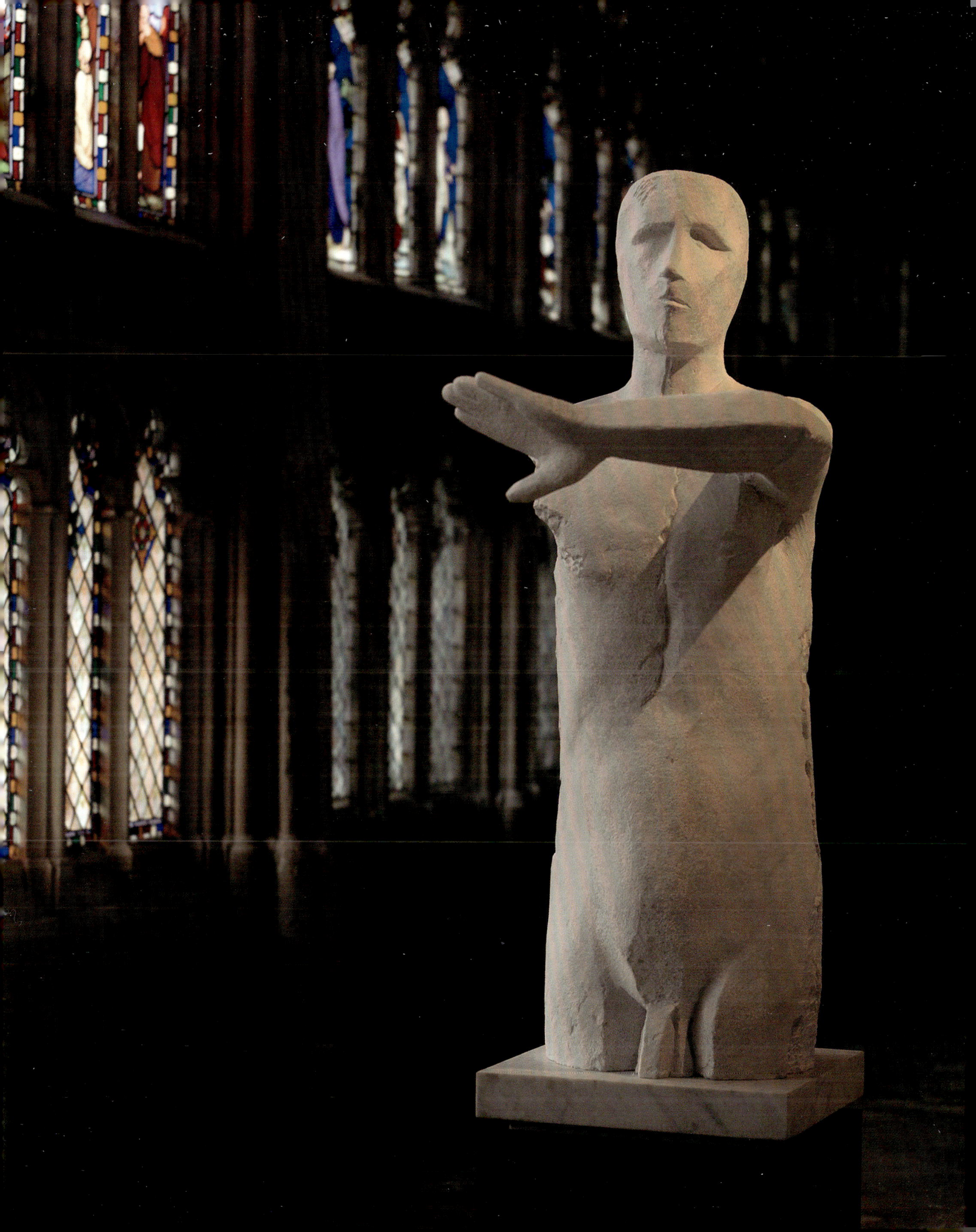

KENNETH ARMITAGE RA 1916-2002

Armitage's later works, symbolic arms and legs, are fully rounded and welcoming. Reach for the Stars, his final work, is both hand and star, supported on an arm that is equally human and architectural. This aspirational piece was inspired by the idea that, "If you reach for the stars you might reach the rooftops."

Reach for the Stars
Kenneth Armitage
Bronze
Unique
915cm high

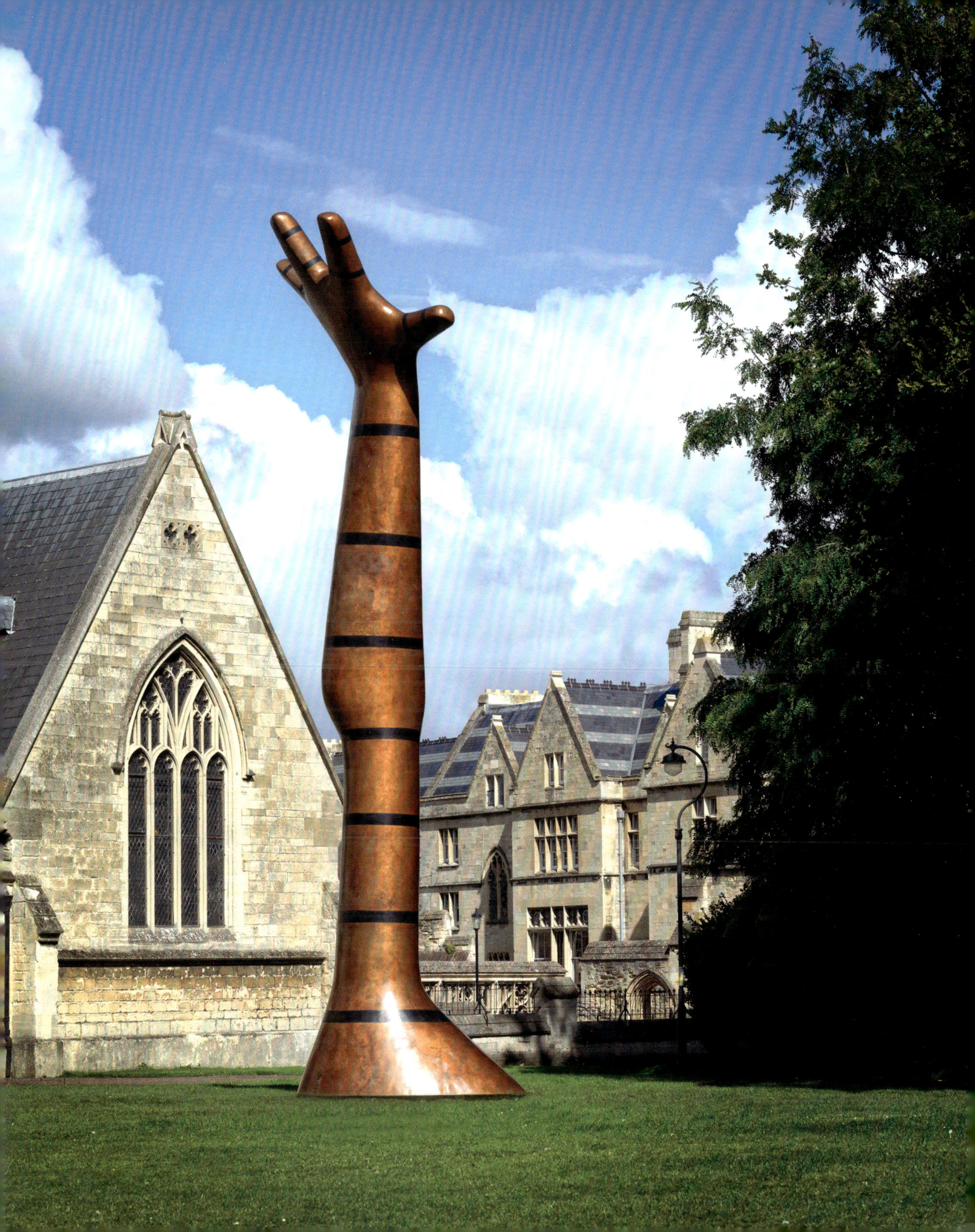

DAVID BACKHOUSE b.1941

'Pilgrim depicts man's search for peace and tranquillity.'

'My themes are simple and universal: the interdependence of nature and humanity, and the search for balance and harmony. The sculptures are meditations on the human condition in our time, reflecting loss and tragedy, hope and delight, and above all the tenacity of the human spirit.'

Pilgrim
David Backhouse
Bronze
Edition of 3
210cm high

Pilgrim is sponsored by Margaret Sheather Ltd

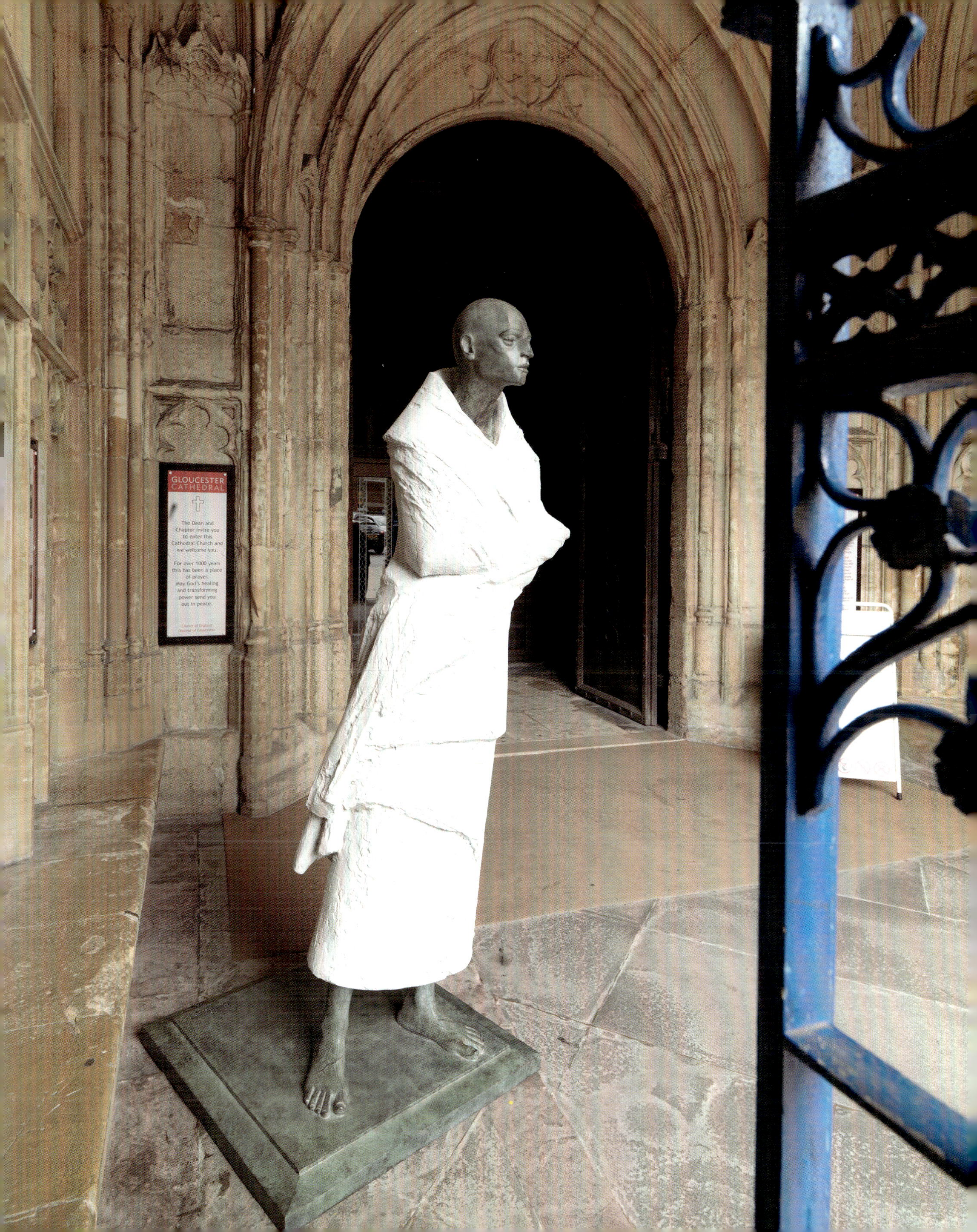
GLOUCESTER
CATHEDRAL
The Dean and Chapter invite you to enter this Cathedral Church and we welcome you.
For over 1000 years this has been a place of prayer.
May God's healing and transforming power send you out in peace.

DAVID BAILEY b.1938

'I like bronzes - there's absolutely no 'Photoshop' on them!'

'I always try to make my fashion photos like Cole Porter songs and my portraits like the Blues. These sculptures are the nearest I can get to the Blues.'

Adam
David Bailey
Bronze
Edition of 6
57cm high

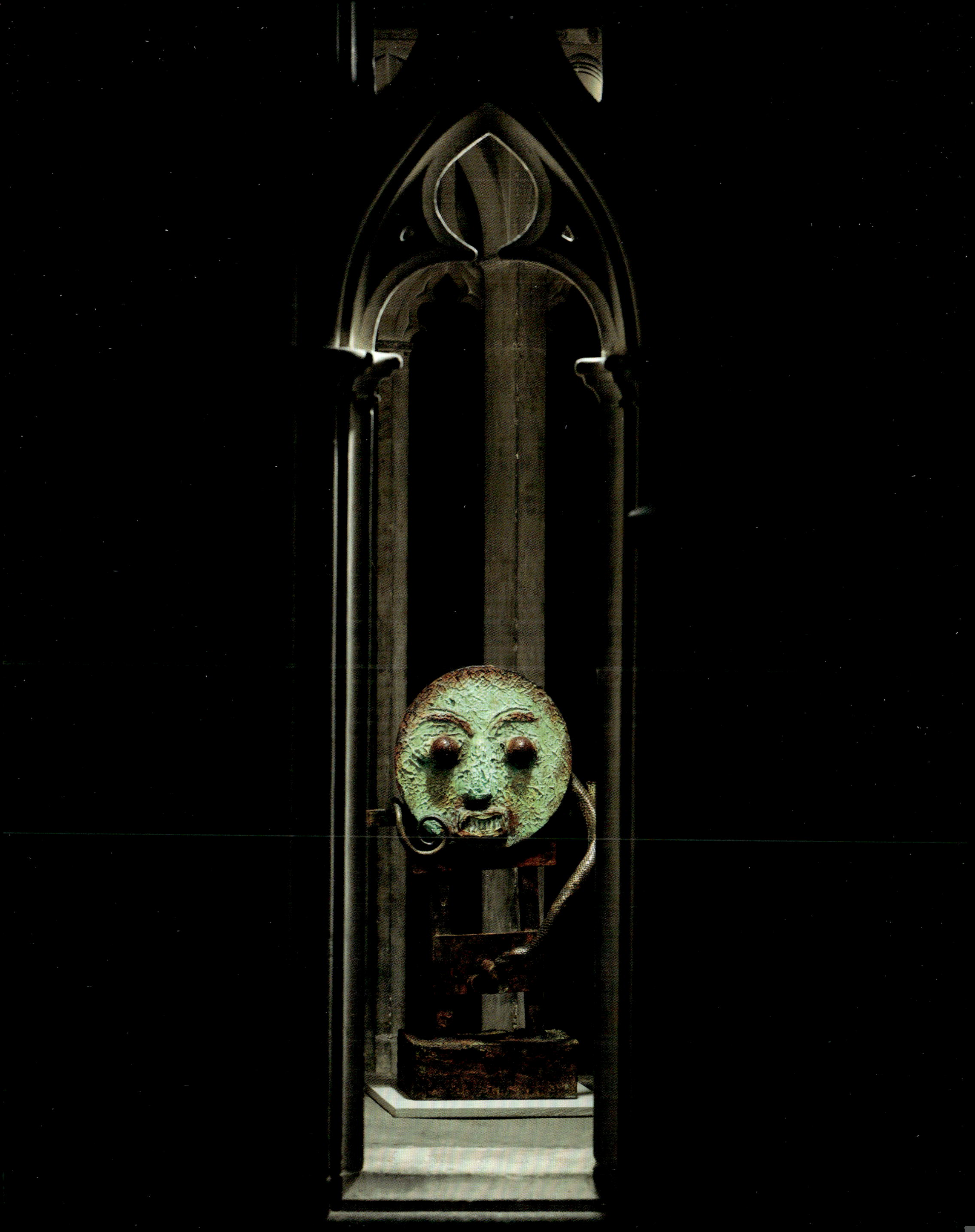

XMan

David Bailey

Bronze

Edition of 6

72cm high

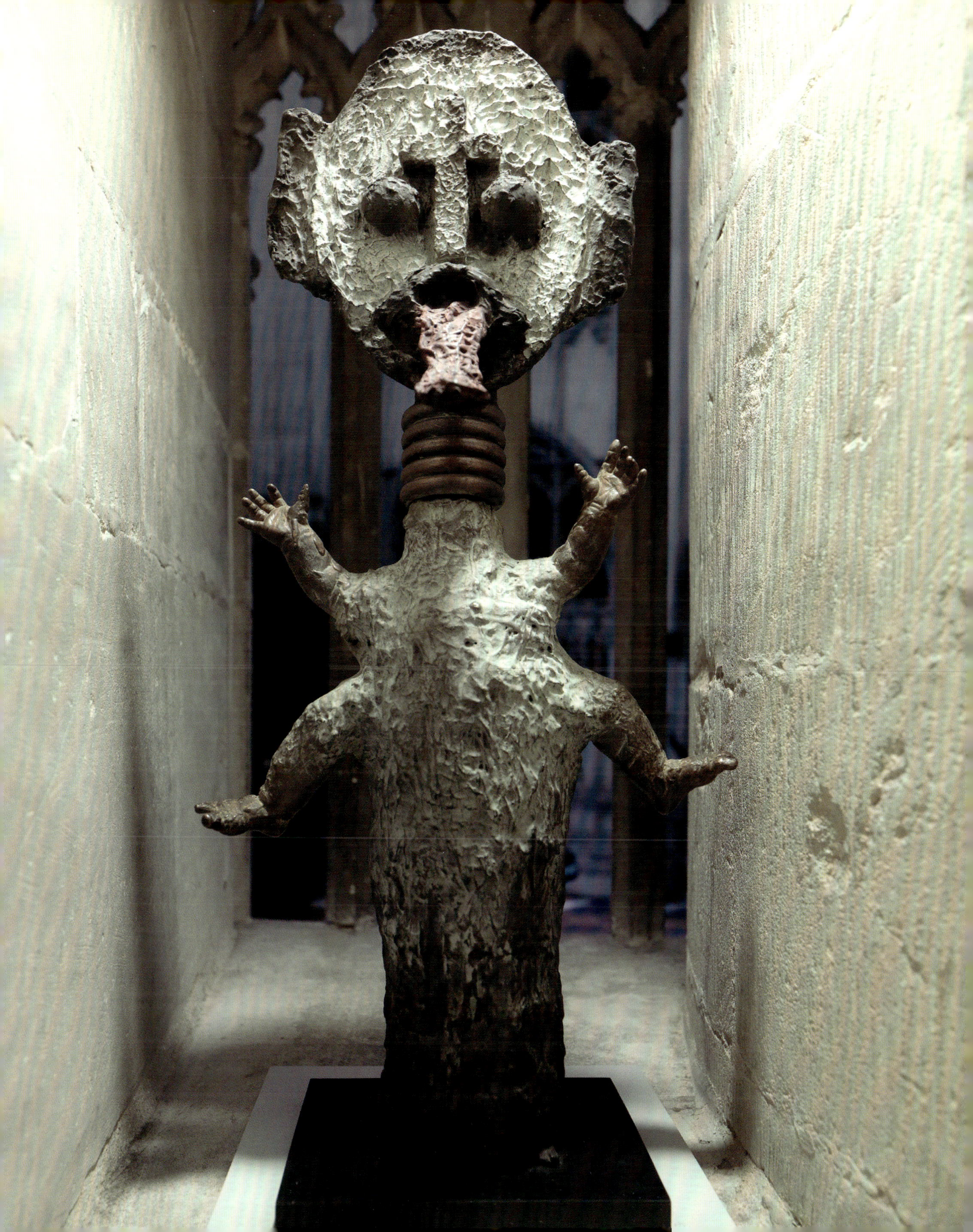

BRUCE BEASLEY FRBS b. 1939

The subject of Beasley's work is natural form but the language and vocabulary of his expression is abstraction. His sculptures reconcile the apparent contradictions of the tectonic and the organic, the constructed and the evolved, the planned and the accidental. They are neither representative nor narrative but, first and foremost, pure form that evokes nature without resembling it.

Breakout II
Bruce Beasley
Bronze
Edition of 9
145cm high

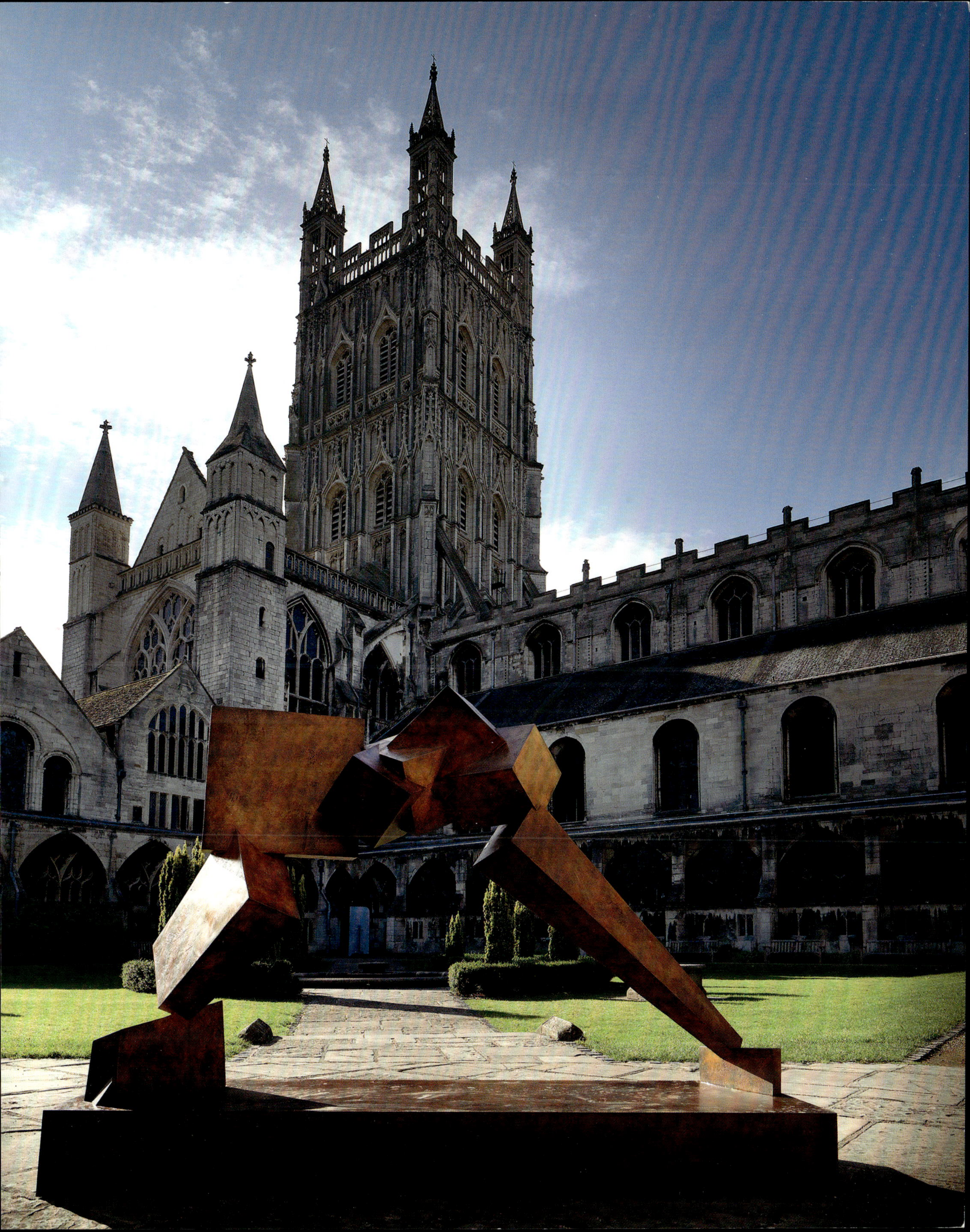

Horizon II

Bruce Beasley

Bronze

Edition of 9

66cm high

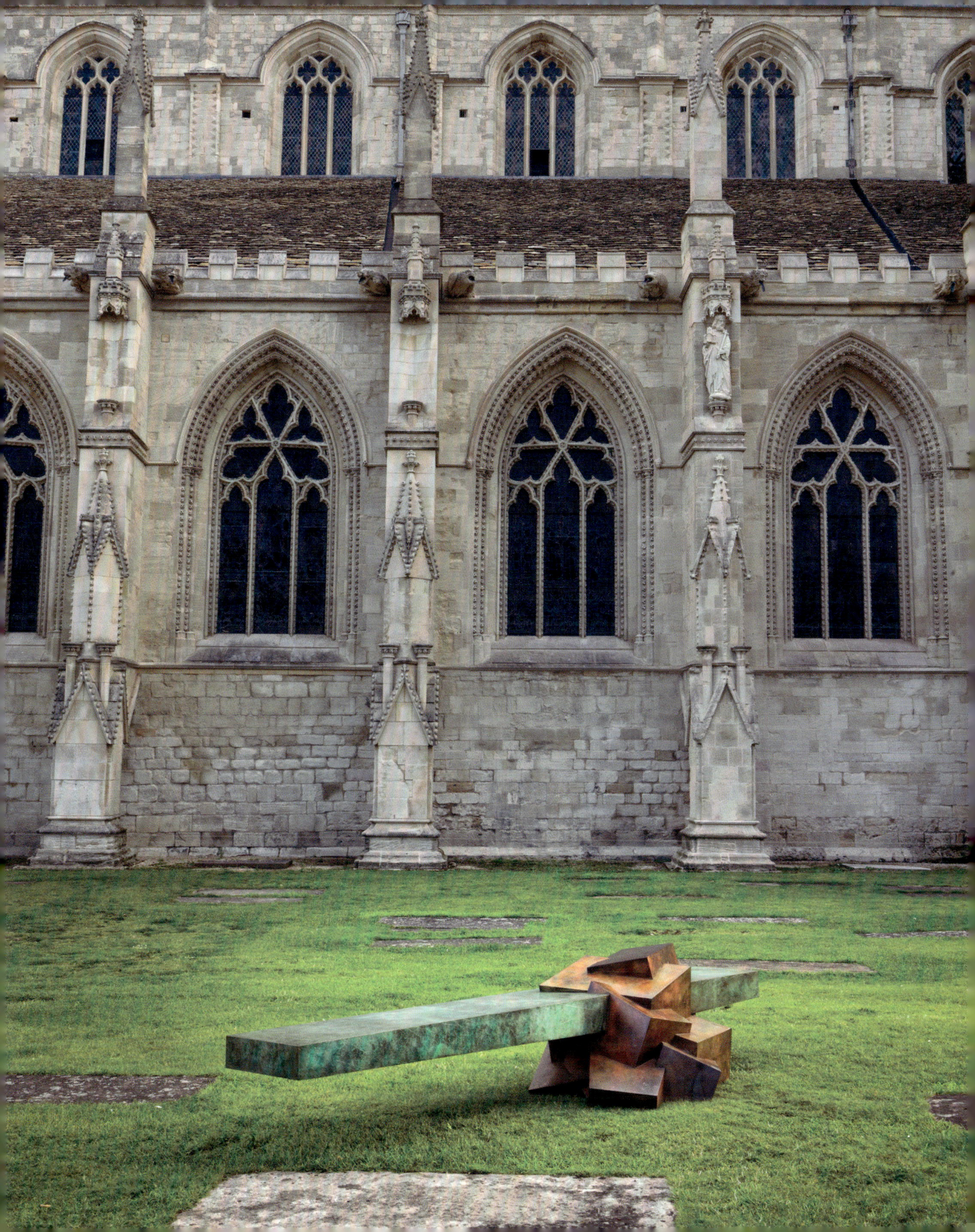

NICK BIBBY b.1960

Perhaps the most iconic of all extinct creatures, the Dodo was one of twelve lost species from the Mascarene Islands painstakingly reconstructed as part of the Bones to Bronze project.

'It has become incredibly important to me to 'bring these animals back to life', to try and produce sculptures that look as though they are just about to fly off, walk or crawl away the moment you turn your back, not some dusty, lifeless museum piece. Over the three years that I spent working on this project, I became increasingly aware of how close we came to actually seeing these wonderful creatures, only a few hundred years at most, less in some cases, an eye blink of geological time. I dream about them sometimes, but when I wake they are all still irretrievably lost.'

Dodo
Nick Bibby
Bronze
Edition of 10
77cm high

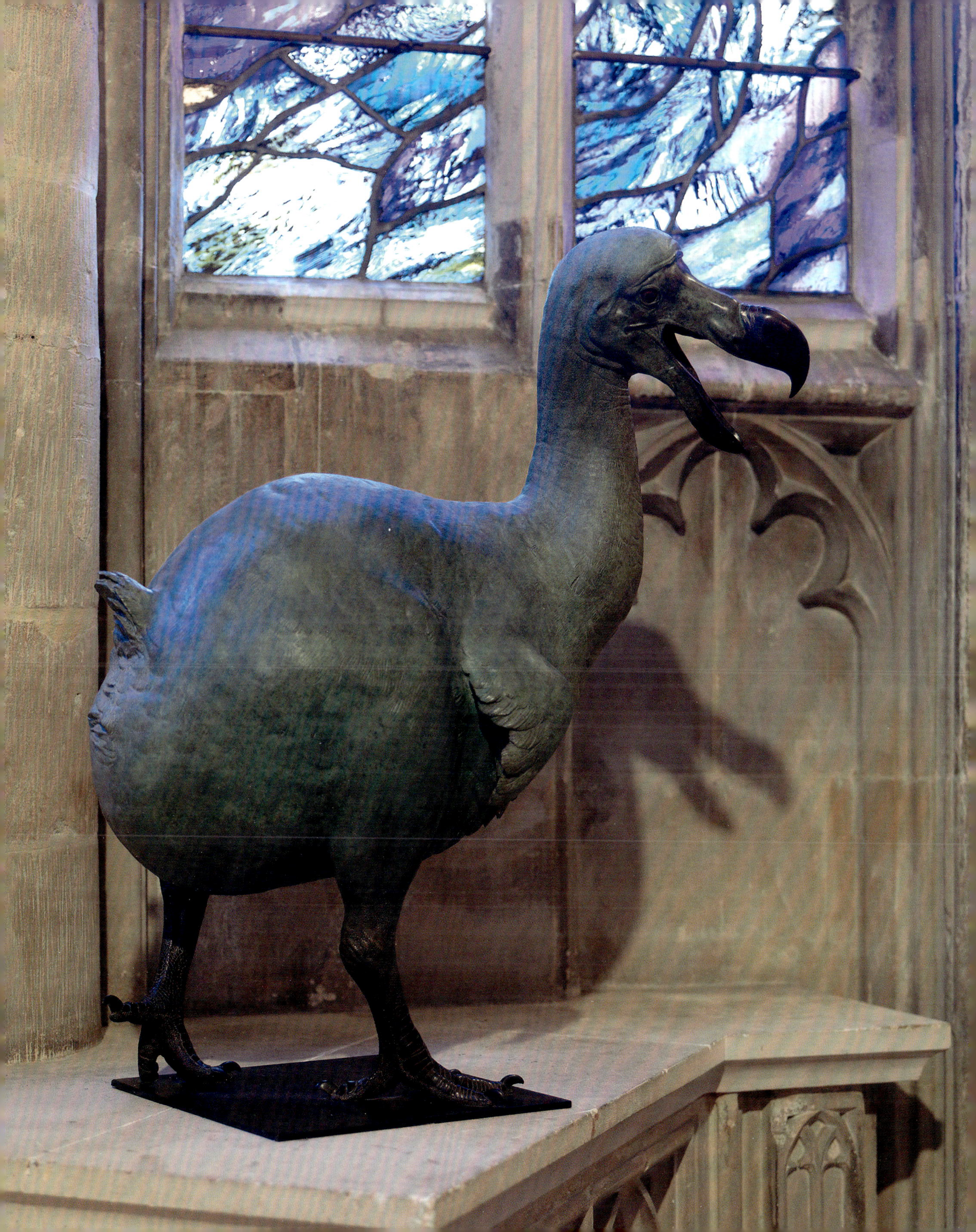

HAMISH BLACK FRBS b.1948

'The simple act of blowing air across the top of a bottle is child's play: the familiarity of filling the chest, then overfilling the bottle with more air and at a speed faster than the bottle's inner space can cope with as it drags out the familiar drone of the bottle's void. It's this enormous elastic space of sound compared to the smallness of the bottle that interests me.

I started by casting the bottle, thinking if I could take the inside and pull it outside, I might get somewhere. The result was the inside on the outside but still attached at the neck. The two cast together was complicating things, so I concentrated on the inside as this is where the sound had come from. A computer animation of a sound wave scribes a vertical line that shortens or lengthens according to the sound's pitch across its horizontal time-line. Employing a similar interval, I cut slices through the cast void of the bottle across its length from neck to bottom and laid them out like a winning hand of cards.

When joined from start to finish at their points of contact, the parts appear stretched between two circles that act as rockers in response.'

sounds like o
Hamish Black
Bronze
Unique
18cm high

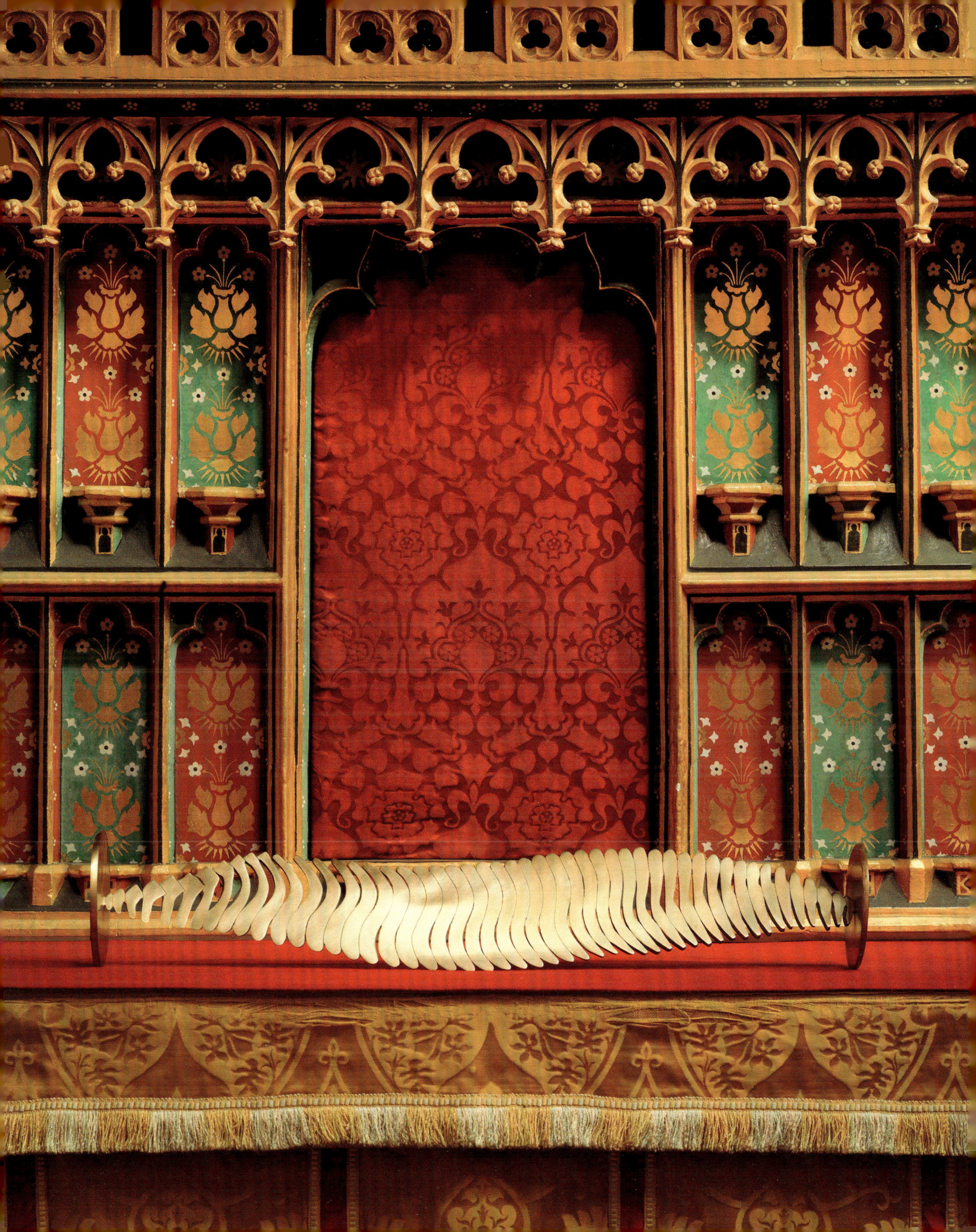

HELAINE BLUMENFELD FRBS b.1942

'The essence of what it is to be human, I believe, is located in the soul. Not an entity that can be seen or measured – but a force that suffuses us, illuminates us and which we can nurture. I was particularly inspired to explore this idea after a walk in an ancient olive grove not far from my studio in Pietrasanta. The trees were eroded and very lyrical, clustered in groups of three or four. Where the wind had moulded them, they seemed to have taken on a mythological quality, as if human souls had embedded themselves in these trees. I went back to the studio and started working obsessively with clay. I did hundreds of these groupings of forms and fired them. I would call this series SOULS, an expression of the search to discover this essential quality which gives meaning and vision in our lives.'

Souls
Helaine Blumenfeld
Bronze
Edition of 3
195cm high

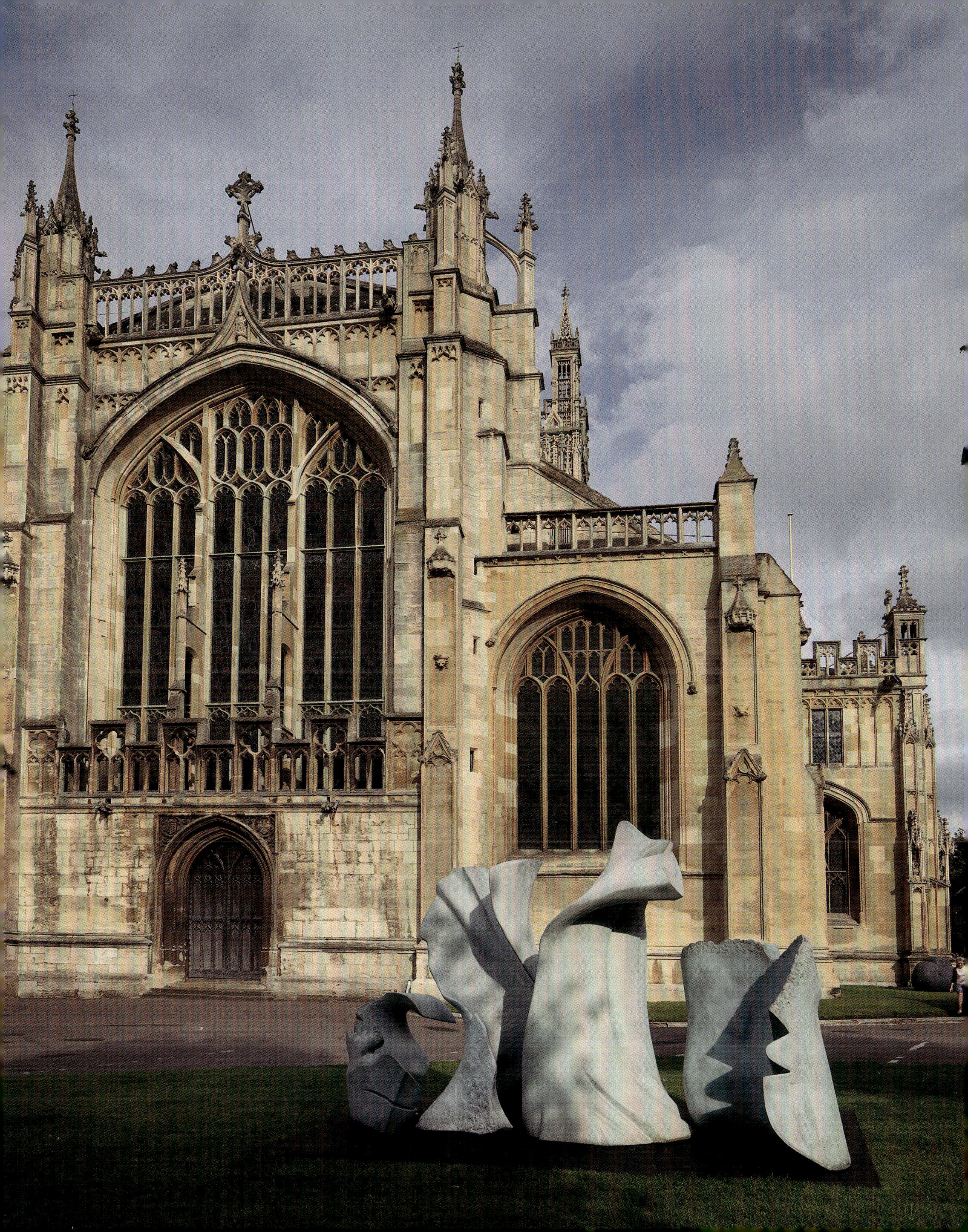

DON BROWN b.1962

Don Brown is a figurative sculptor who is best known for his continuing series of sculptures of his wife and muse, Yoko, in a range of poses and attitudes.

Brown's sculptures of Yoko have long been accompanied by an interest in still life, reflected both in his sculptures and drawings. One sculpture of Yoko shows her shrouded entirely in fabric - a work that becomes as much a study in inanimate material as a figurative portrait.

The idea of glimpsing a body within a still life object is central to Plum, a bronze plum enlarged and elevated on a steel rod atop a plinth almost in the manner of a bust. The symmetrical creviced orb subtly evokes aspects of the human form such as the buttocks or navel. The plum's suggestive contours echo the transposed objects of surrealism or what Magritte termed 'elective affinities' between dissimilar forms. And so Brown's 'still life' works are inescapably corporeal, sharing much with his more explicitly figurative pieces.

Plum, 2008
Don Brown
Bronze
Edition of 6
78cm high
Copyright: The Artist, courtesy Sadie Coles HQ, London

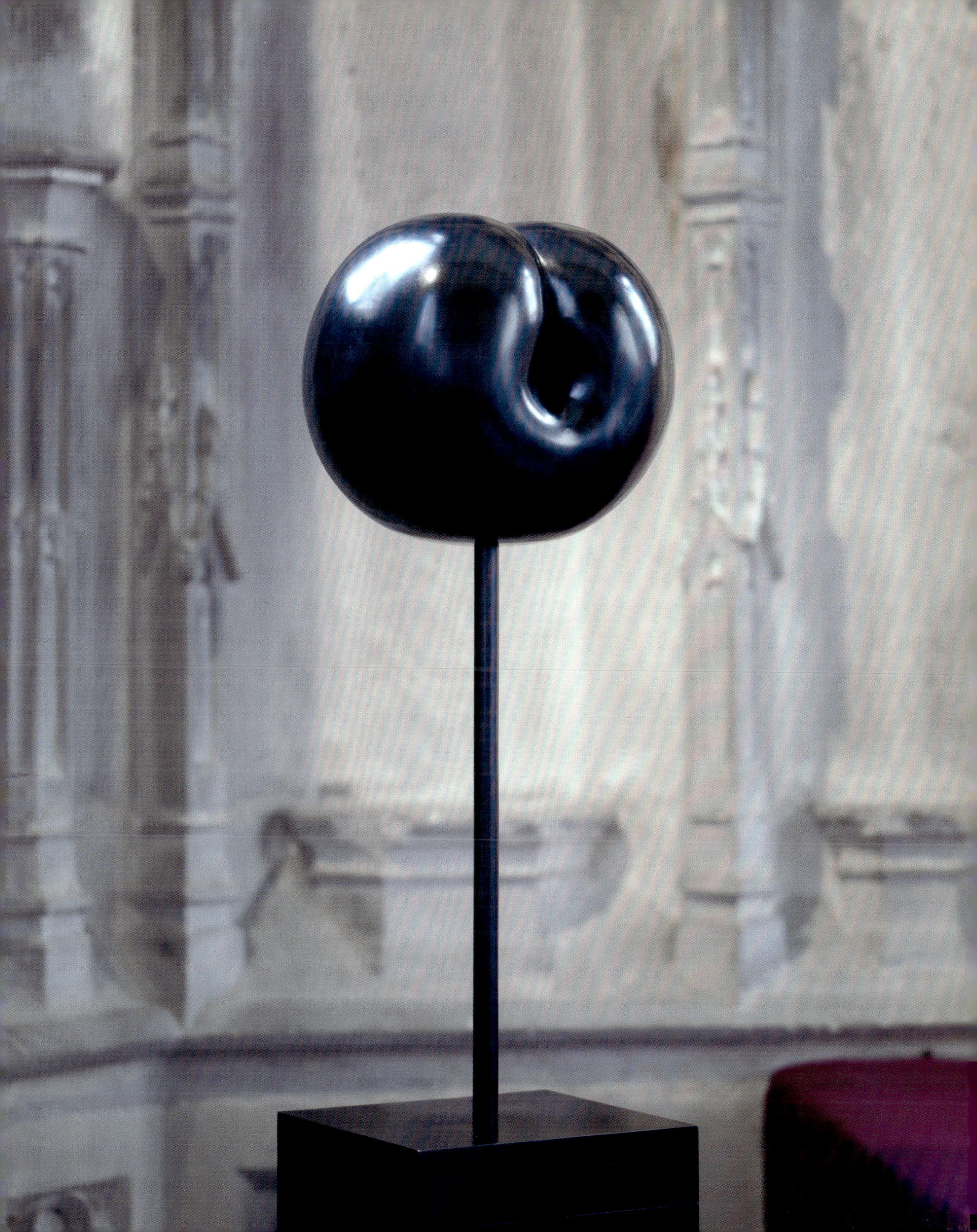

RALPH BROWN RA 1928 - 2013

The title for Display No More In Vain the Lofty Banner comes from All is Vanity, by Anne Finch, Countess of Winchelsea, 1661-1720:

"Trail all your pikes,
dispirit every drum,

March in a slow
procession from afar,

Ye silent, ye dejected men of war!

Be still the hautboys, and
the flute be dumb!

Display no more, in
vain, the lofty banner,

For see! where on the
bier before ye lies

The pale, the fall'n,
th'untimely sacrifice

To your mistaken shrine, to
your false idol honour!"

Brown took this poem on the glorification and futility of war as inspiration for this ironic 'heroic style' sculpture which seeks to express a timeless message still resonant today.

Display No More In Vain the Lofty Banner

Ralph Brown

Bronze

Edition of 5

209cm high

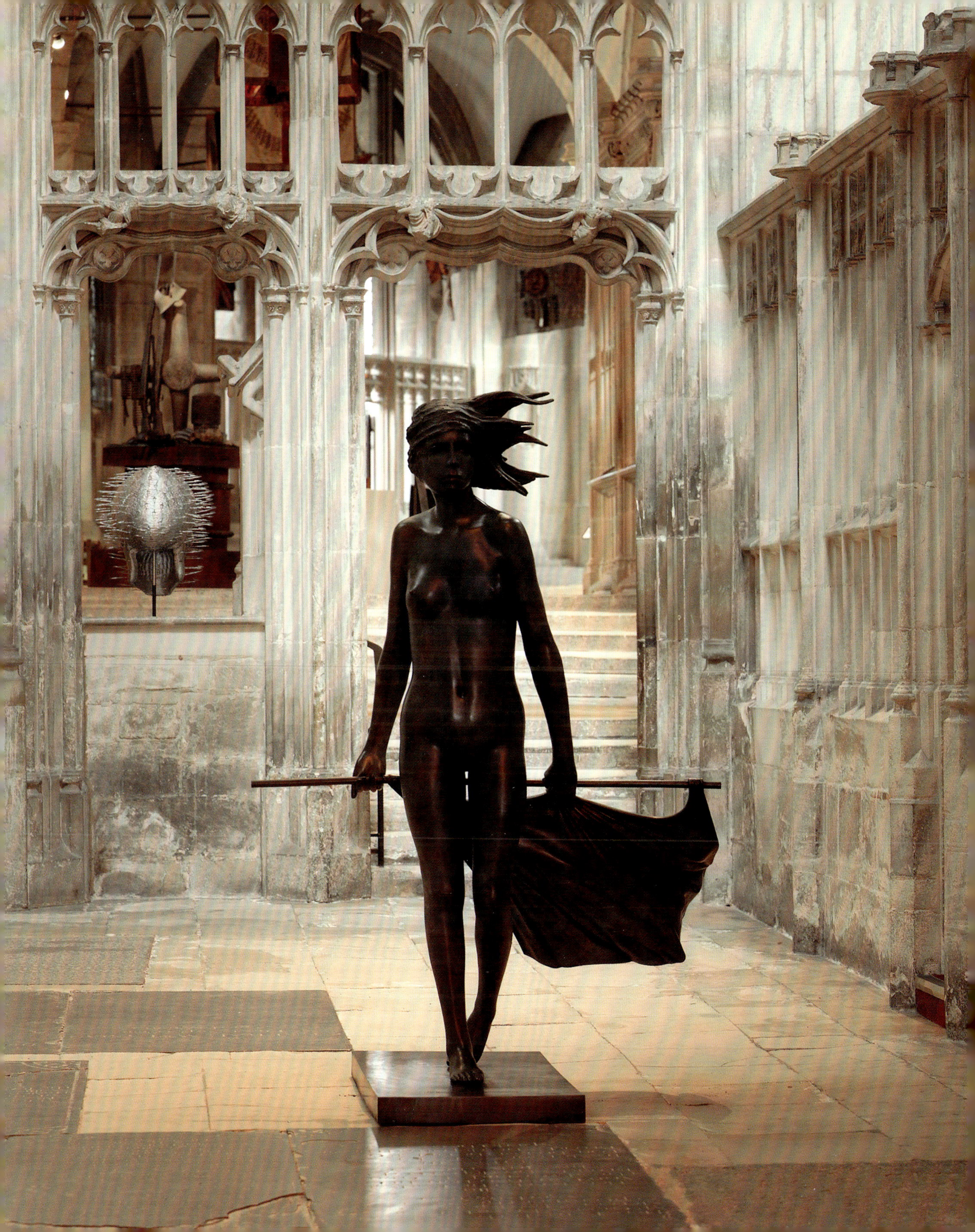

Pomona

Ralph Brown

Bronze

Edition of 5

98cm high

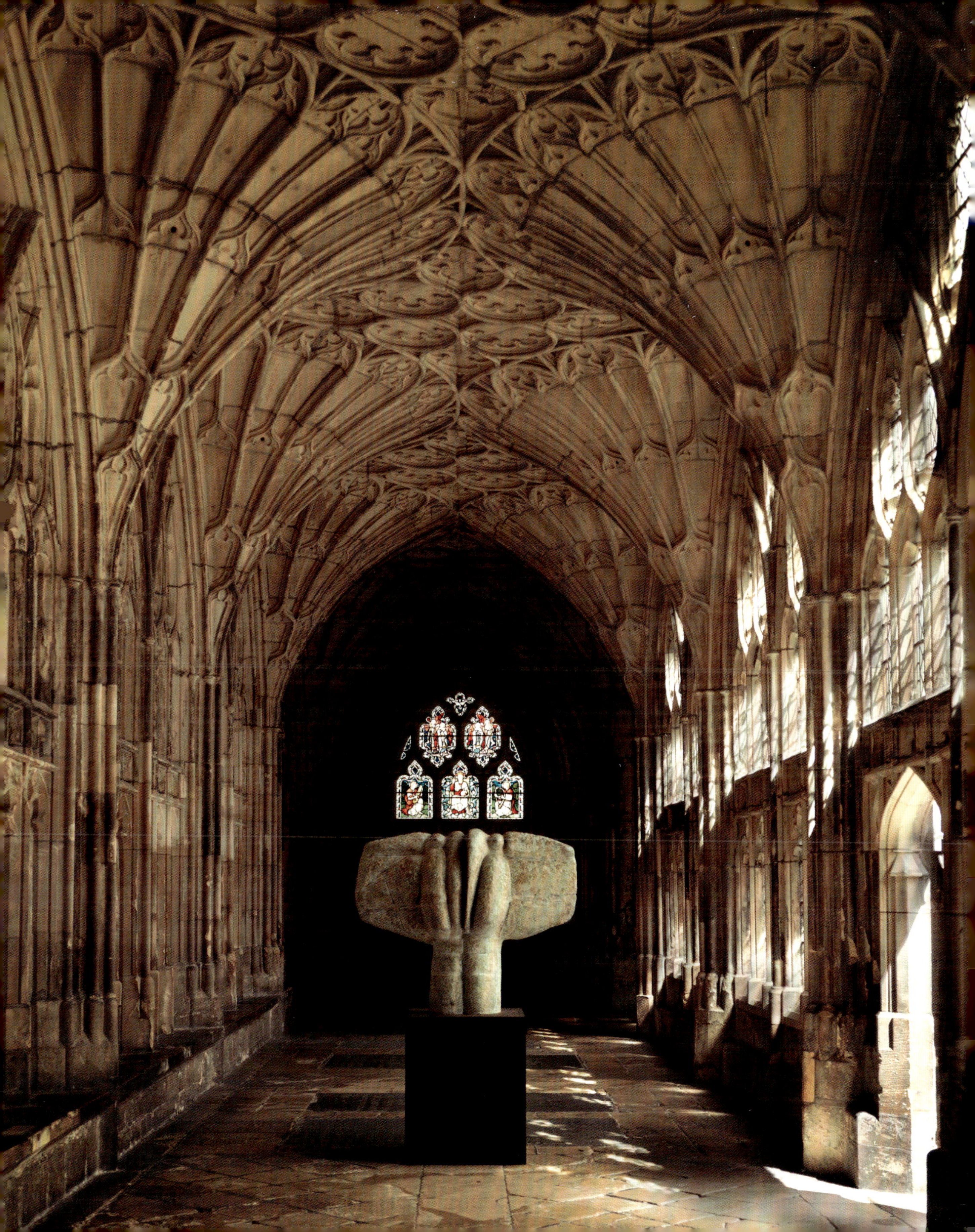

JON BUCK FRBS b.1951

'There is no doubt that colour plays a major role in the impact and identity of this sculpture. Tennyson's words "Nature, red in tooth and claw" were in part a response to Darwin's theories of natural selection and as such it continues to be a phrase that reflects our attitude and the primacy we give to the colour red. In Art History, red is commonly associated with danger, passion, beauty and anger but perhaps we attribute such potency to this colour because it is synonymous with blood, the vital, life-giving fluid flowing within us and most living creatures.

The sculpture as a whole is totemic; Nature is both within us and outside us. Inscribed into the surface on one side is the outward appearance of a generic man and on the other is an inner mindscape of symbols drawn from a natural lexicon of beasts and birds. Metaphors and symbols from nature are an ancient and lyrical way by which Man has attempted to express his own fears and aspirations but it is perhaps surprising just how often we turn to that same resource in poetry and art today.'

Brookside metal

In Man's Nature is sponsored by Brookside Metal Company Limited

In Man's Nature

Jon Buck

Bronze

Edition of 5

240cm high

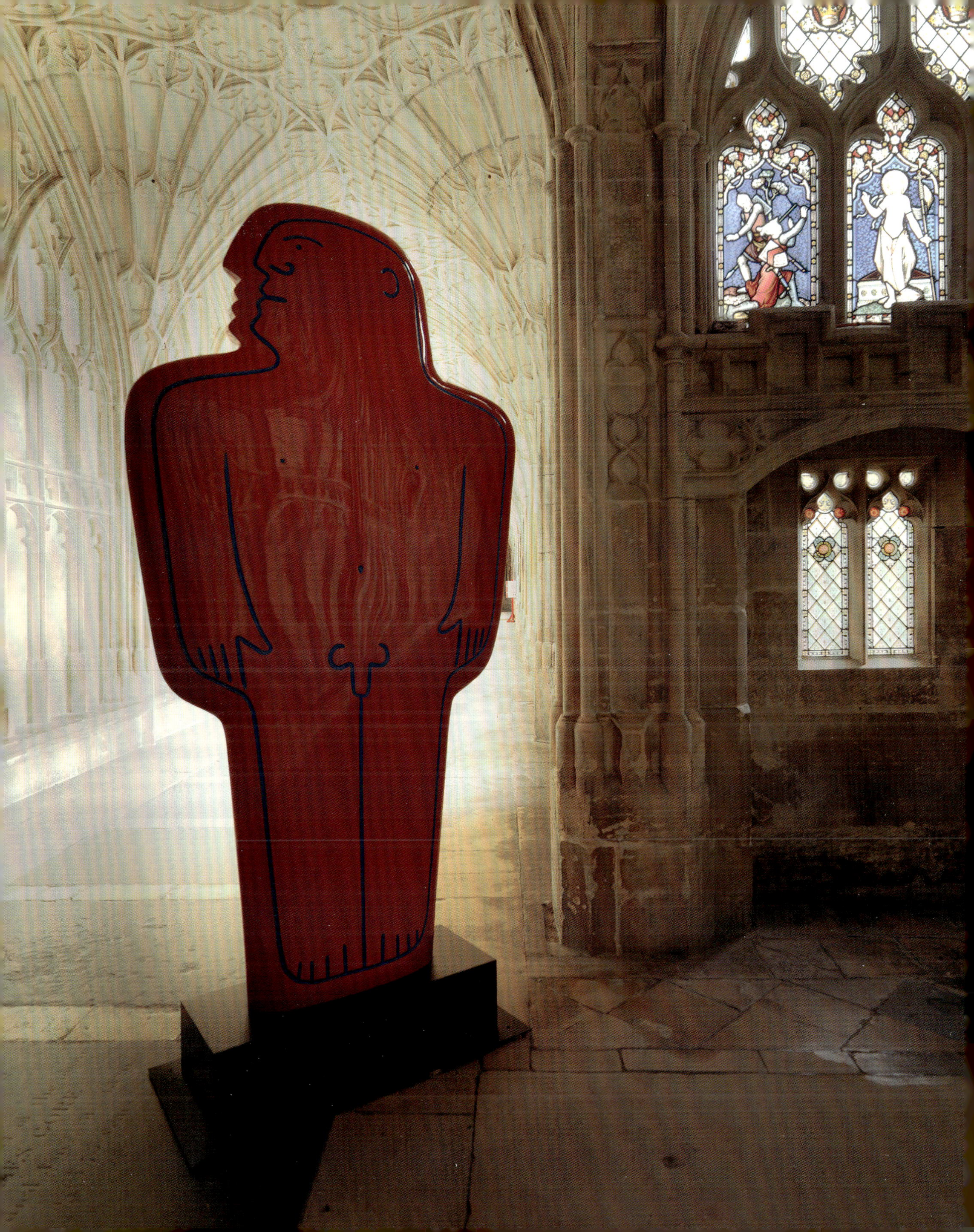

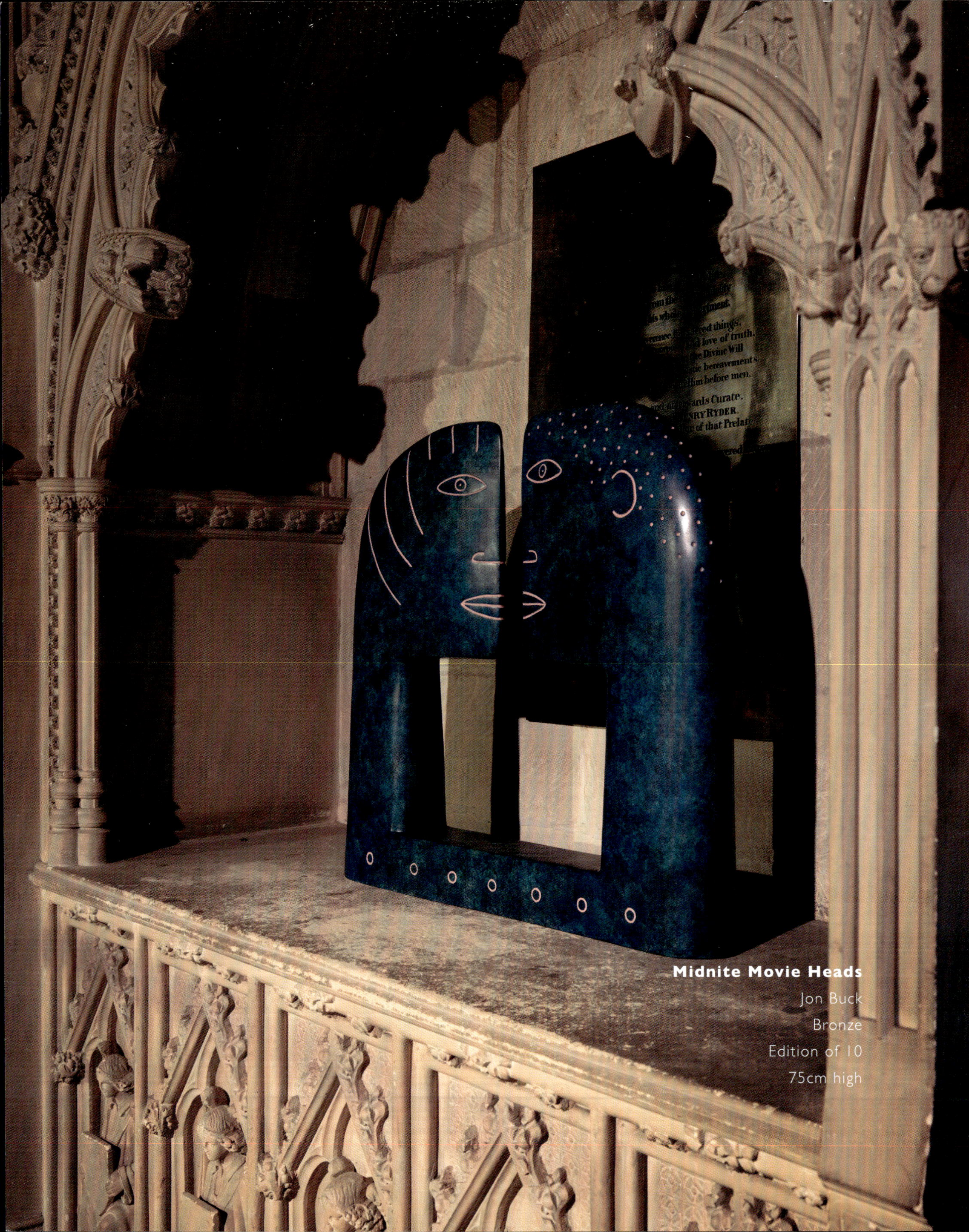

Midnite Movie Heads
Jon Buck
Bronze
Edition of 10
75cm high

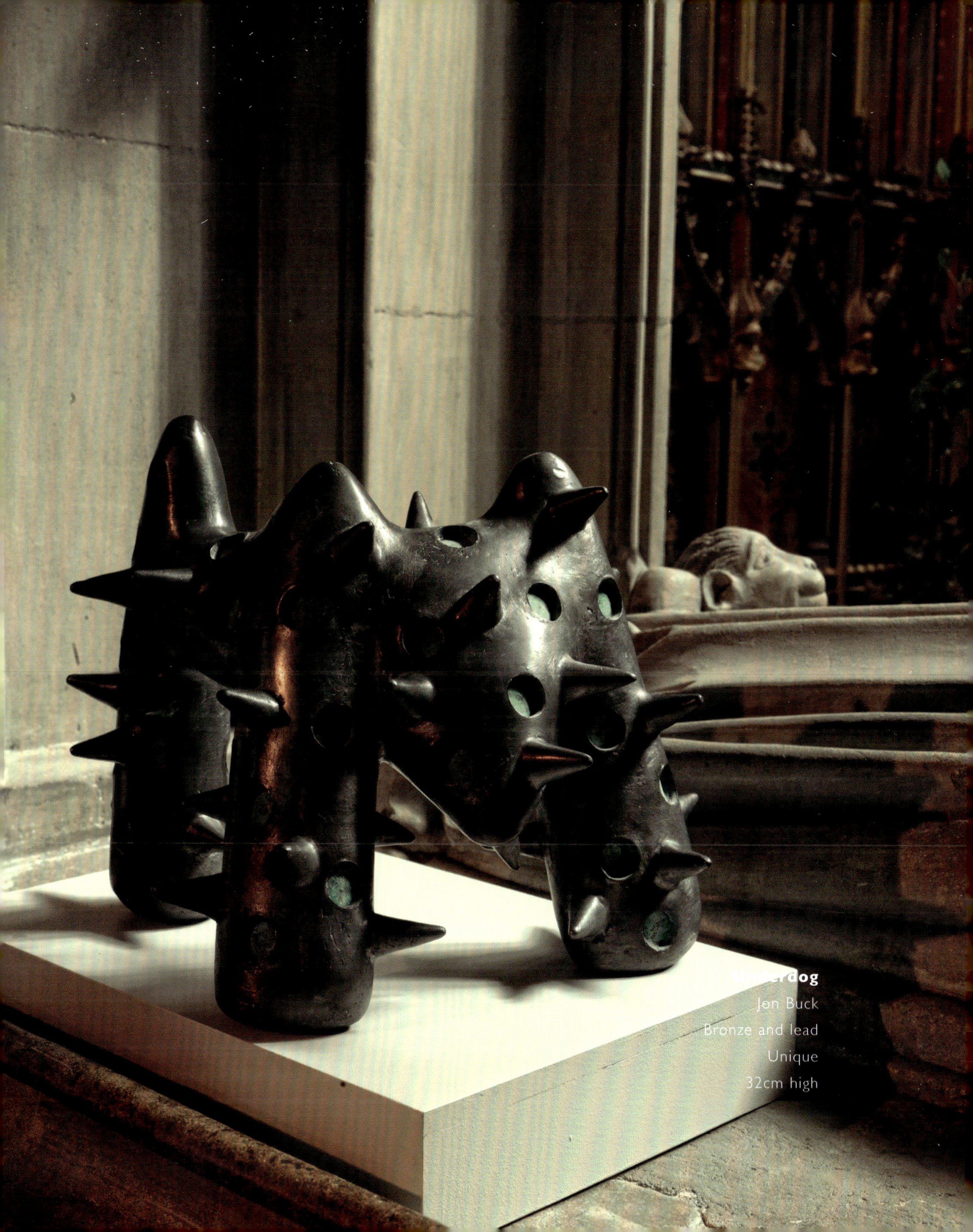

Underdog
Jon Buck
Bronze and lead
Unique
32cm high

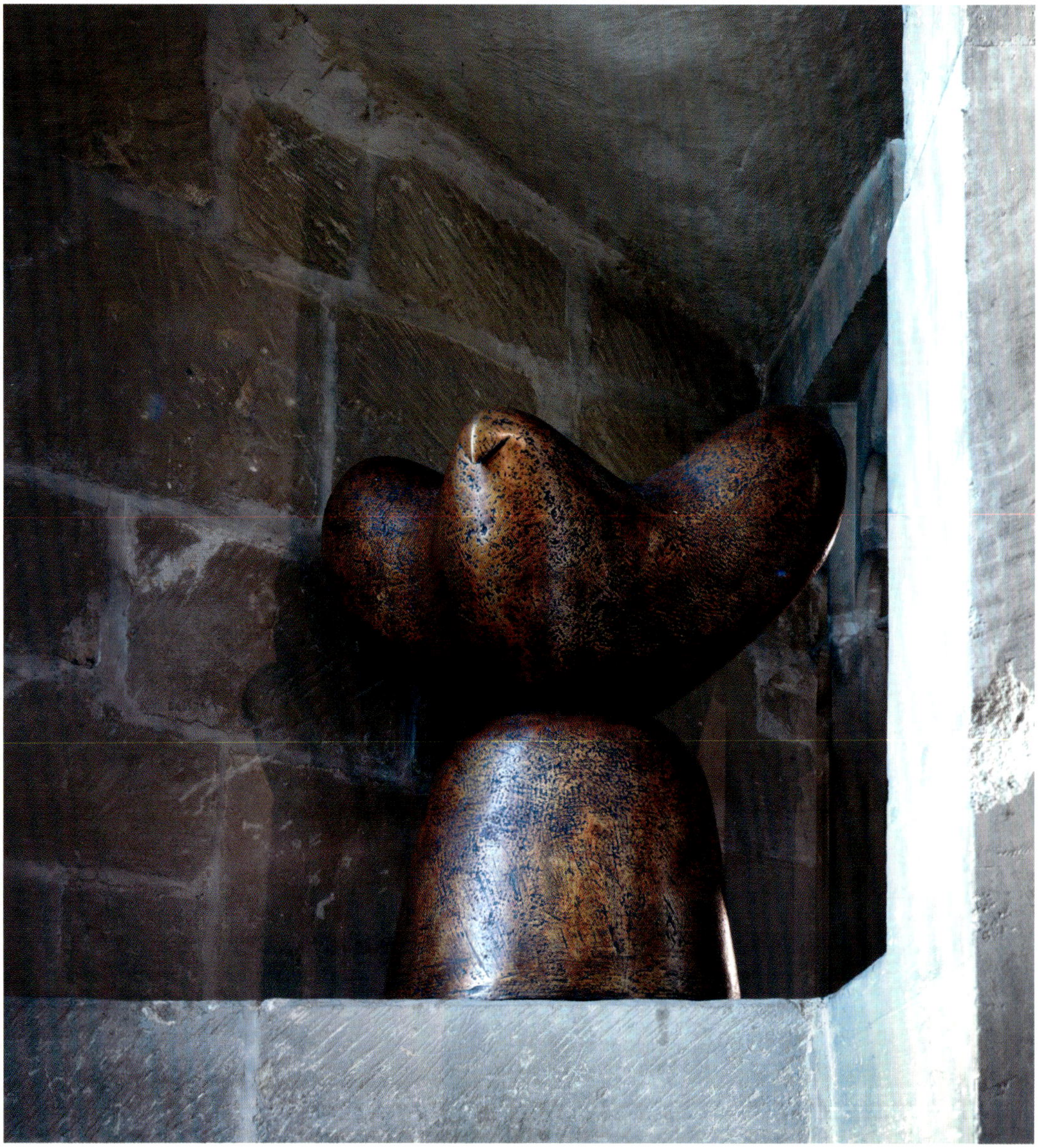

Bombird
Jon Buck
Bronze
Edition of 10
60cm high

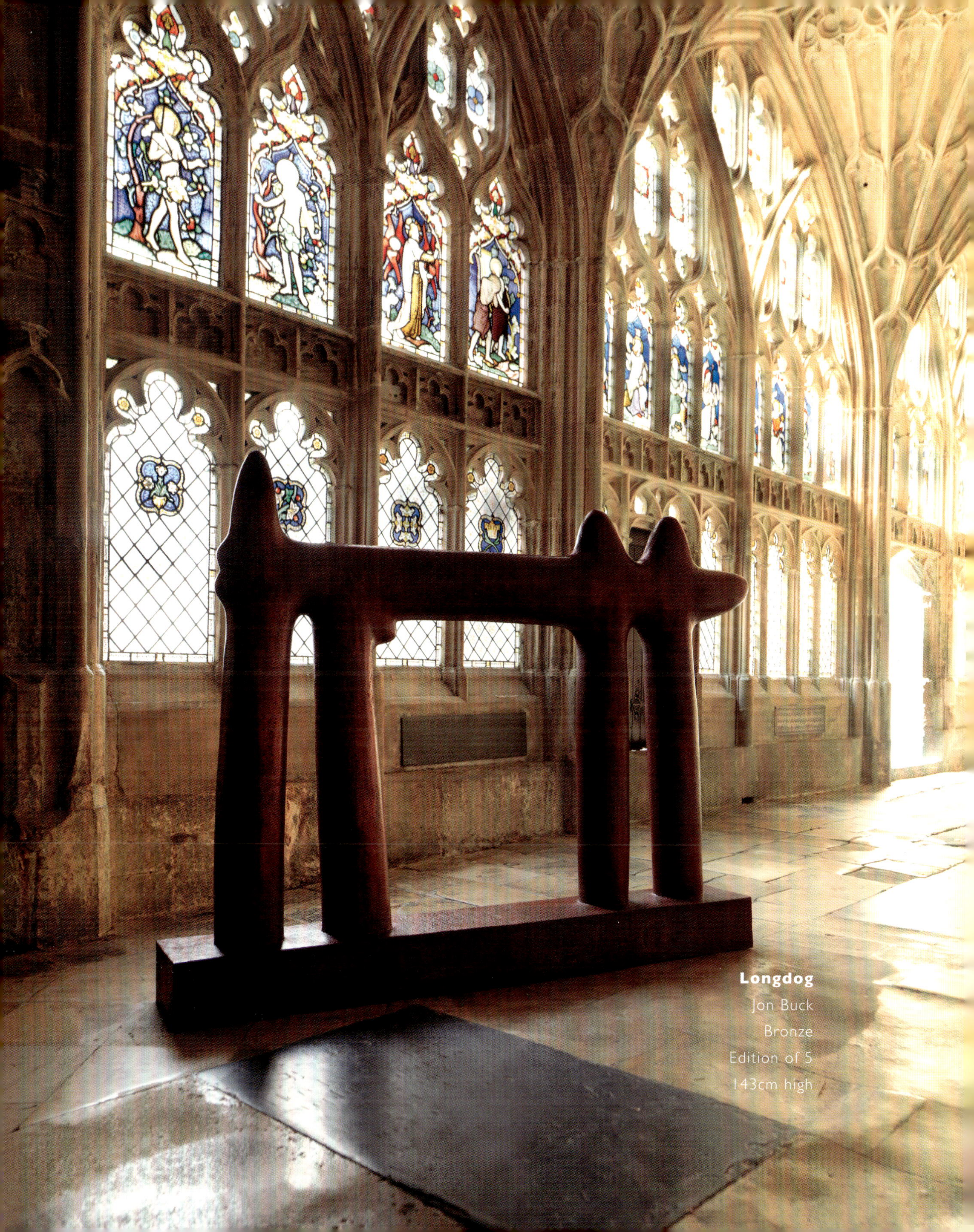

Longdog
Jon Buck
Bronze
Edition of 5
143cm high

REMBRANDT BUGATTI 1884 – 1916

Rembrandt Bugatti was a naturally gifted sculptor who developed his powerful and expressive language from an early age. His subjects were mostly animals which he patiently and carefully observed and portrayed with great sensitivity and respect.

Bugatti's earlier works were strongly impressionistic yet convincing studies of specific animals. This style gradually matured into a more angular and expressionist intensity which conveyed mood and emotion as well as anatomy and realism.

Siberian Tiger is a powerful and moving sculpture in which the vigour and power of the pacing beast is expressed through the energetic, slabbed surface of the bronze. The spirit of the tiger is articulated through the passion and virtuosity of its maker.

Siberian Tiger
Rembrandt Bugatti
Bronze
Edition of 8
172cm high

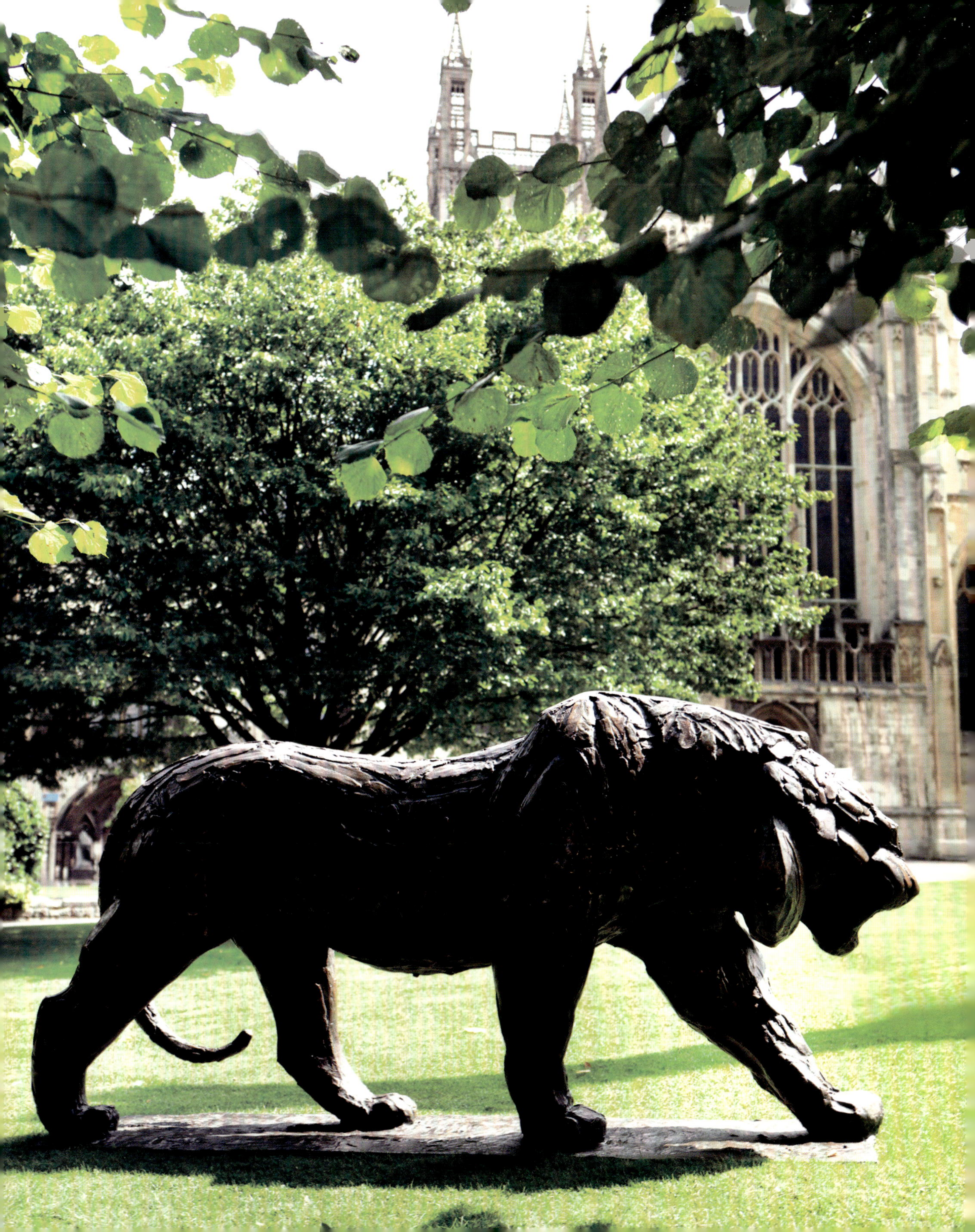

DANIEL CHADWICK b.1965

"An installation in response to the Cathedral space.

Harmonic waves of energy are passed into the system. The energy is transmitted from rod to rod and out to the furthest discs. The natural frequency of the system as a whole prevents the waves finding equilibrium with the elements."

Constellation 2014

Daniel Chadwick

Stainless steel, acrylic sheet, motor and timer.

Unique

400cm height

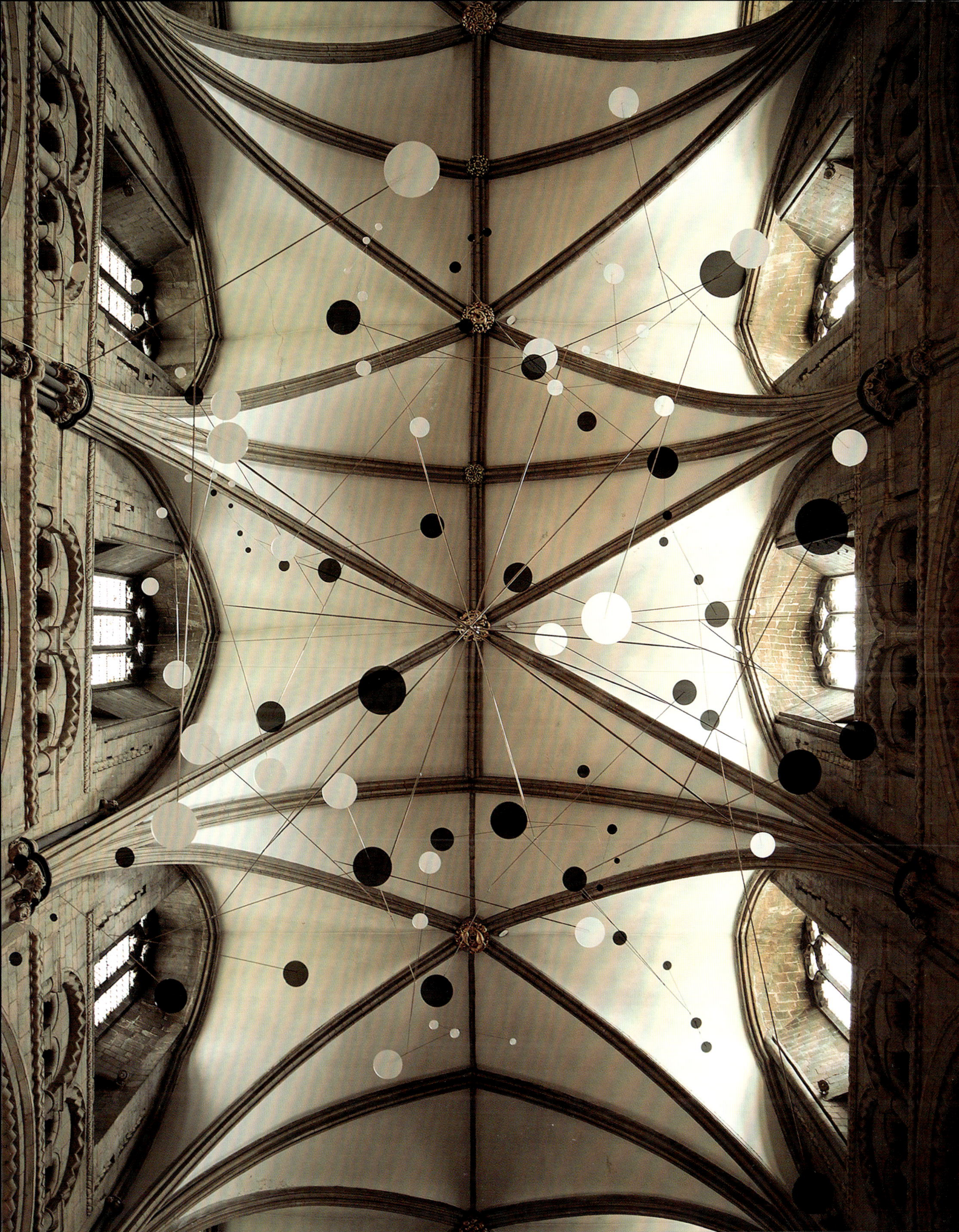

LYNN CHADWICK RA 1914 - 2003

Throughout Lynn Chadwick's long and productive career, 'the couple' was an enduring subject to which he returned many times. In Jubilee IV, one of a series of dynamic cloaked couples made between 1977 and 1985, the wing-like drapery of earlier pieces has evolved into billowing cloaks which flow boldly out behind the figures as they stride vigorously forward into the wind.

As in all Chadwick's work, the crucial presence of the piece comes from its particular stance and the relationship between the two figures as well as his characteristic skill in balancing sculptural concerns of line, texture, mass, weight, geometry and movement.

Jubilee IV
Lynn Chadwick
Bronze
Edition of 6
285cm high

Lead sponsor
willans
Willans LLP | solicitors
Jubilee IV is sponsored by Willans llp

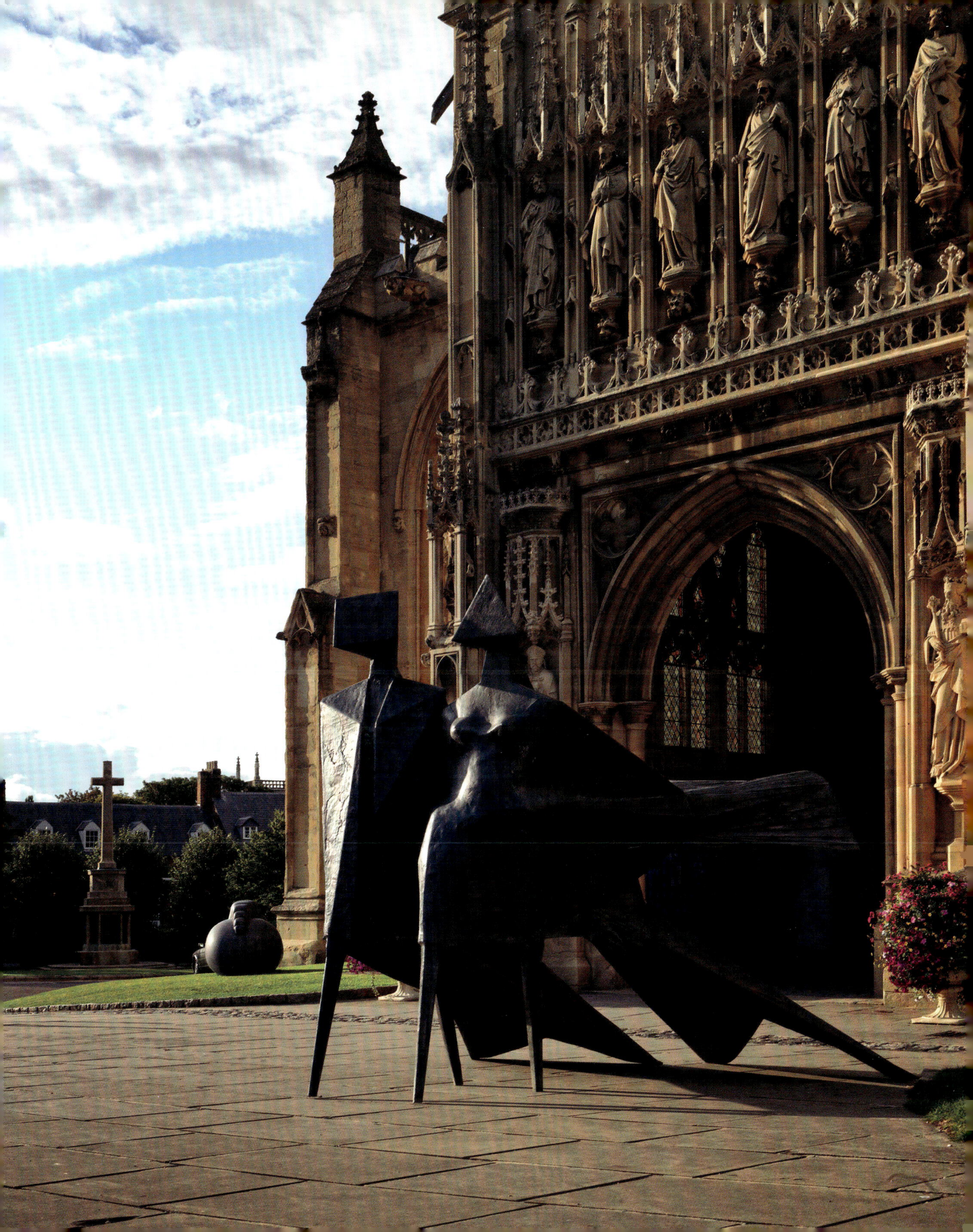

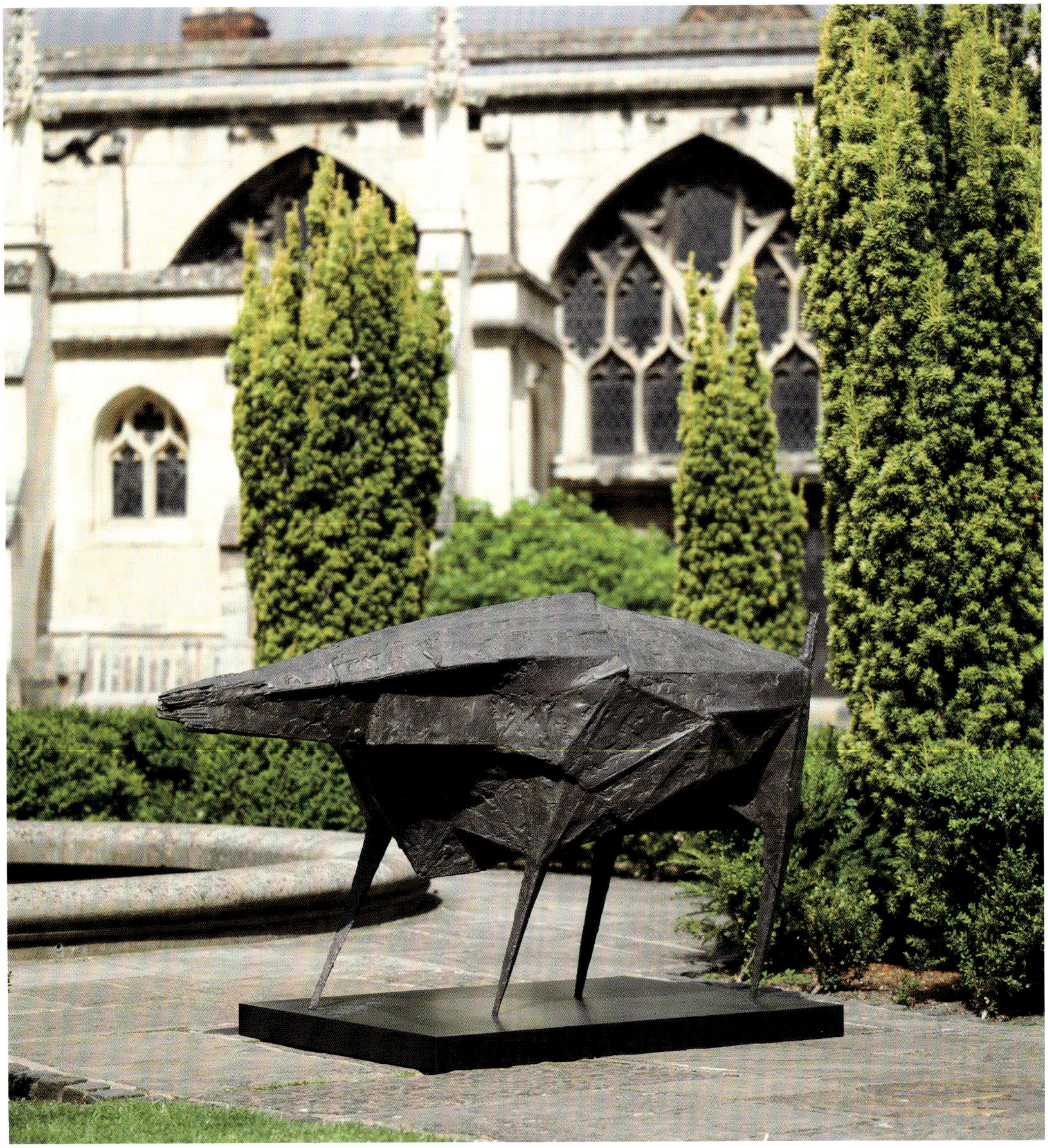

Black Beast

Lynn Chadwick

Bronze

Edition of 4

101cm high

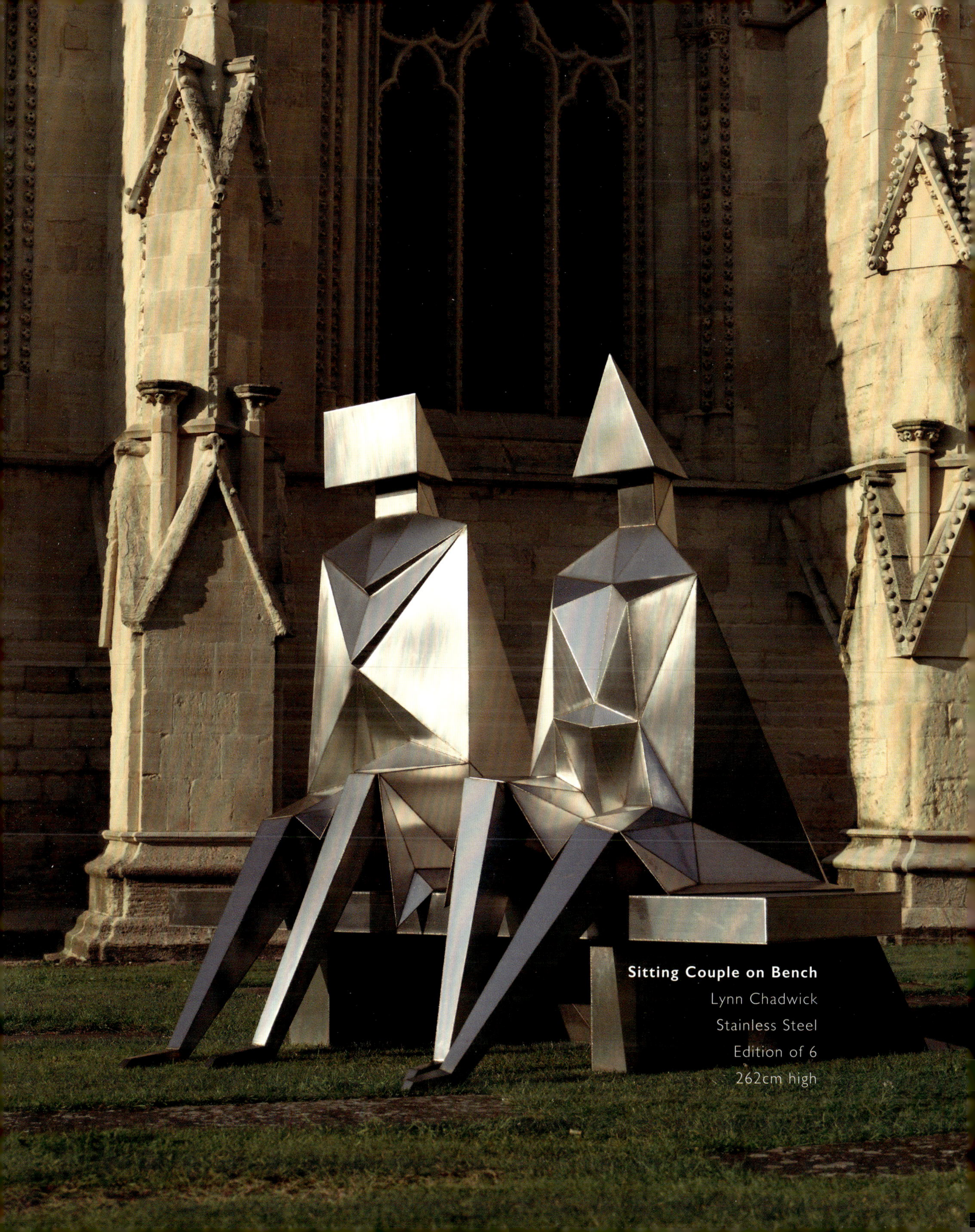

Sitting Couple on Bench
Lynn Chadwick
Stainless Steel
Edition of 6
262cm high

ANN CHRISTOPHER RA FRBS b.1947

'Solitary presence, demanding contemplation, Beyond Silence expresses my belief that silence is not empty space but an opportunity to allow time for thoughts and feelings to surface into the conscious mind. Sculpture should have a power and presence - not unlike that of an ancient standing stone - and this sculpture incorporates my long-standing influences and interests in stone and rock formations as well as architecture, flight and precision engineering. In Beyond Silence, it is the lines, cutting deeply into and visually holding the form, which become important.'

Beyond Silence
Ann Christopher
Bronze
Edition of 3
226cm high

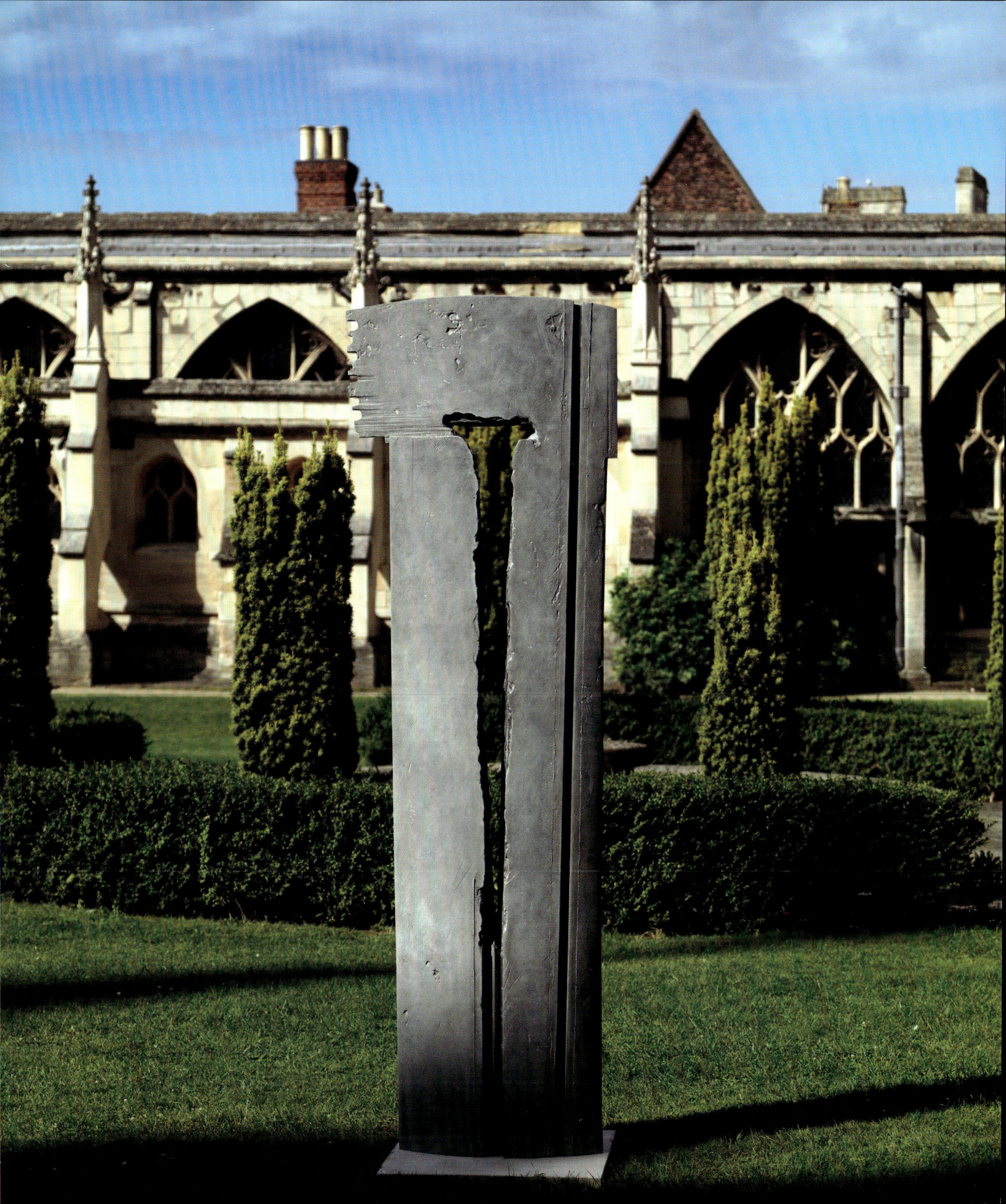

Split Shadow
Ann Christopher
Plaster
Unique
275cm high

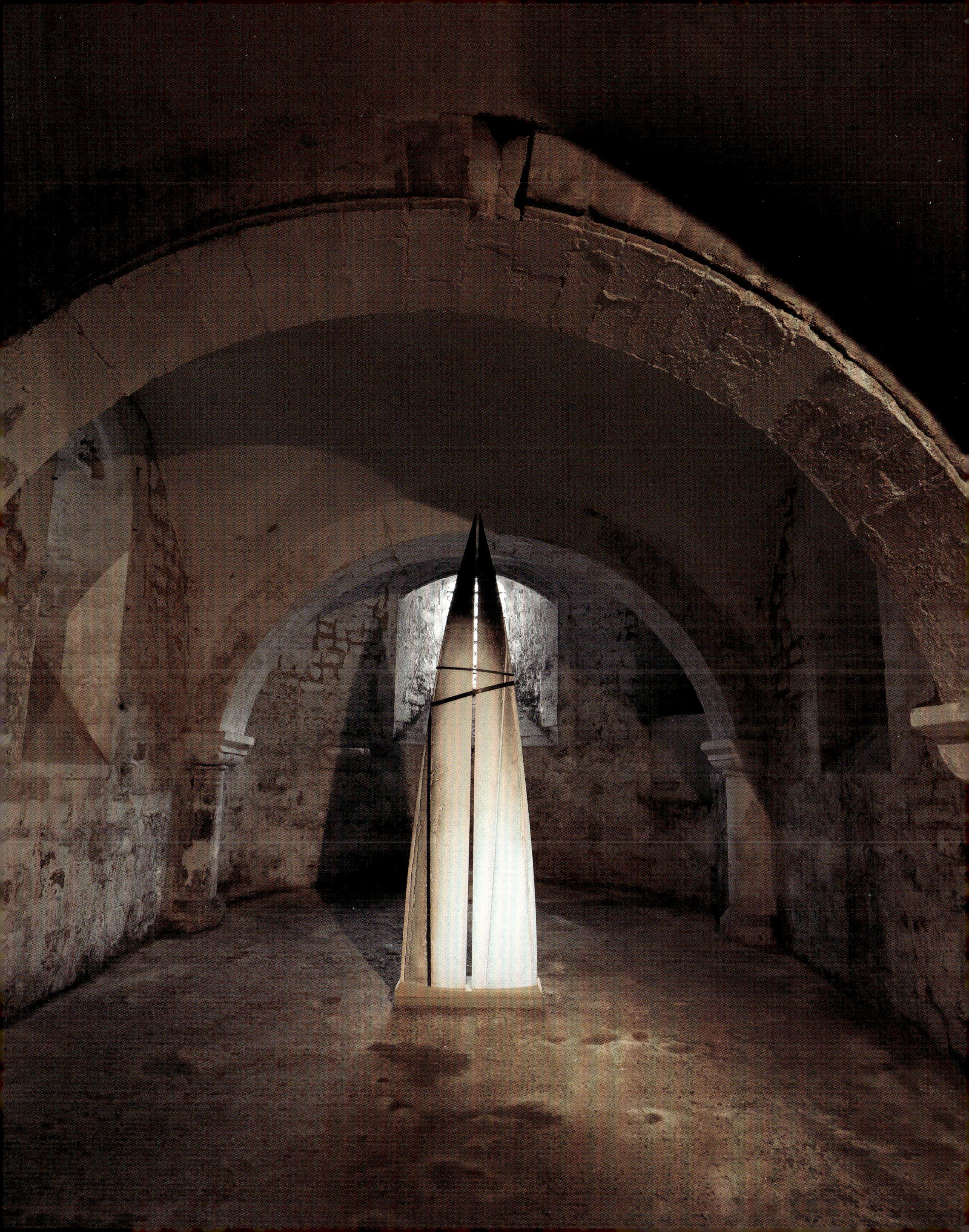

BRIAN CLARKE b.1953

Caesar Released From the Prison of Ambition
Brian Clarke
Bronze and oil paint
Unique
133.5cm high

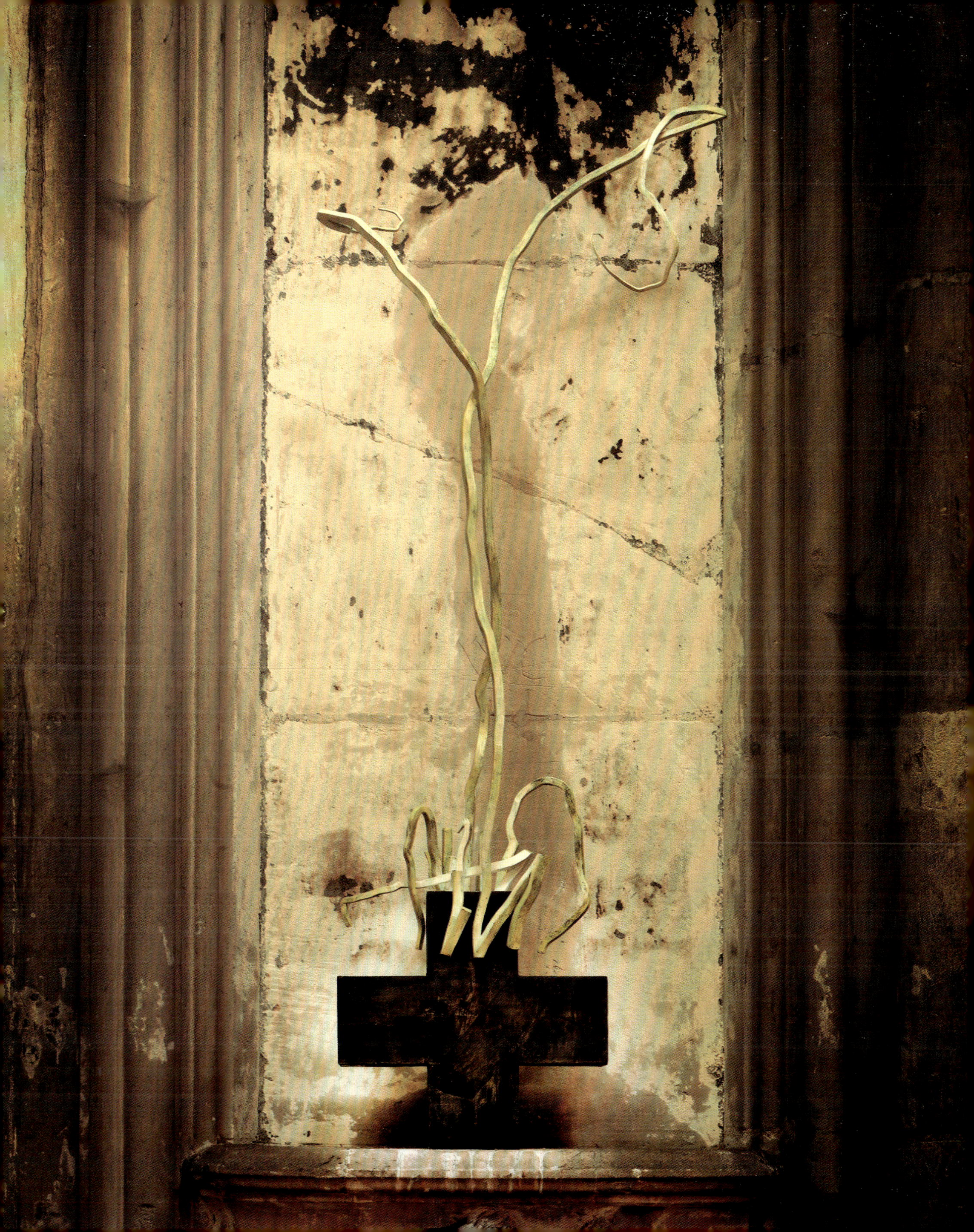

GEOFFREY CLARKE RA b.1924

Clarke made three major works for the 1963 outdoor sculpture exhibition in Battersea Park. Some of the earliest pieces to be made using his pioneering method of casting aluminium from polystyrene, these works embody both vulnerability and strength, a tension created by the polarity between the hardness and solidity of metal and the brittleness and lightness of polystyrene. They hint at defunct artillery machines left behind in the aftermath of some terrifying conflict. Now abandoned, they have become objects of curiosity and contemplation.

Battersea II
Geoffrey Clarke
Aluminium
Unique
76cm high

Battersea III
Geoffrey Clarke
Aluminium
Unique
122cm high

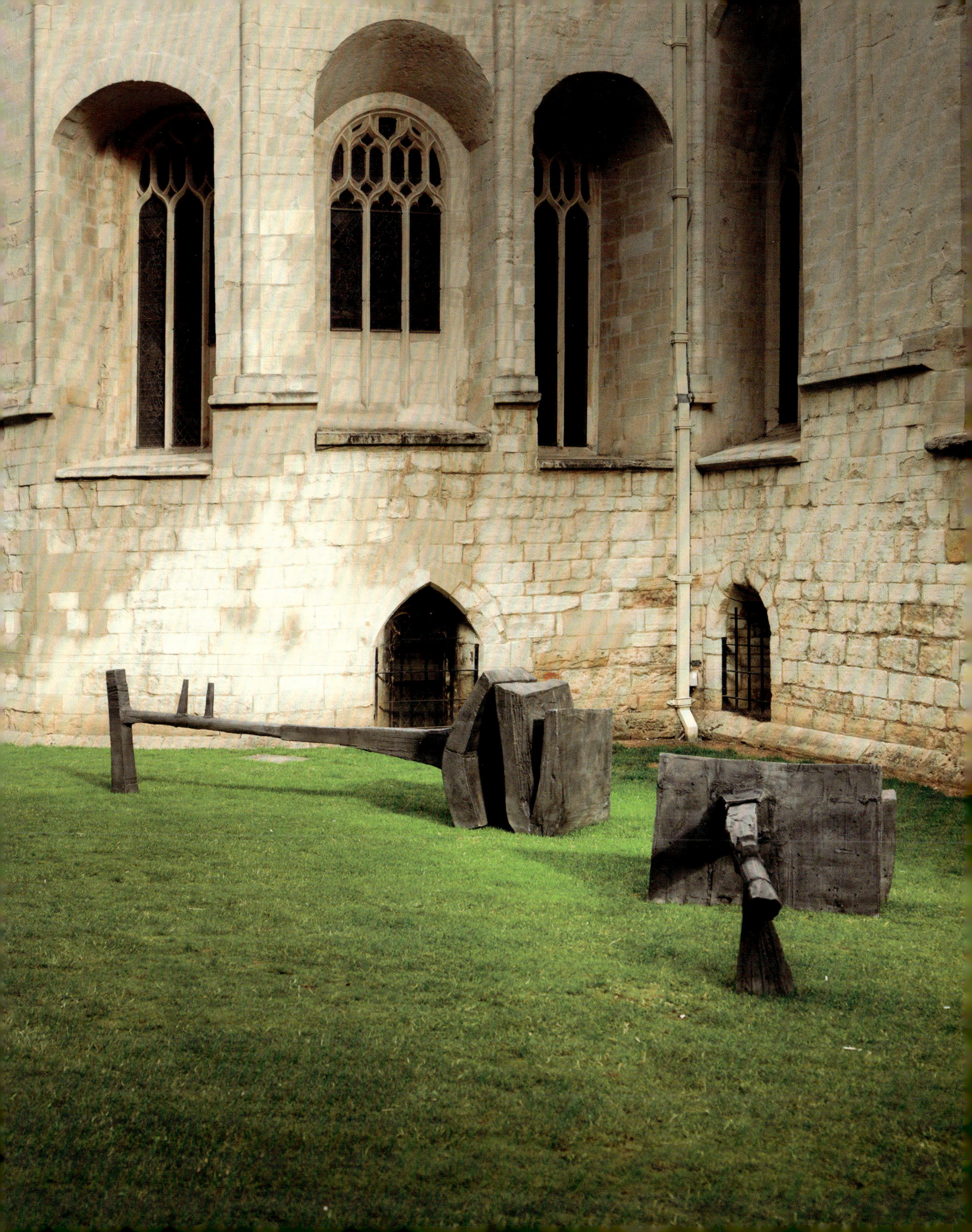

Taunton Deane Crematorium:
Test Panel 1963

Geoffrey Clarke

Cast aluminium and coloured glass

Unique

213cm high

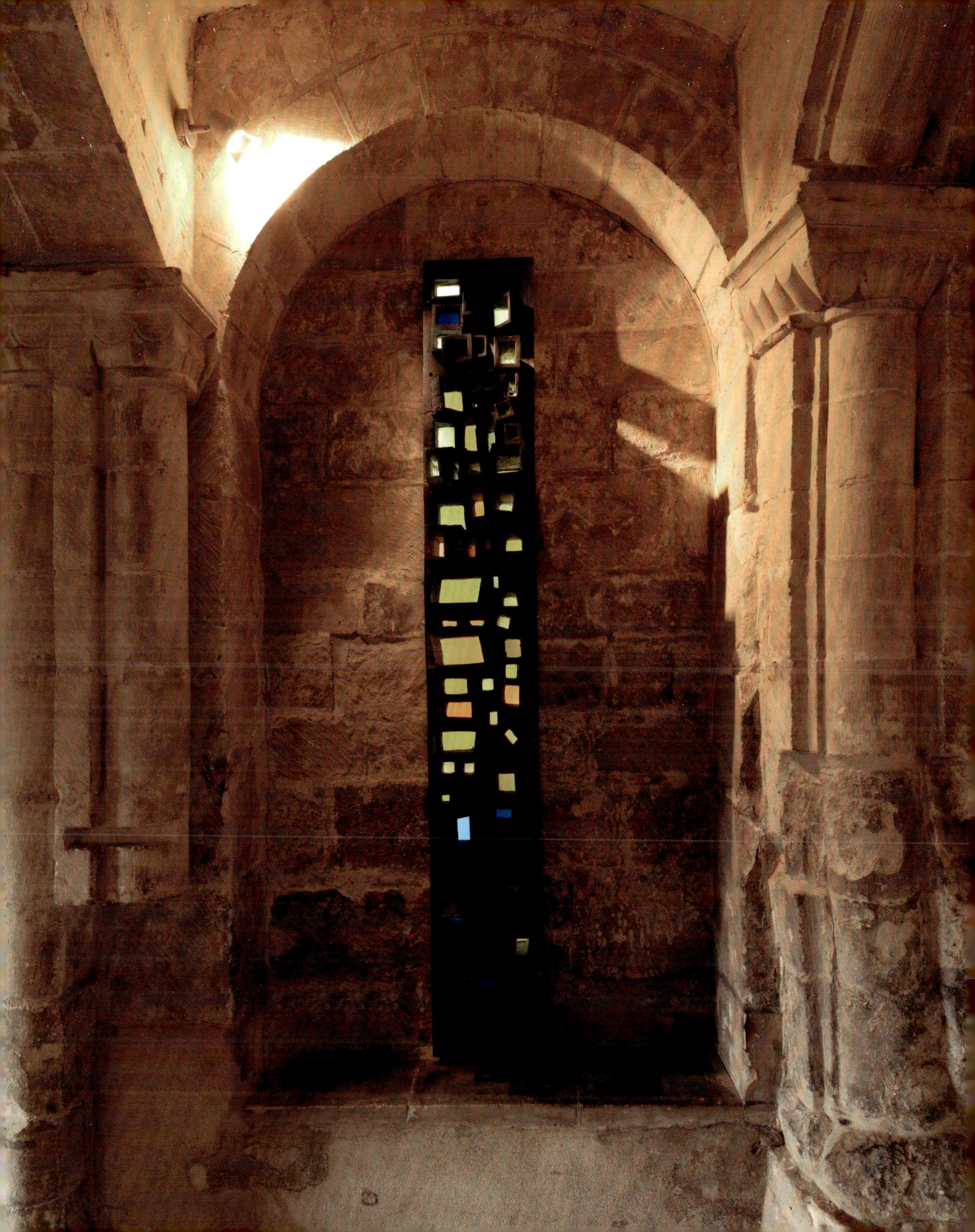

MICHAEL COOPER FRBS b.1944

Cooper's sensuous animal and human forms are carved in marble or stone before being cast into bronze. His empathy for his subjects allows his chisel to reveal not only the inner calm and beauty of the stone but also the essence of the animal itself. Cooper's sculptures are dignified, self-assured, independent and respectful. They have a deep and quiet energy perhaps imparted by the long hours of 'chipping' which bring them forth from the stone.

His work brings the third dimension vividly to life through the irresistible urge to feel and caress surface and form and this abstract, almost musical pleasure is essential to the appreciation of his sculptures.

Snail
Michael Cooper
Bronze
Edition of 6
92cm high

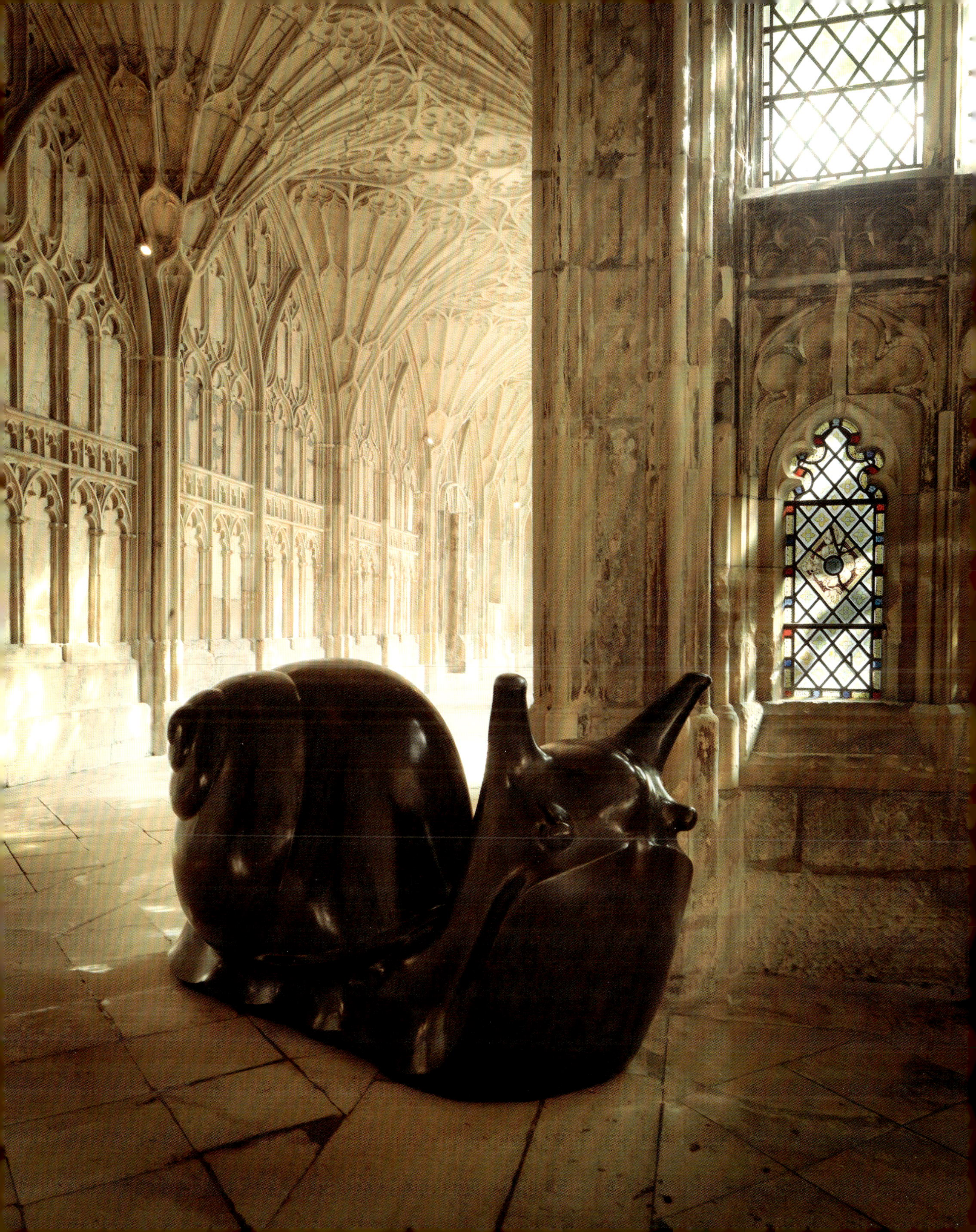

Tortoise

Michael Cooper

Bronze

Edition of 6

80cm high

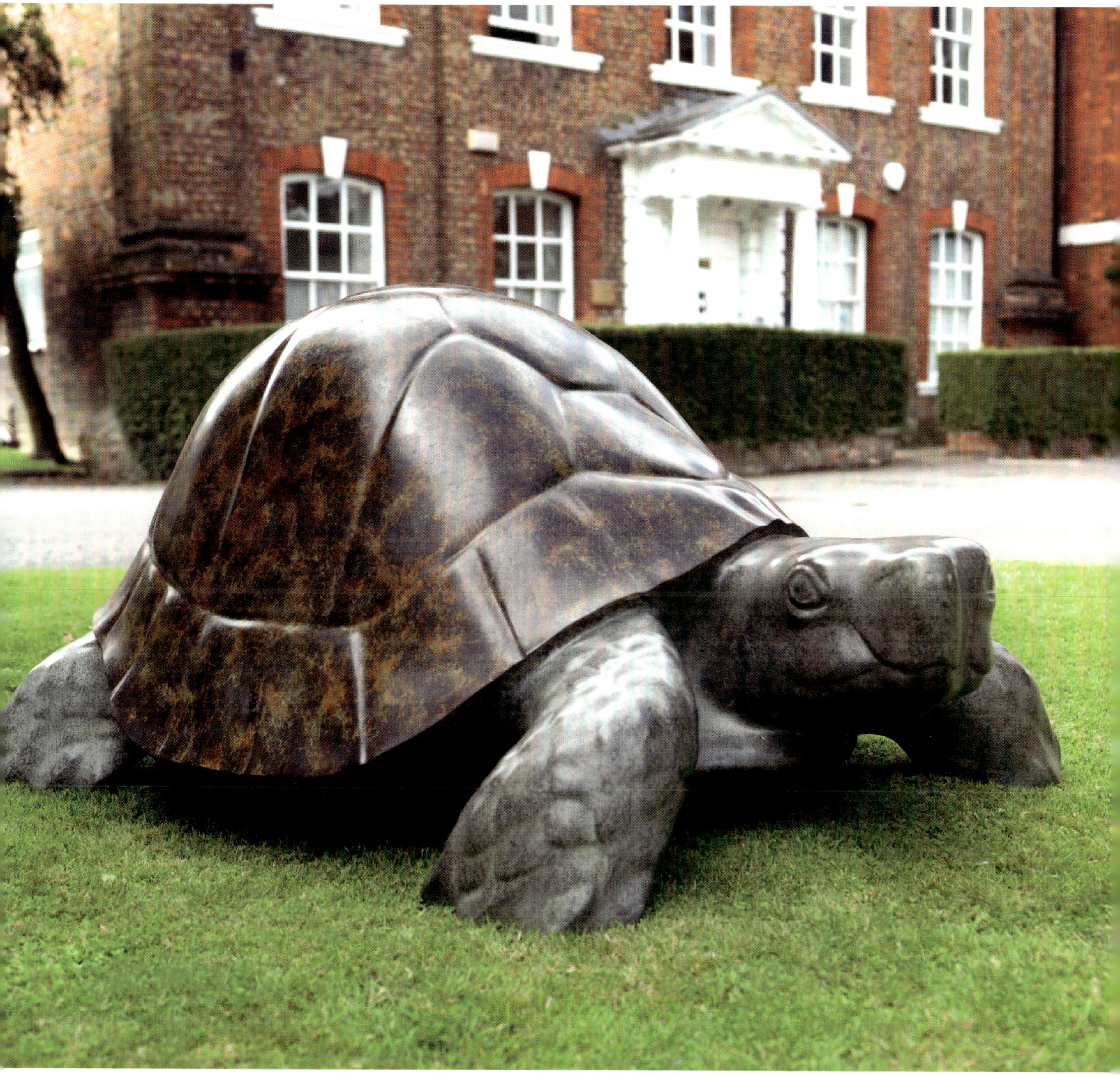

TERENCE COVENTRY b.1938

Coventry has walked his stretch of the Cornish coastal path for the last fifty years, closely observing the jackdaws, ravens, gannets and other avian residents of the remote headland. The faceted sculptural form of Monumental Gannet Head, reduced to a series of geometric planes, dynamically expresses the power and elegance of this magnificent bird.

'I spend a lot of time walking the dogs and we live in a beautiful place here, right on the edge of the cliffs. When I'm walking I'll often stumble over something because I'm looking at the birds and taking in the things that you see naturally but observing them more precisely.'

Monumental Gannet Head
Terence Coventry
Bronze
Edition of 5
205cm high

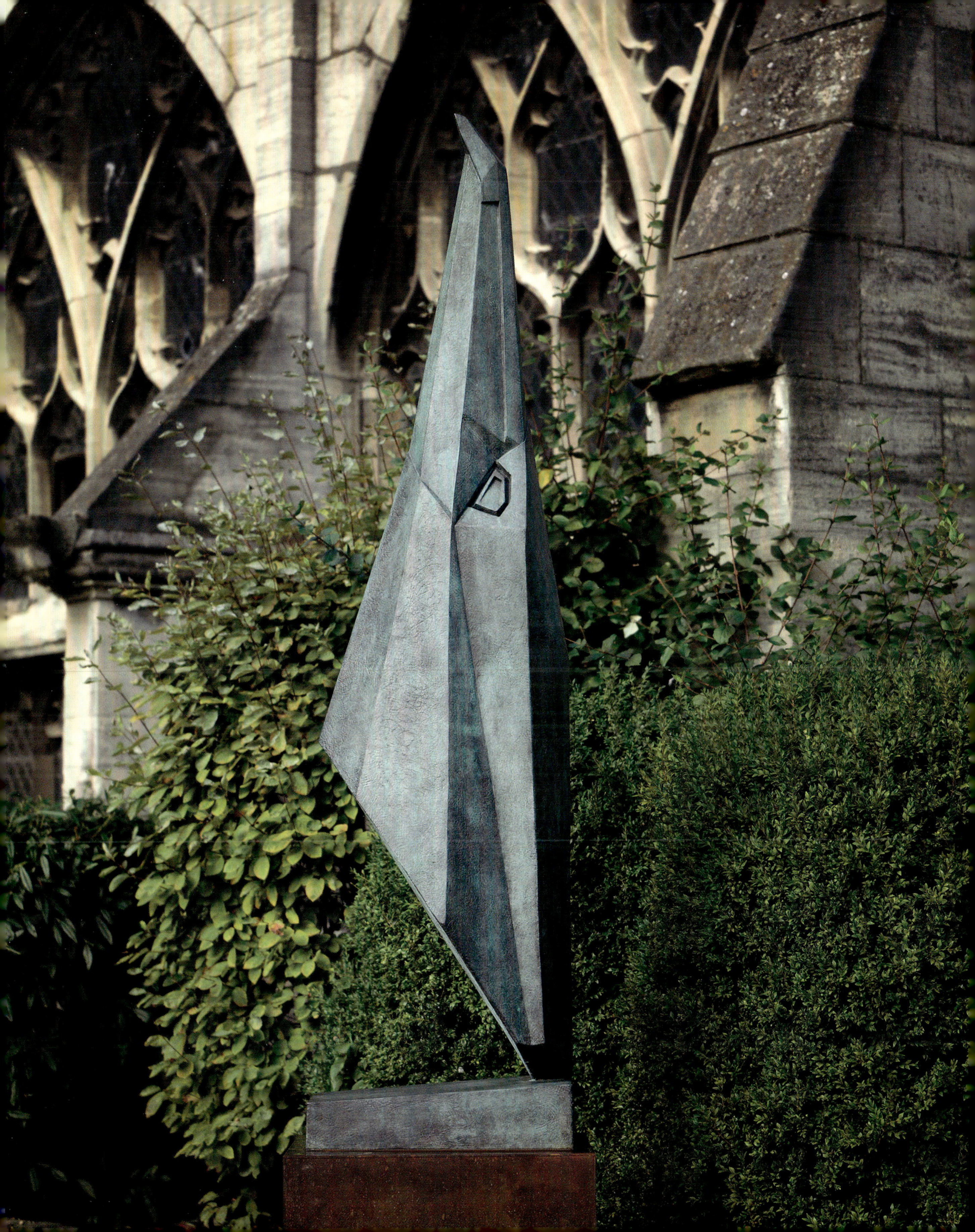

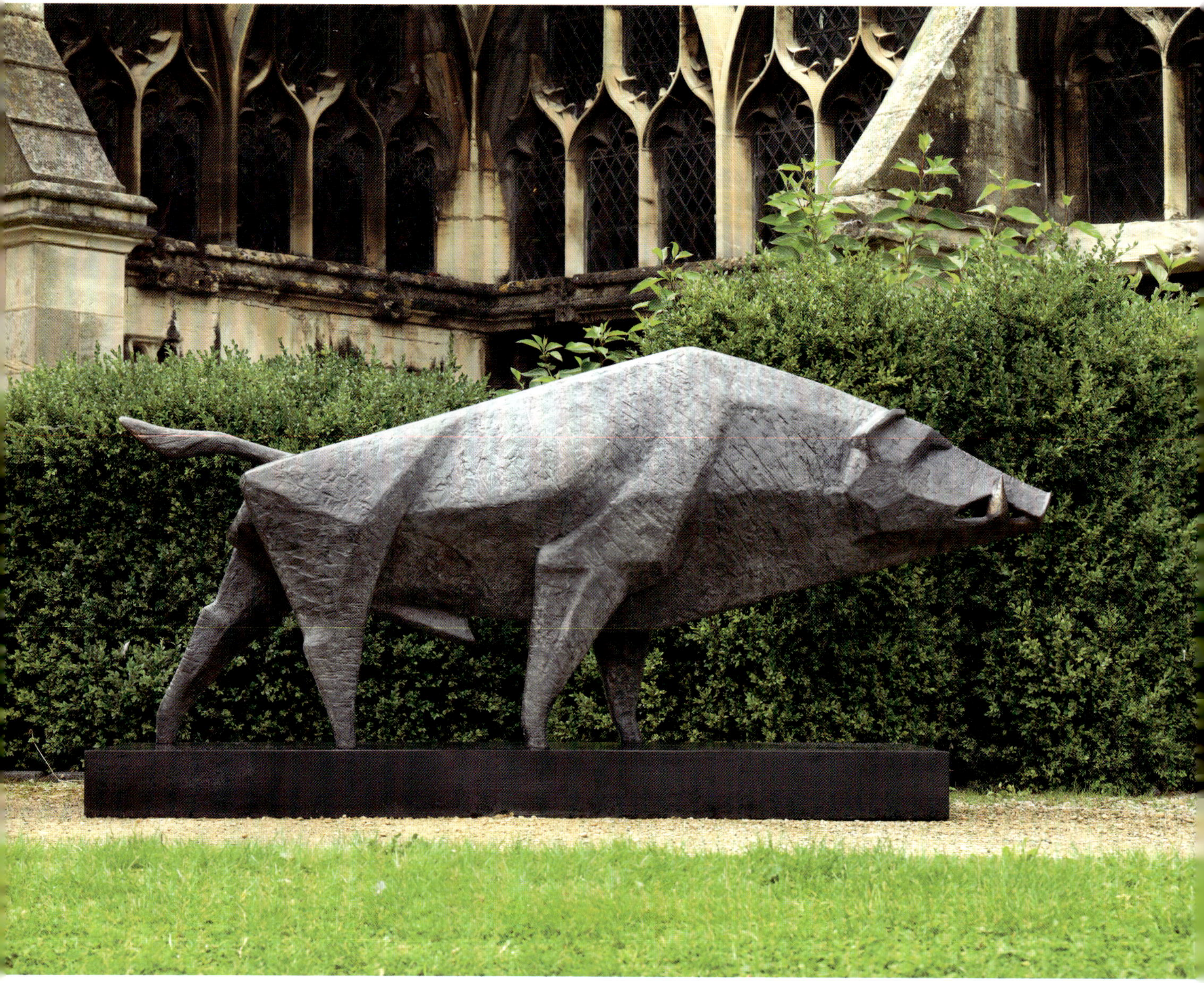

Boar II

Terence Coventry

Bronze

Edition of 5

100cm high

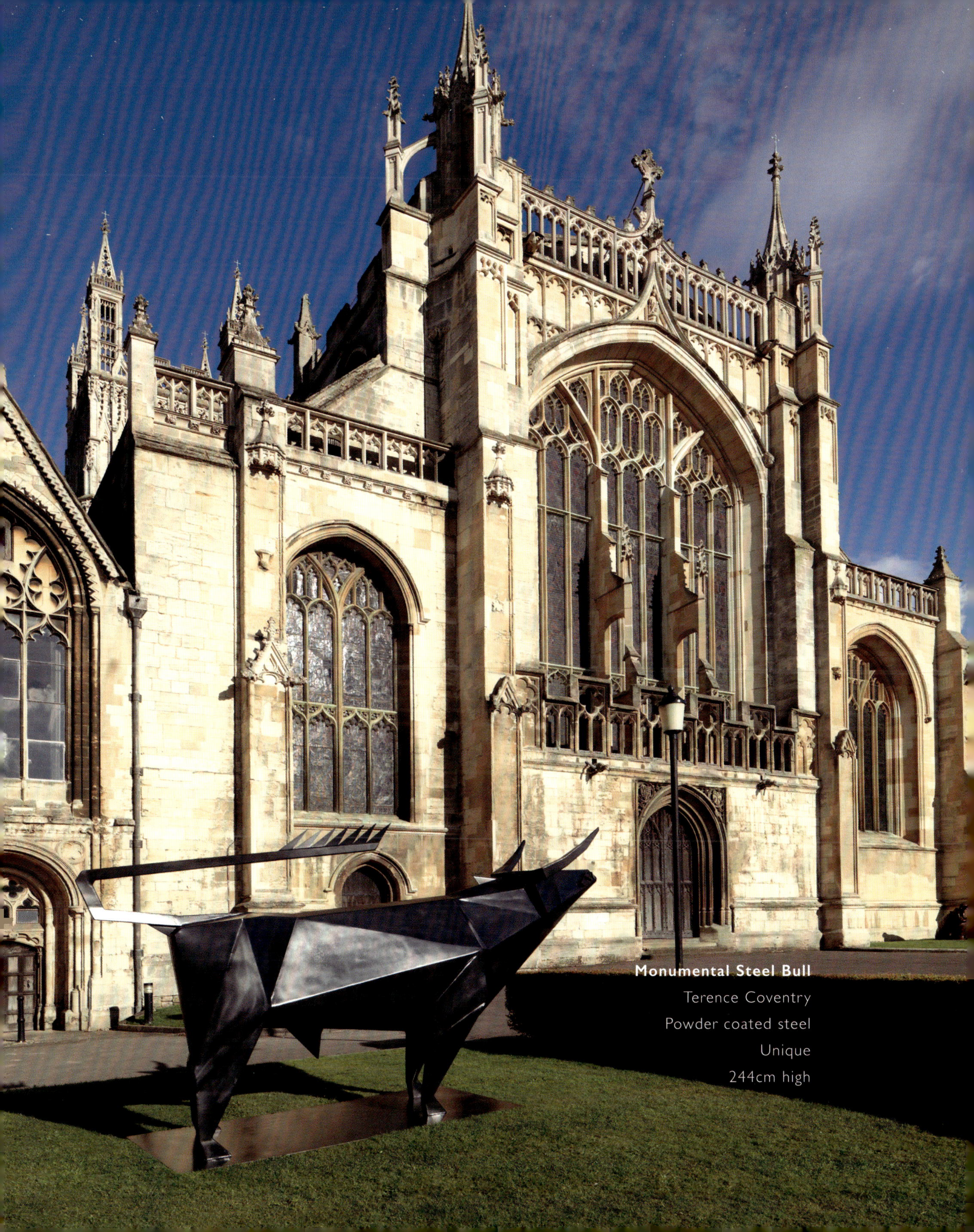

Monumental Steel Bull
Terence Coventry
Powder coated steel
Unique
244cm high

Lying Hound

Terence Coventry

Bronze

Edition of 7

52cm high

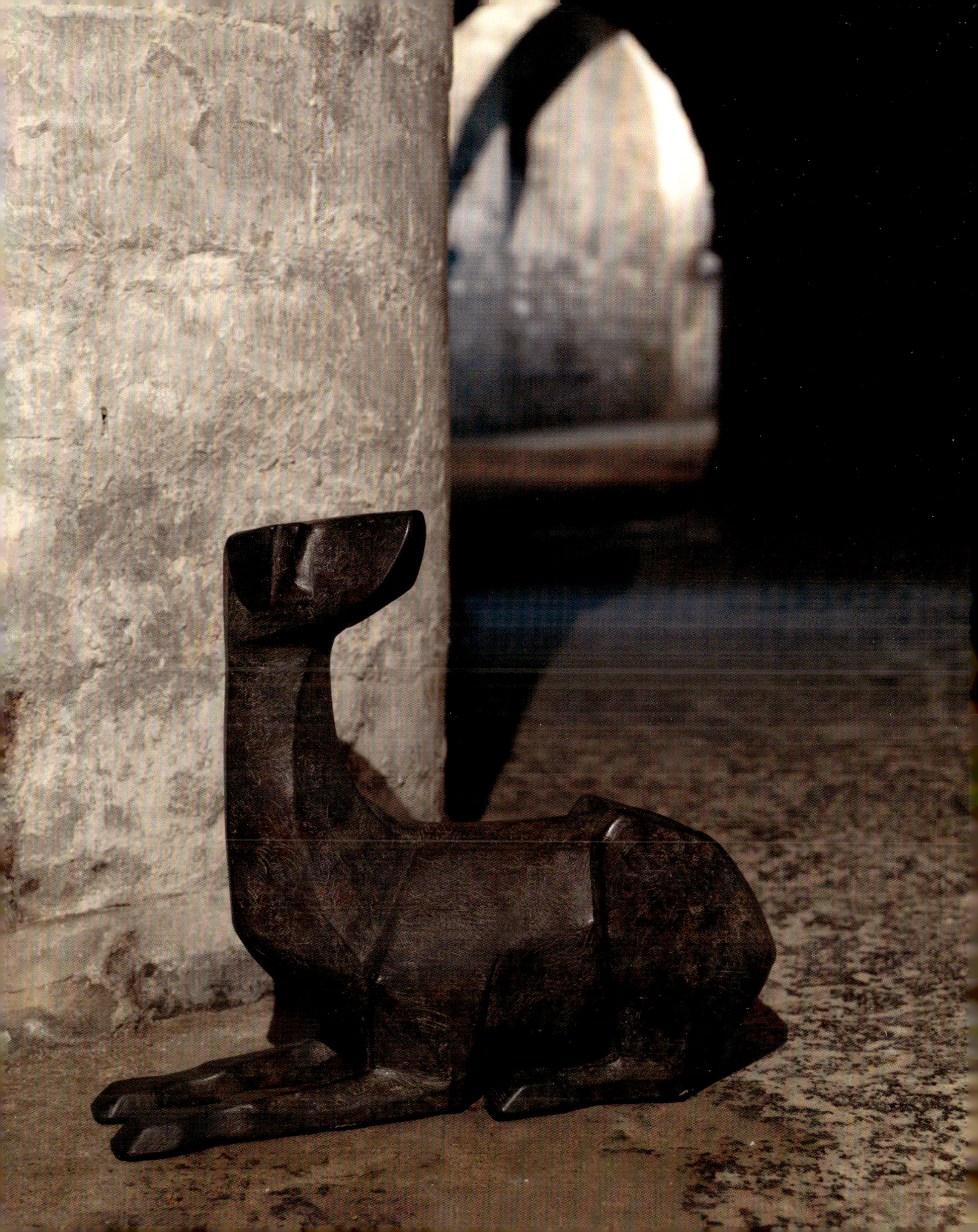

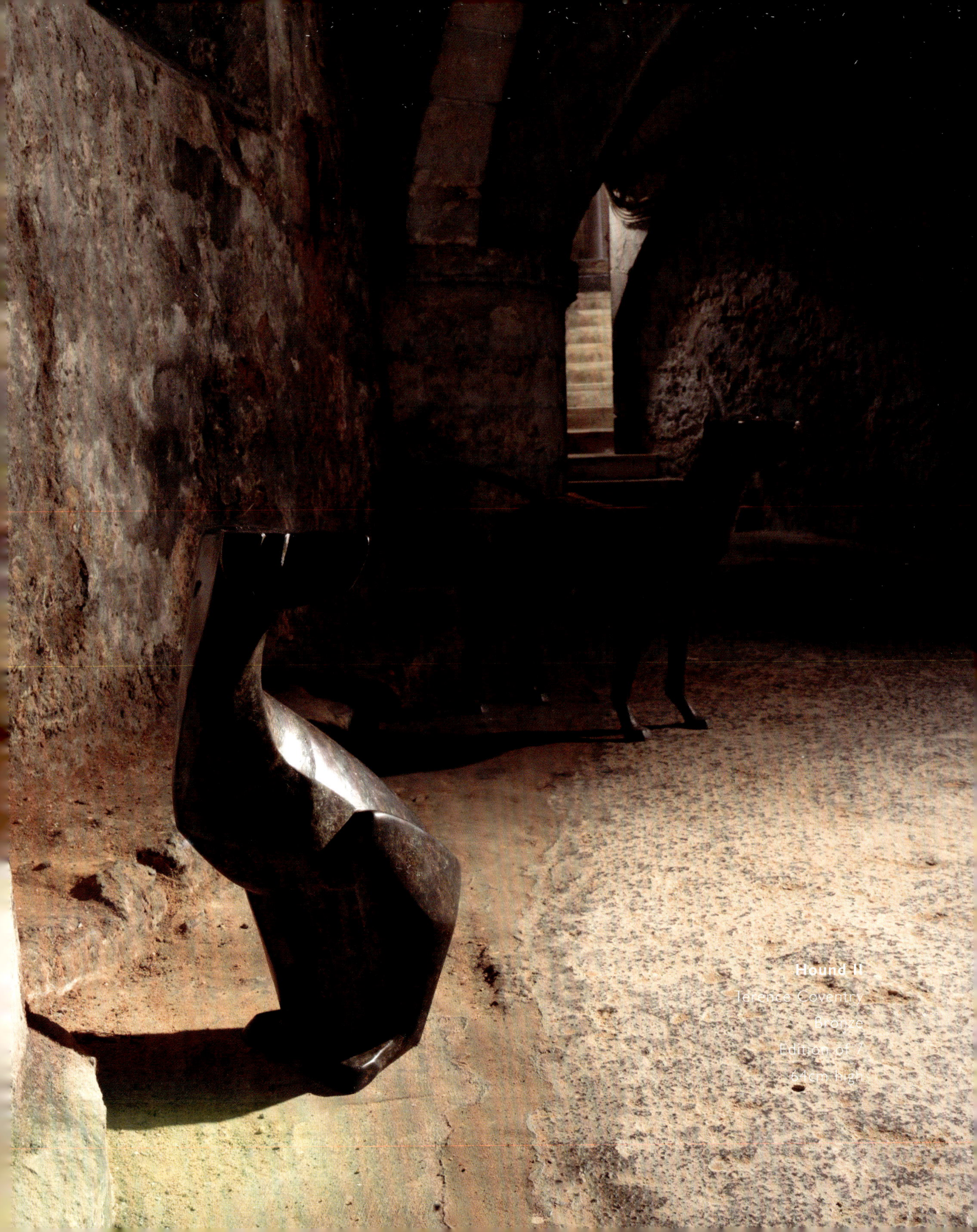

Hound II
Terence Coventry
Bronze
Edition of 7
64cm high

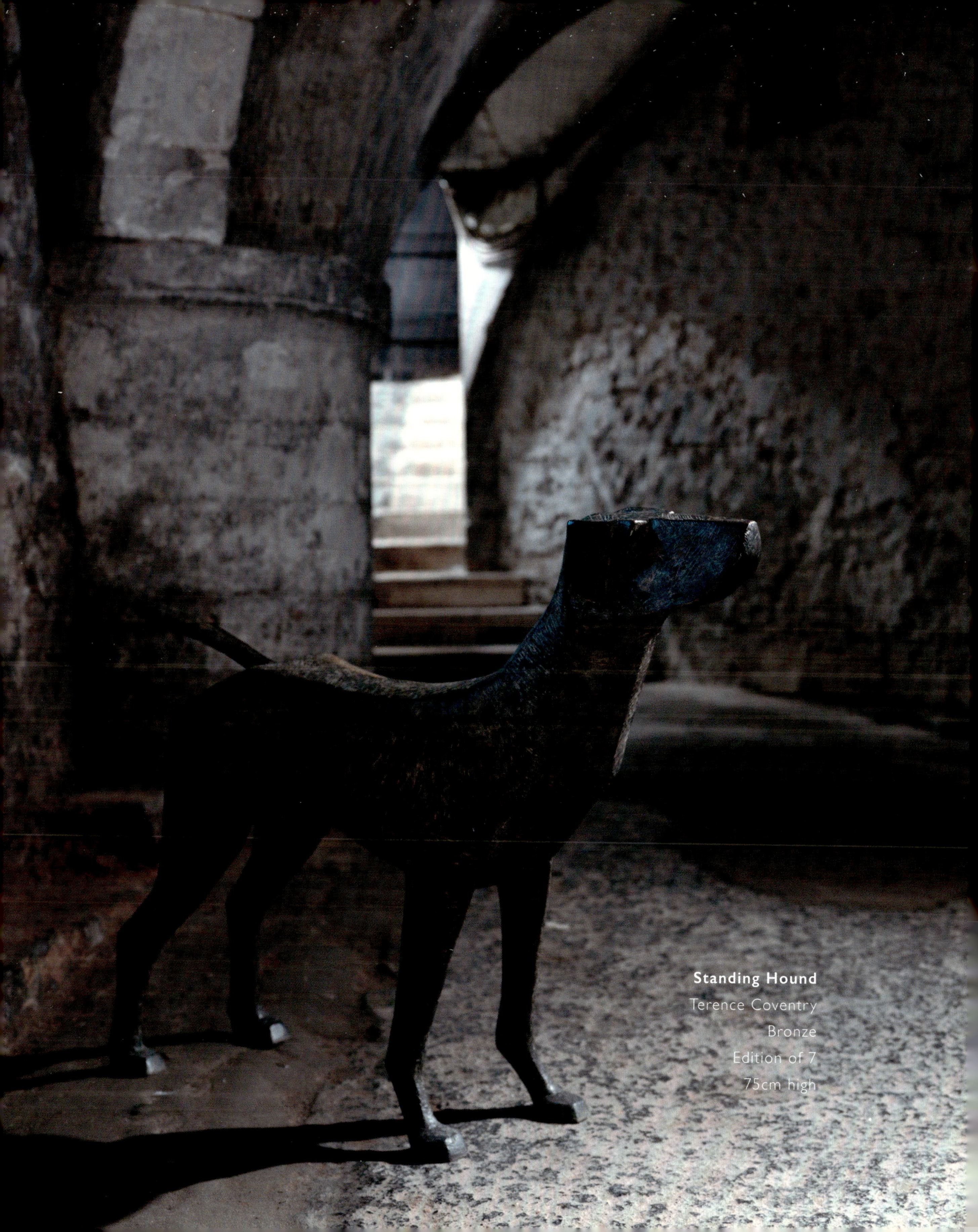

Standing Hound
Terence Coventry
Bronze
Edition of 7
75cm high

STEVE DILWORTH b.1949

'The whalebone box is heavy, and no wonder, as it is lined with a lead box and inside this I sealed water, seawater taken during a storm. A reliquary originally intended for a quiet place but borrowed by Iain Sinclair to give an imagined pilgrimage purpose, though it has since waited patiently on his mantlepiece in Hackney, growing heavier as Sinclair grows older. Now enjoying a short break in Gloucester, an essence of storm in a quieter place.'

Whalebone Casket
Steve Dilworth
Whalebone, lead and storm water
Unique
18cm high

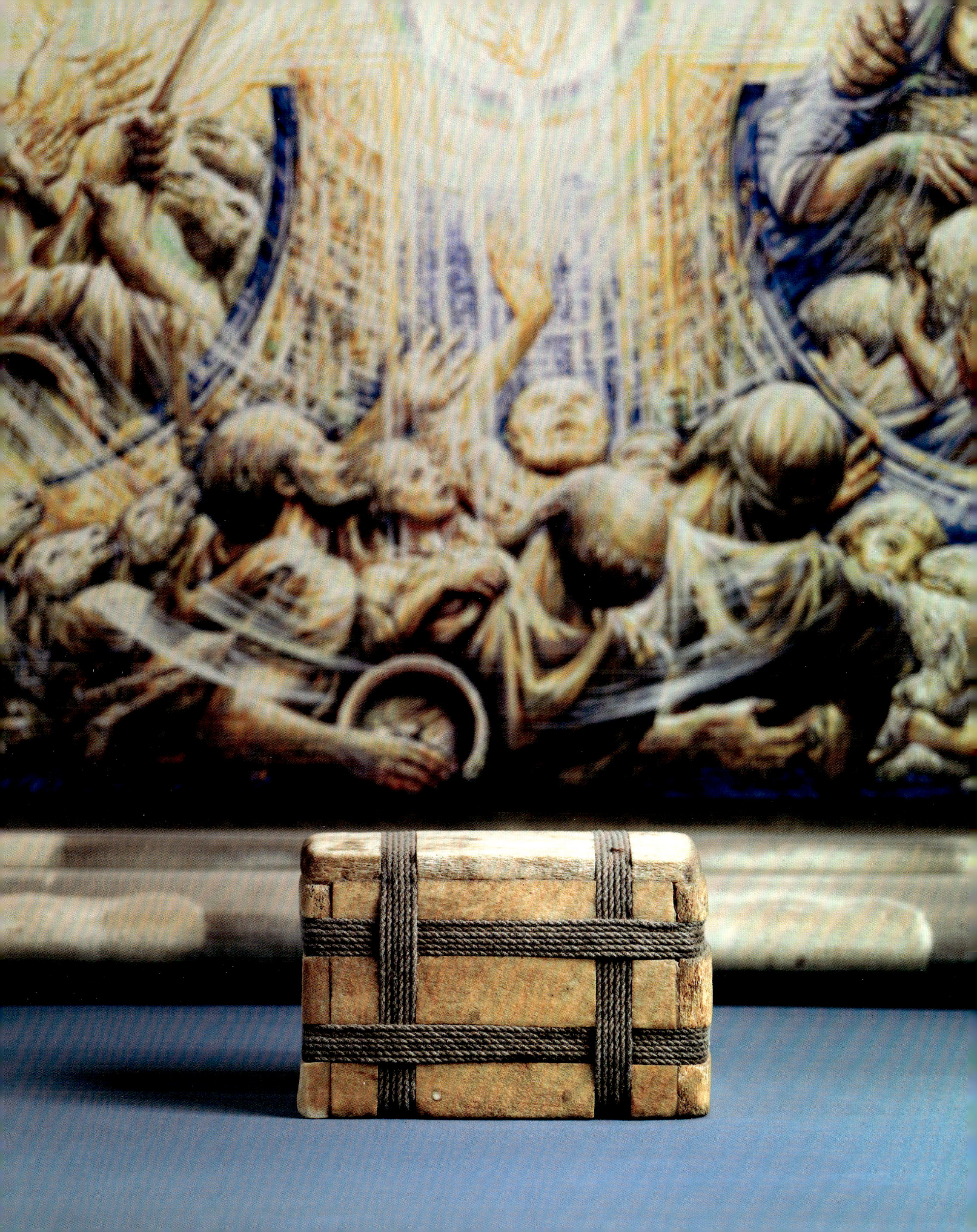

Owl

Steve Dilworth

Oak, horn and enclosed Owl

Unique

17.5cm high

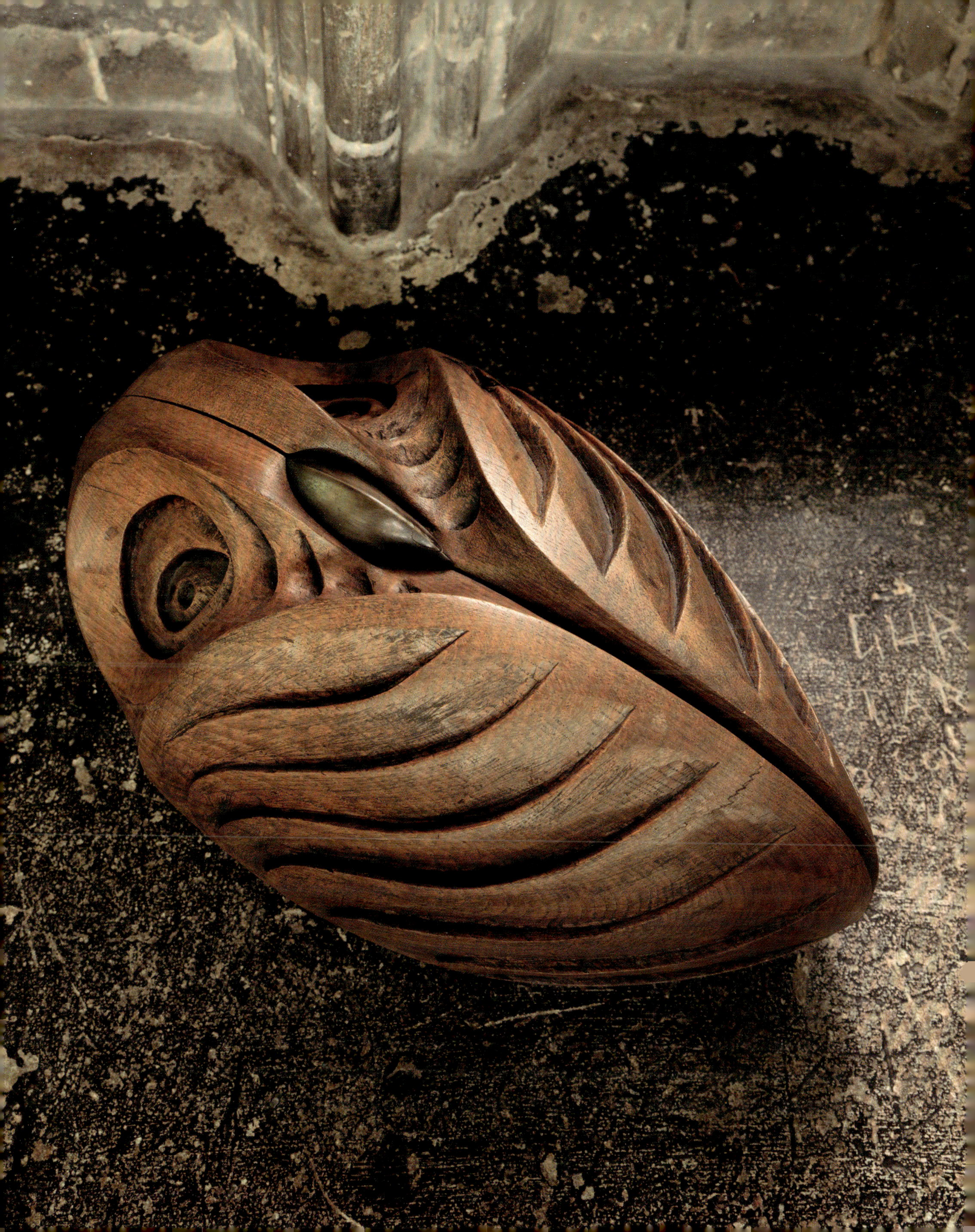

ANGUS FAIRHURST 1966-2008

Untouched is one of three sculptures of ponds made in the mid-2000s. The mottled black banks and sparse rushes were originally modelled in clay and then cast in bronze. As with all of his works in bronze, Fairhurst worked on wax moulds in the foundry before they were finally cast. These works are among many in which he 'recreated' nature in the inescapably artificial confines of a gallery (in 2004 at Tate Britain's 'In-A-Gadda-Da-Vida' exhibition, the ponds appeared alongside wallpaper depictions of trees). They reflect Fairhurst's deep-running love of nature at the same time as they wryly imply the impossibility of freezing it in perpetuity.

Implying pristineness and seclusion in its title, the work invokes romantic ideals of nature while casting viewers in the role of Narcissus. Another work made in the same period, The Birth of Consistency (2004), showed a gorilla – one of the recurring motifs of Fairhurst's work – contemplating itself in a similar mirrored pool and wrenching the reflective surface towards itself. The concept of 'undoing' pervaded Fairhurst's practice – absence was an ever-present motif.

Untouched

Angus Fairhurst

Bronze and stainless steel

Edition of 3

70cm high

Copyright: The Estate of Angus Fairhurst, courtesy Sadie Coles HQ, London

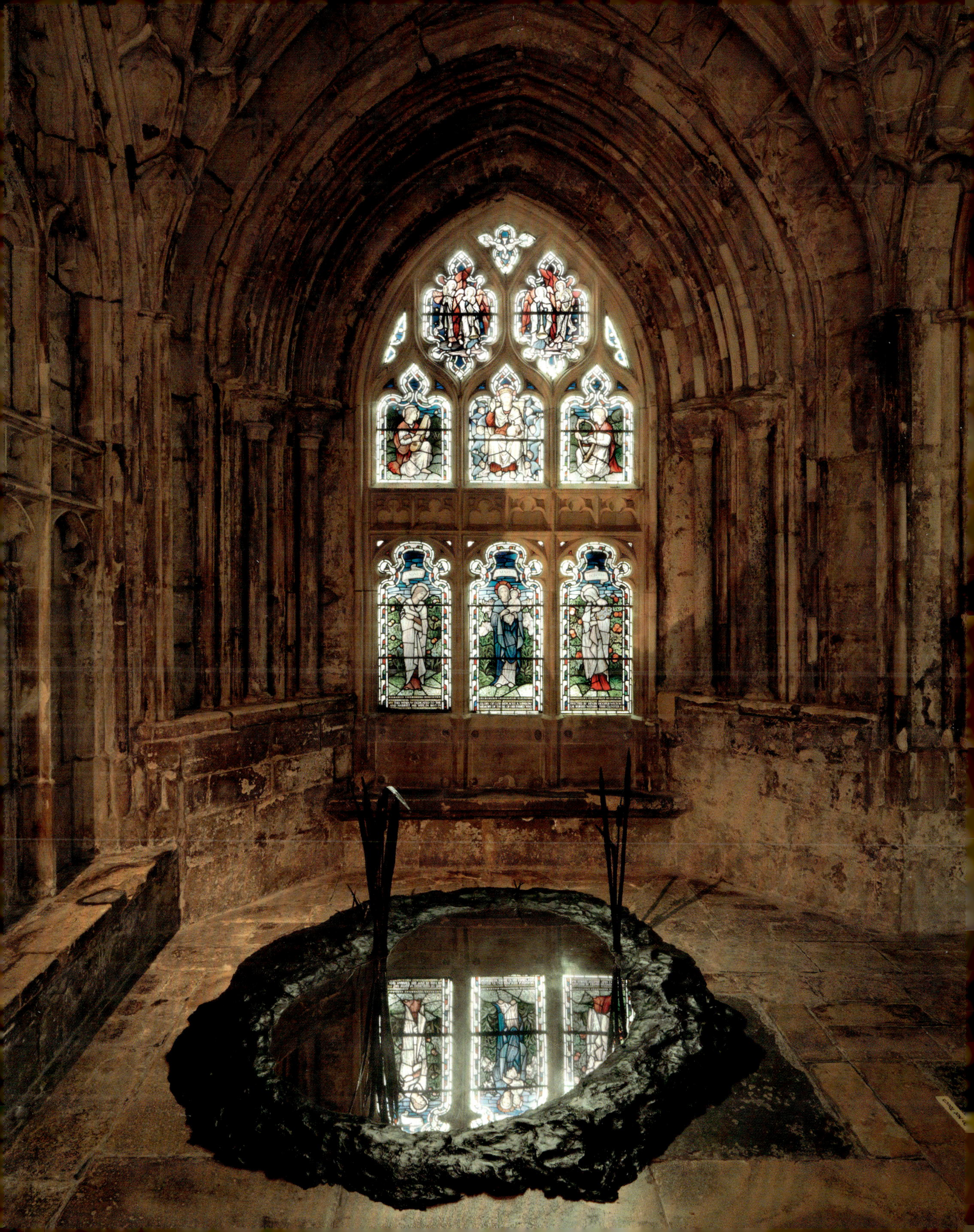

ABIGAIL FALLIS b.1968

Fallis has always been concerned with transforming surfaces and the process of making. She experiments with diverse materials including papier mâché, fish skeletons, neon and bronze. Fundamentally interested in topical issues that affect our daily lives, her work is characterised by a quirky sense of humour, coupled with powerful messages on the environment and our consumerism-led society.

'Dodo - Death of the Author refers to Lewis Carroll's 'Alice in Wonderland' where the Dodo was intended as a caricature of Carroll himself – his stammer is said to have led him to pronounce his name "Dodo-Dodgson". Tenniel, the illustrator, decided to draw hands onto the Dodo so that he could take a sweet from Alice.'

Dodo – Death of the Author
Abigail Fallis
Steel and papier mâché
Series of 3
79cm high

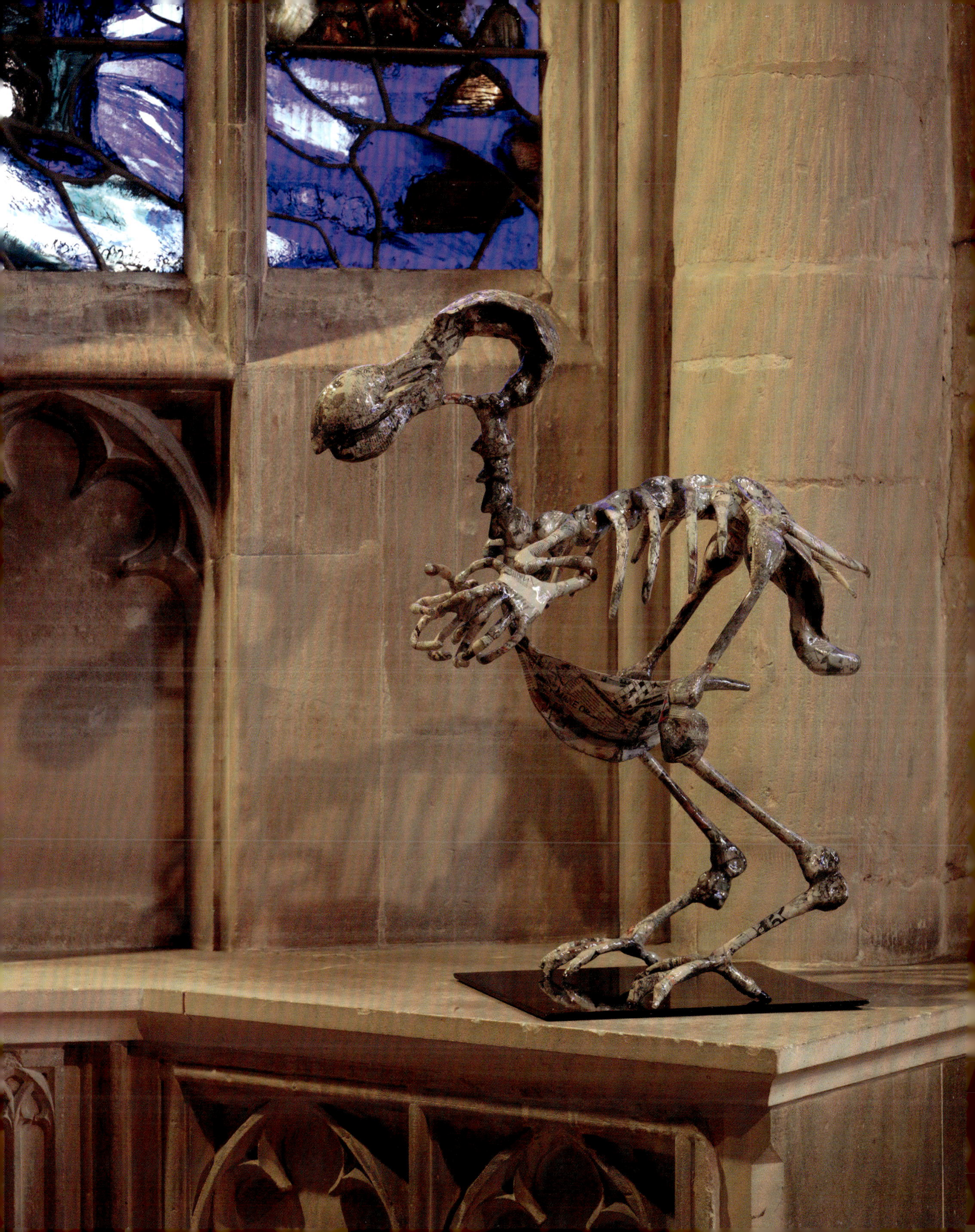

SUE FREEBOROUGH b.1941

'Through the Mitochondrial DNA of women in East Africa, scientists in the 80's discovered that Africa was the seat of all humanity. This mDNA is only passed down to the next generation by the mother and so a line can be traced from people of today, through their mDNA, to a single woman who lived about 150,000 years ago in East Africa, and named by the scientists as Mitochondrial Eve. Mitochondria exist in every cell of the body as a vital energy source and are in all living things. My sculpture is a totem object symbolising the unity of human evolution through the female body and acknowledges our kinship with all living creatures.'

Mitochondrial Eve
Sue Freeborough
Bronze
Edition of 5
166cm high

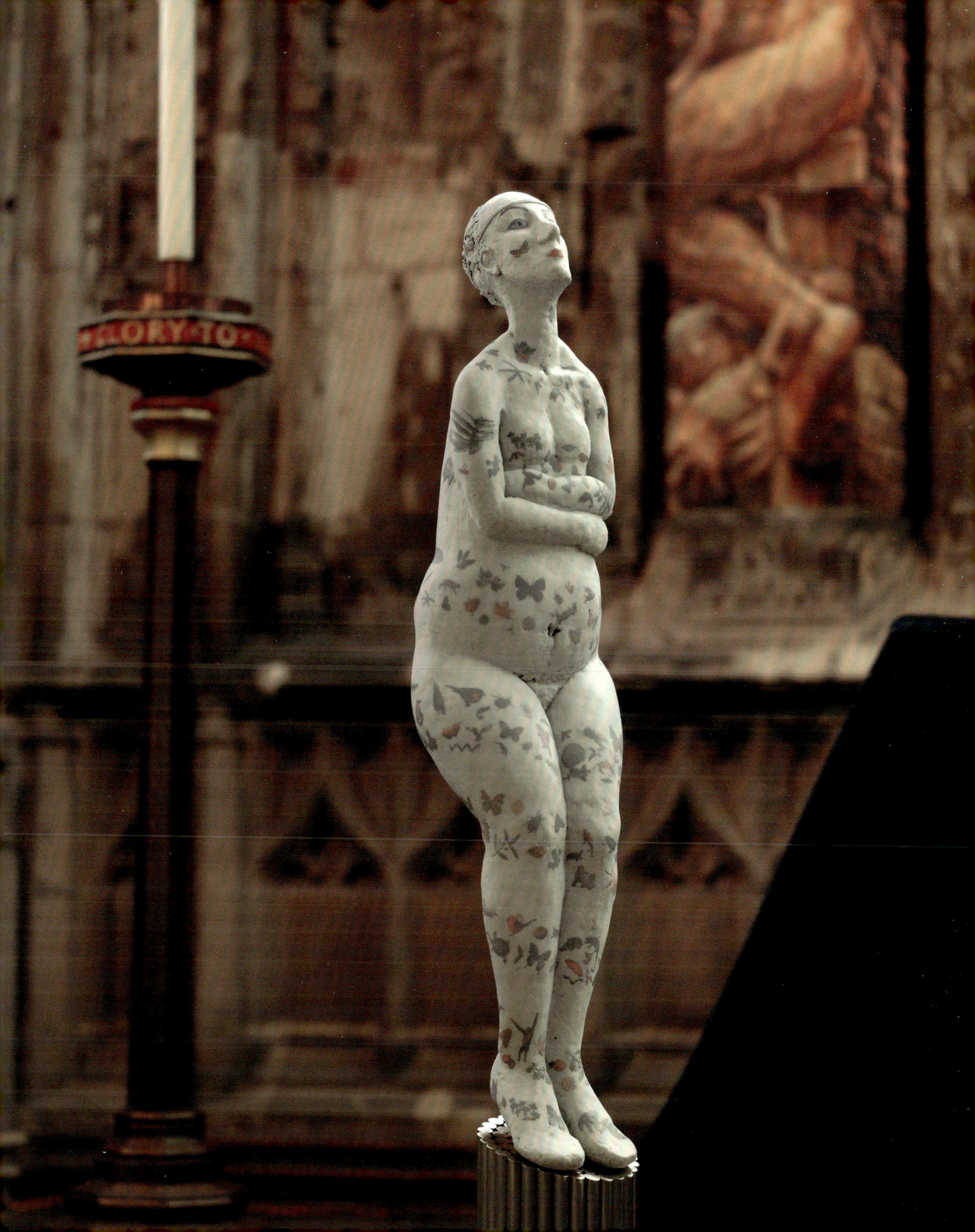
GLORY TO

Let there be Spaces in your Togetherness

Sue Freeborough

Bronze

Edition of 5

119cm high

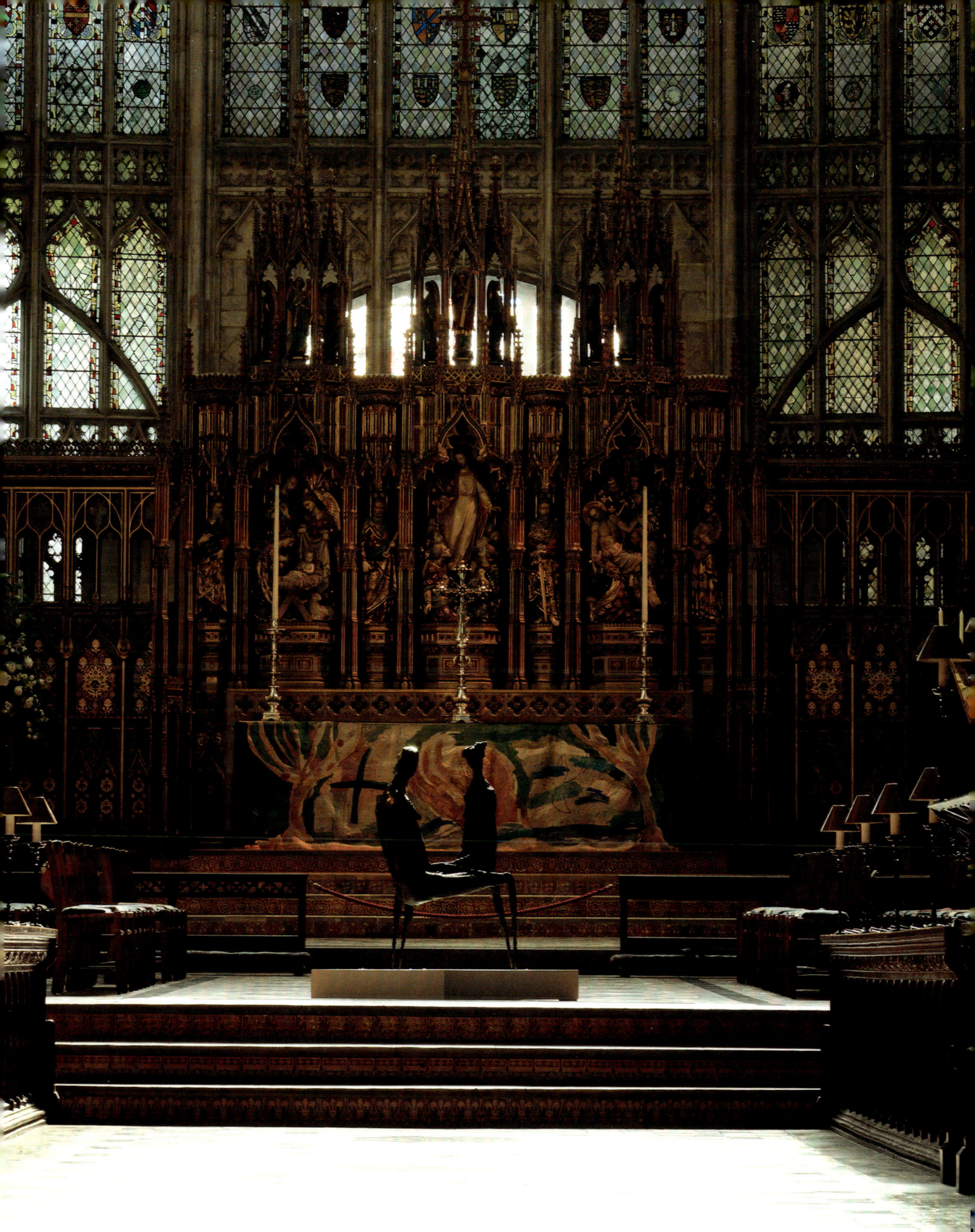

ANTONY GORMLEY RA b.1950

'POSE, like the other five expansion works shown in the exhibition MODEL at White Cube Bermondsey, London in 2012, translates the darkness of the body into substance.

I started to make works that translate body volume into expanded rectangular masses in 2011. The centroids remain in the same relationship but the volumes expand and fuse.

They are an attempt to explore the body as a place rather than as an object using the formal language of the built environment. Hovering in an intermediate zone between anatomy and geometry, they attempt to reconcile the internal experience of the body with the containing condition of architecture.

If POSE were shown vertically, it would assume the languid classical pose of a Venus. Horizontally, the work's dramatic cantilever comes into dialogue with funerary sculpture but resists the inevitable pull of the earth on the body.'

POSE, 2012

Antony Gormley

Cast iron

68.3 x 213.2 x 55.4

© the Artist
courtesy White Cube

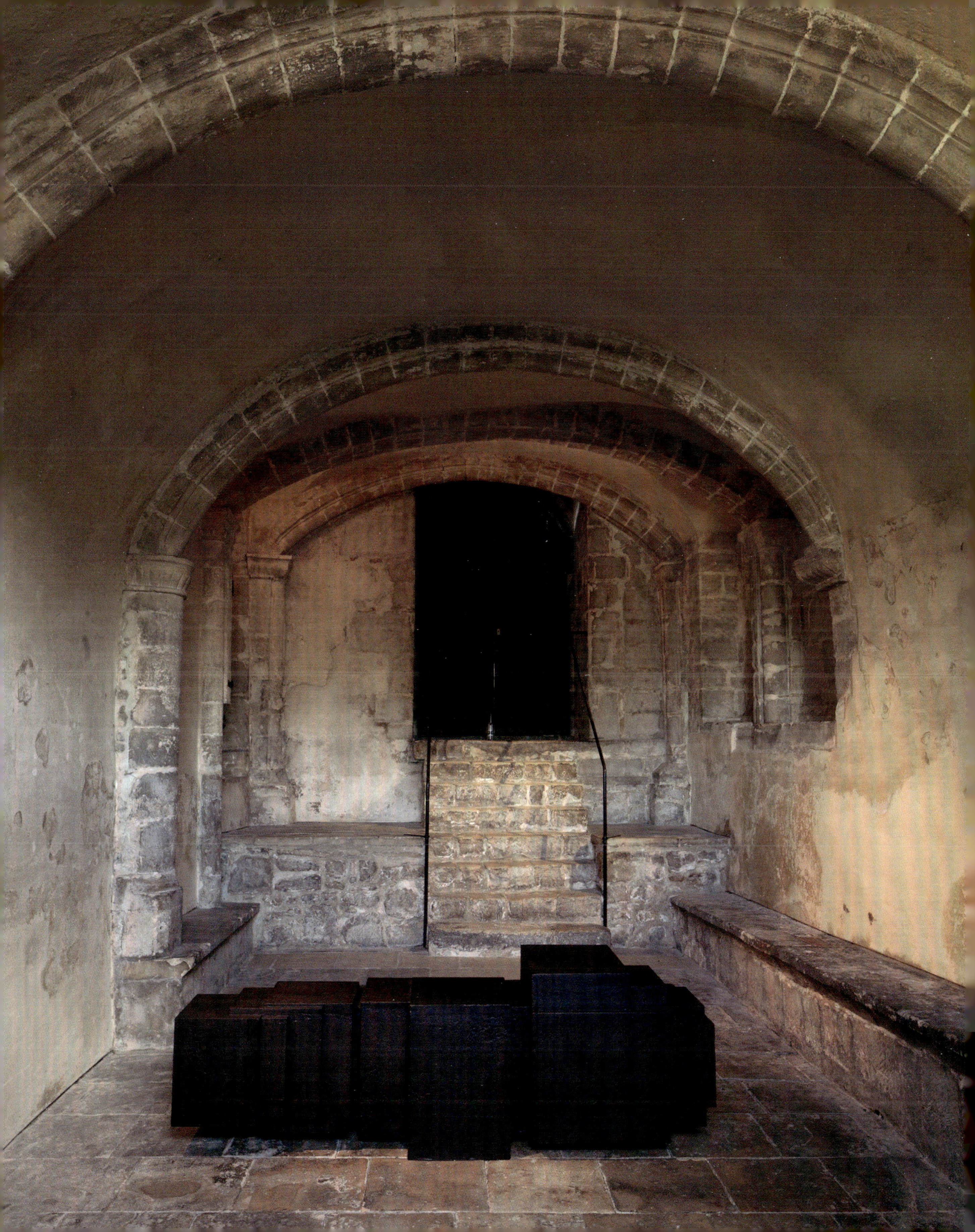

STEVEN GREGORY b.1952

'I am using the familiar shape of a wreath, symbolic of death, a wheel of cast bronze human skulls, vertebrae, rib cages, femurs, tibias and other skeletal elements. They represent the transitory nature of the human condition and suggest the wheel of life as time ticks remorselessly by, evoking ceaseless movement, the unstoppable passage of time which death alone can symbolize.

Rather like an artefact excavated from an archaeological dig, changed by the passage of time, I wanted to create a decayed and aged appearance, so the sculpture is un-waxed in order for nature to actively do its bit to gently alter and develop the patina.'

Tick Tock
Steven Gregory
Bronze
Unique
140cm high

© Steven Gregory, administered by DACS 2014

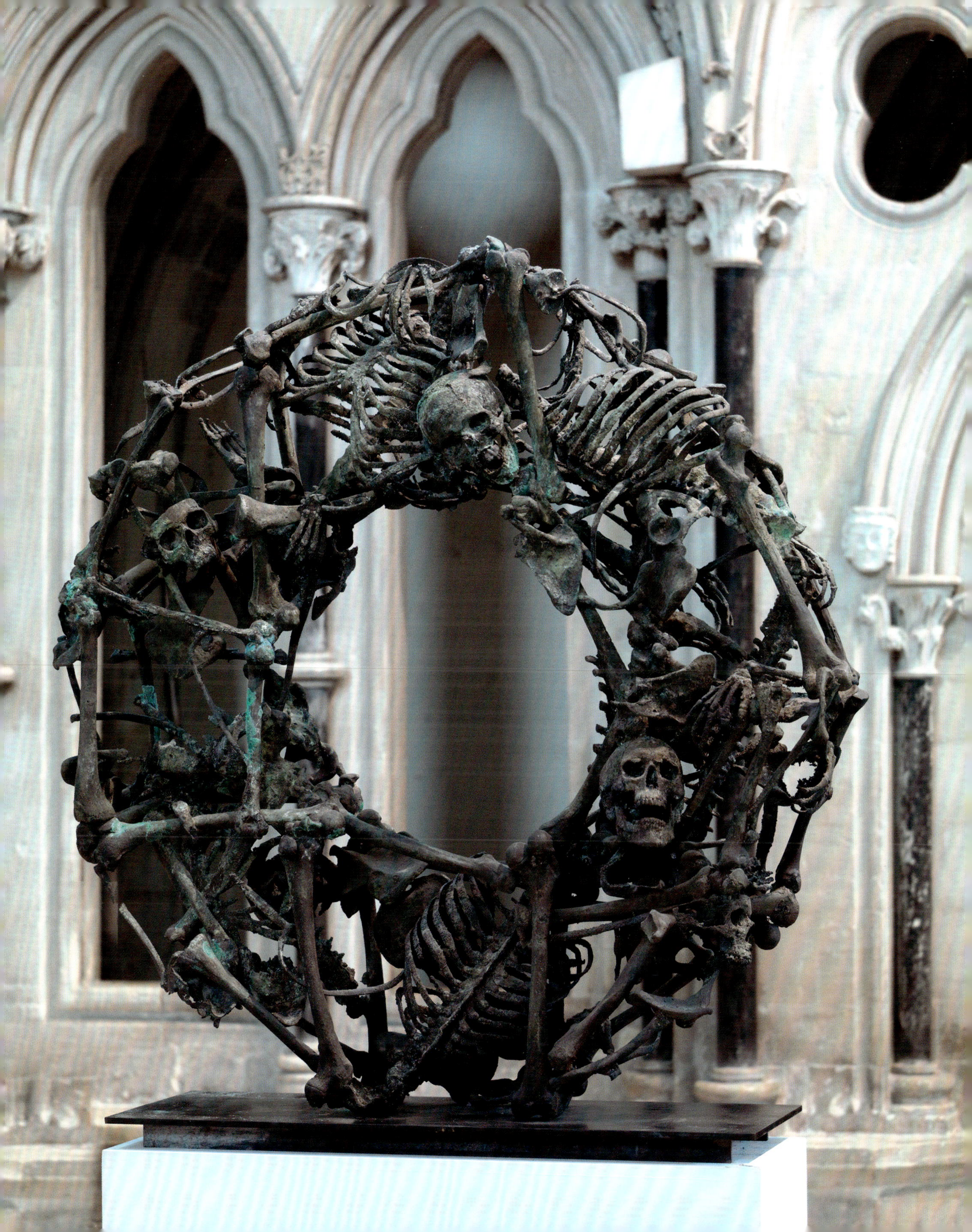

NIGEL HALL RA b.1943

'Time spent in the South of France has resulted in many drawings of the plants of the region, in particular the parasol pines. Despite my work being resolutely non-figurative, throughout my life I have made studies of the natural & man-made world around me. These are made from a simple enjoyment of the forms I come across but are not at the forefront of my mind when engaged in my studio activities. They must, however be making their presence felt at some subconscious level, for the sculptures that make up the Southern Shade series share with the drawings an involvement with interwoven linear elements, some free in space and others entangled in a shadow interior which echoes the shaded canopy of the trees and their complex latticework of branches.

The various elements that comprise the works are expressed as potentially separate parts implying the possibility of shifting & changing.

As with all my sculpture, I attempt to make the works light on their feet, countering the drag of gravity with a visual uplift, just as nature strives to do.'

Southern Shade I
Nigel Hall
MDF
Unique
235cm high

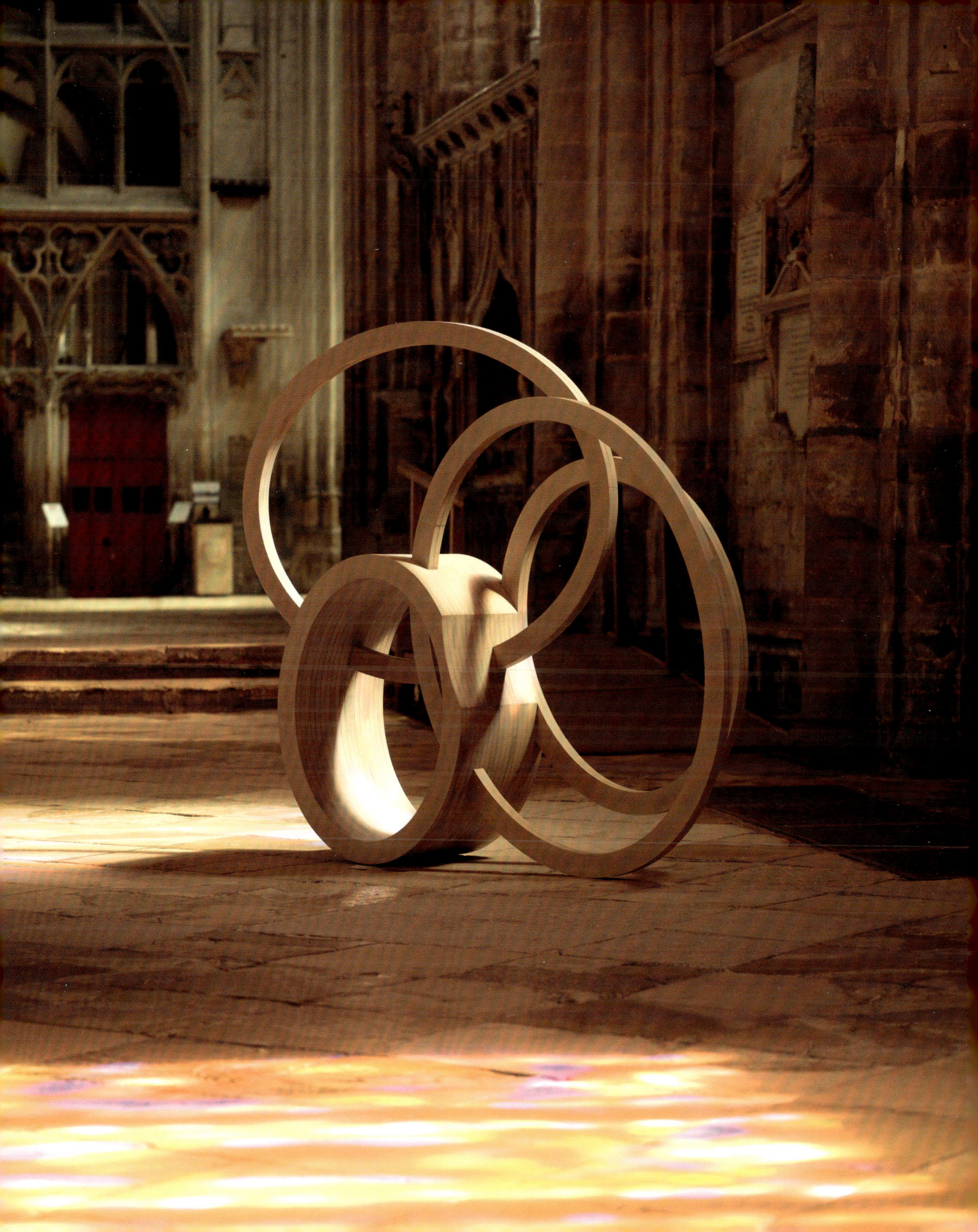

Southern Shade III
Nigel Hall
MDF
Unique
166.5cm high

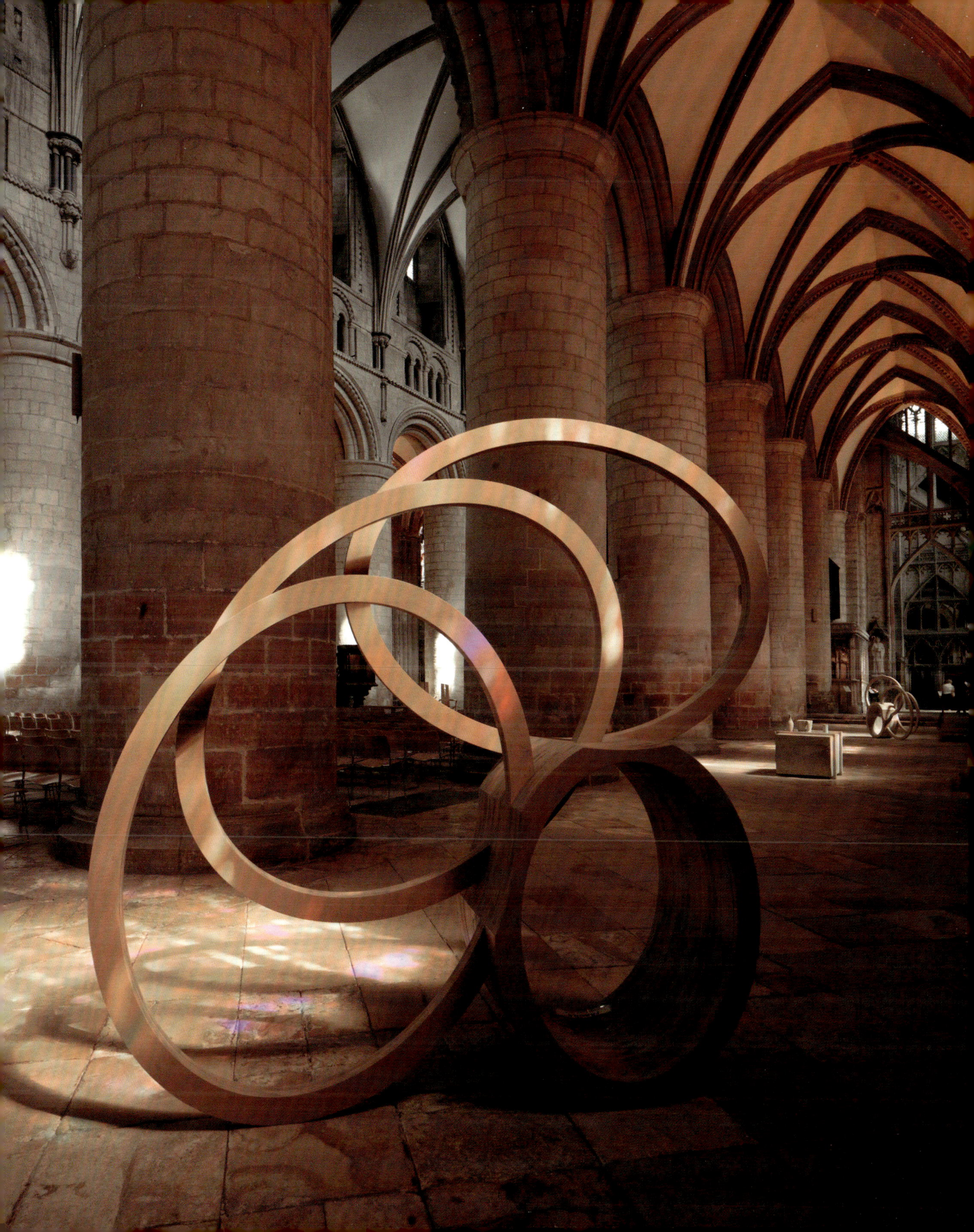

MARCUS HARVEY b.1963

'I have made about 20 or so paintings and sculptures of footballs and I'm not quite sure why. I never especially liked playing football as a kid. I preferred rugby.

I like Alan Clarke's defence of football hooliganism as relating to the behaviour of young men who, should the need arise, be the first to fight in battle in defence of their country. A testing ground if you like. So I take football as a cultural phenomenon more seriously.

Football runs deep. This sculpture is about En-ger-land and the awful rollercoaster of the national game. To have ruled half the world once and to expect to hold the world cup aloft now is something nature refuses to countenance. The poor old deflated leather football of the past holds a great anxiety for the national psyche, to re-flate it is to be too presumptuous by half in a new world order.

I saw Wales versus Germany at Cardiff years ago, more for a day out rather than any real interest in the game. I was actually shocked by the Welsh singing.

Singing not chanting. A powerful plaintive soulfulness bestowed such respect and tenderness for the occasion that I had to distract myself so as not to be seen to be tearful at a football match, and the booming oooohs and aaars, surely they must be those of crowds through the ages, right back to the first organised sporting events of the Greeks and Romans.

This historical arc suggested that the patination of the bronze should recall something archeological, ancient!'

Victoria
Marcus Harvey
Bronze
Edition of 3
104cm high

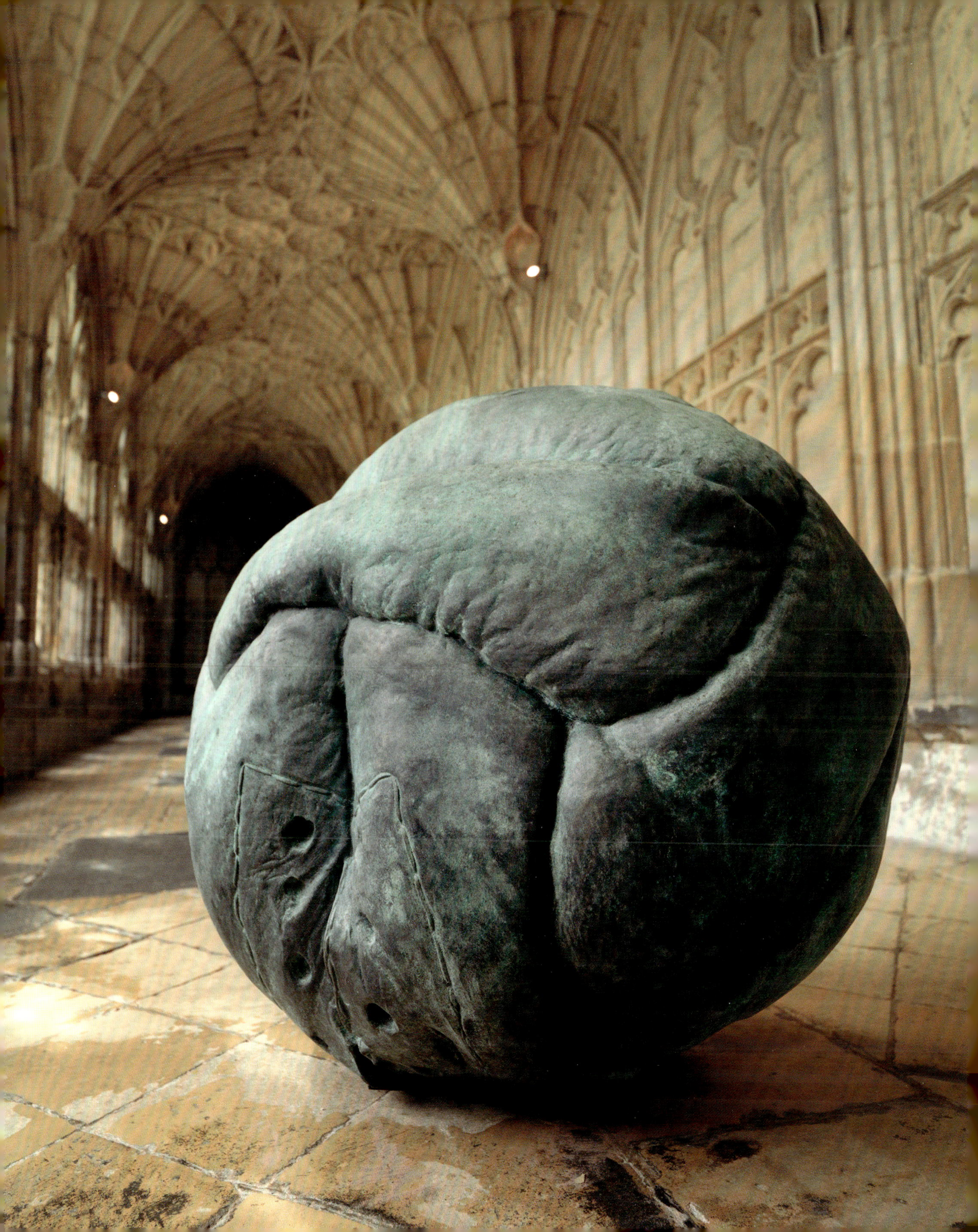

DAMIEN HIRST b.1965

Fallen Angel is taken from Antonio Canova's The Repentant Magdalene (c.1794-96). Whilst the original sculpture's empty palms symbolise Magdalene's sense of spiritual abandonment on the death of Christ, here she is recreated as an angel fallen from grace; a victim of self-harm and drug abuse. As elsewhere in Hirst's work, a point of tension is created between the desperate subject matter and the rich materials utilised.

Throughout his artistic career, Hirst has repeatedly employed religious imagery and motifs. In an interview with Gordon Burn from 2000, Hirst explained: 'I think the science and the art are both lacking in some sort of spirituality. And I think that they're sort of head-butting each other trying to get something like that back. I don't know. I can't quite work it out, but it's something like that. Because there's all these religious references as well. I'm instinctively drawn to these things. If you think art plus the rigour of science equals something spiritual, well, I think it's the other way round... It's an art-science-religion thing that's going on.'

Fallen Angel
2008-2014
Damien Hirst
Gold Plated Silver
Edition of 3
165.6cm high ex. base

© Damien Hirst and Science Ltd. All rights reserved, DACS 2014

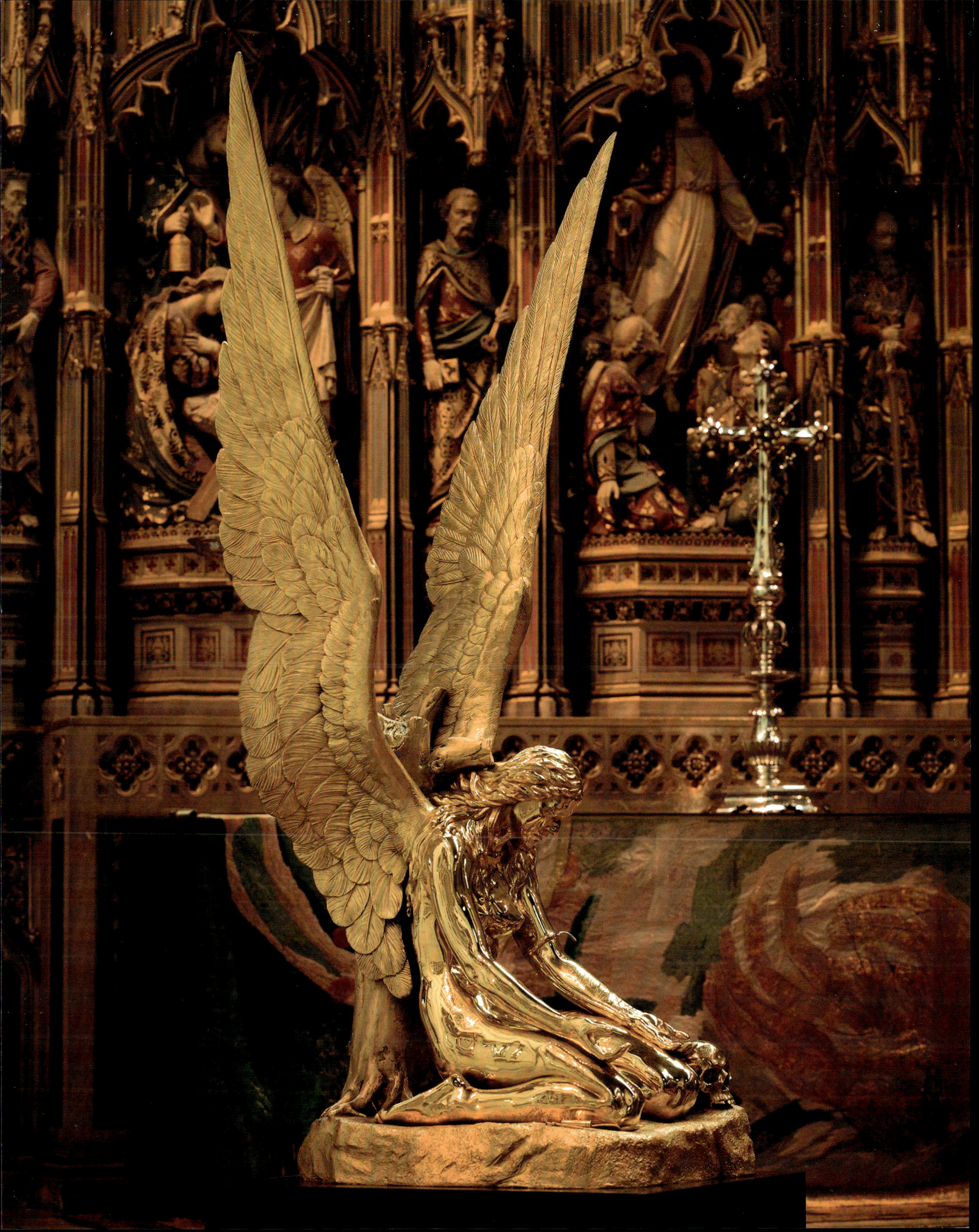

Anatomy of an Angel (Black)

2008

Damien Hirst

Bronze

Edition of 3

185cm high

Private Collection

© Damien Hirst and Science Ltd.
All rights reserved, DACS 2014

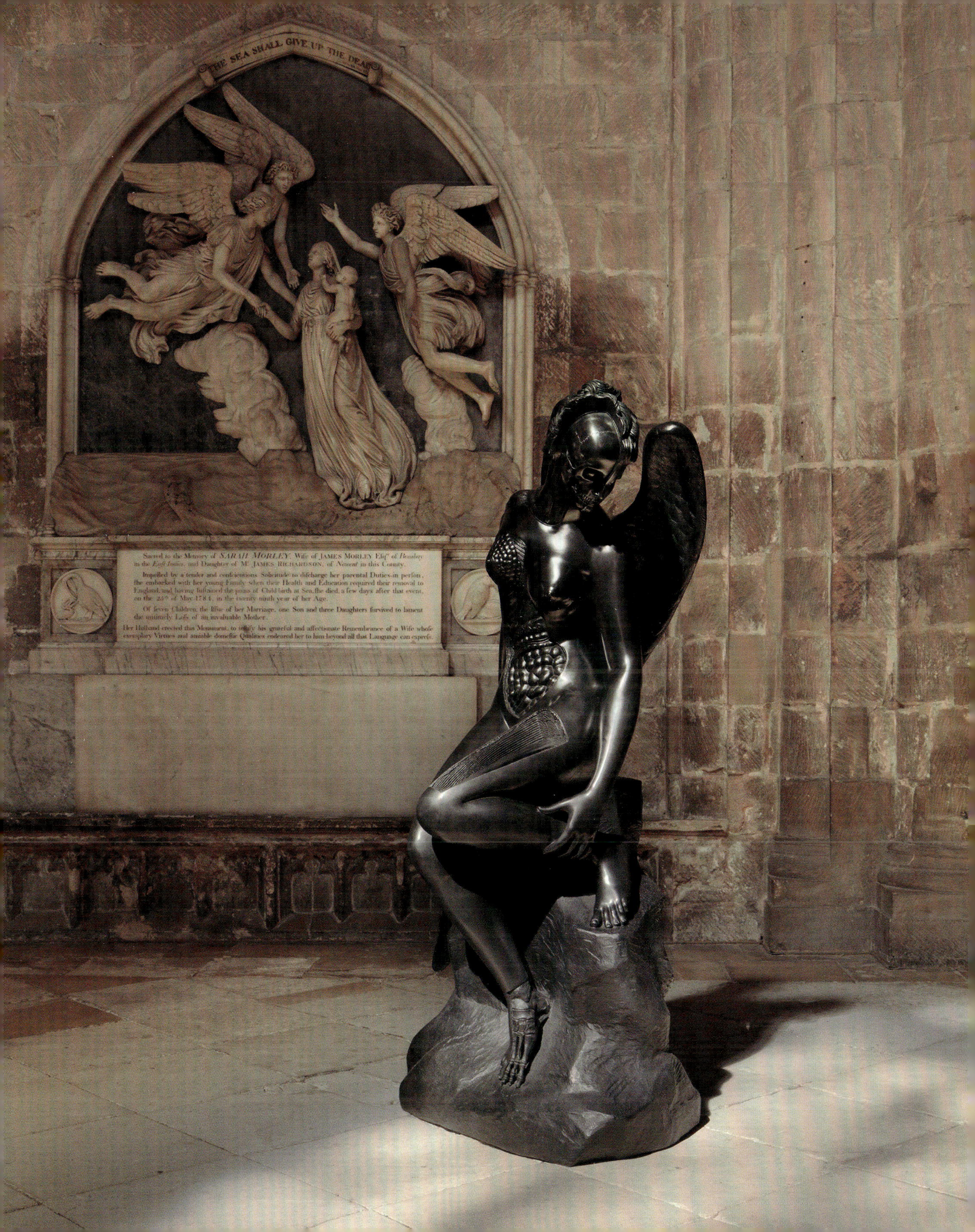
THE SEA SHALL GIVE UP THE DEAD
Sacred to the Memory of SARAH MORLEY, Wife of JAMES MORLEY Esq. of Bombay
Impelled by a tender and conscientious Solicitude to discharge her parental Duties in person,
Of seven Children, the issue of her Marriage, one Son and three Daughters survived to lament
the untimely Loss of an invaluable Mother.

JOHN HOSKIN 1921-1990

"Vital and original...being a very distinct personality, he belongs to the animistic or magical trend in the now recognisable school of English sculpture." Herbert Read on John Hoskin

From the early 1950's, Hoskin started experimenting with metals, producing spindly creatures and insect-like figures with exactly the 'linear, cursive quality' which Read described. Most of his sculptures are unique and constructed from mild steel. Shiny, curved, organic surfaces combine with geometric, black welded forms. In a later shift, working with abstract planar forms, Hoskin turned to the construction of abstract sculpture made from flat and curved steel plates.

'Welding is like knitting with fire.' John Hoskin

Big V
John Hoskin
Welded Steel
Unique
103cm high

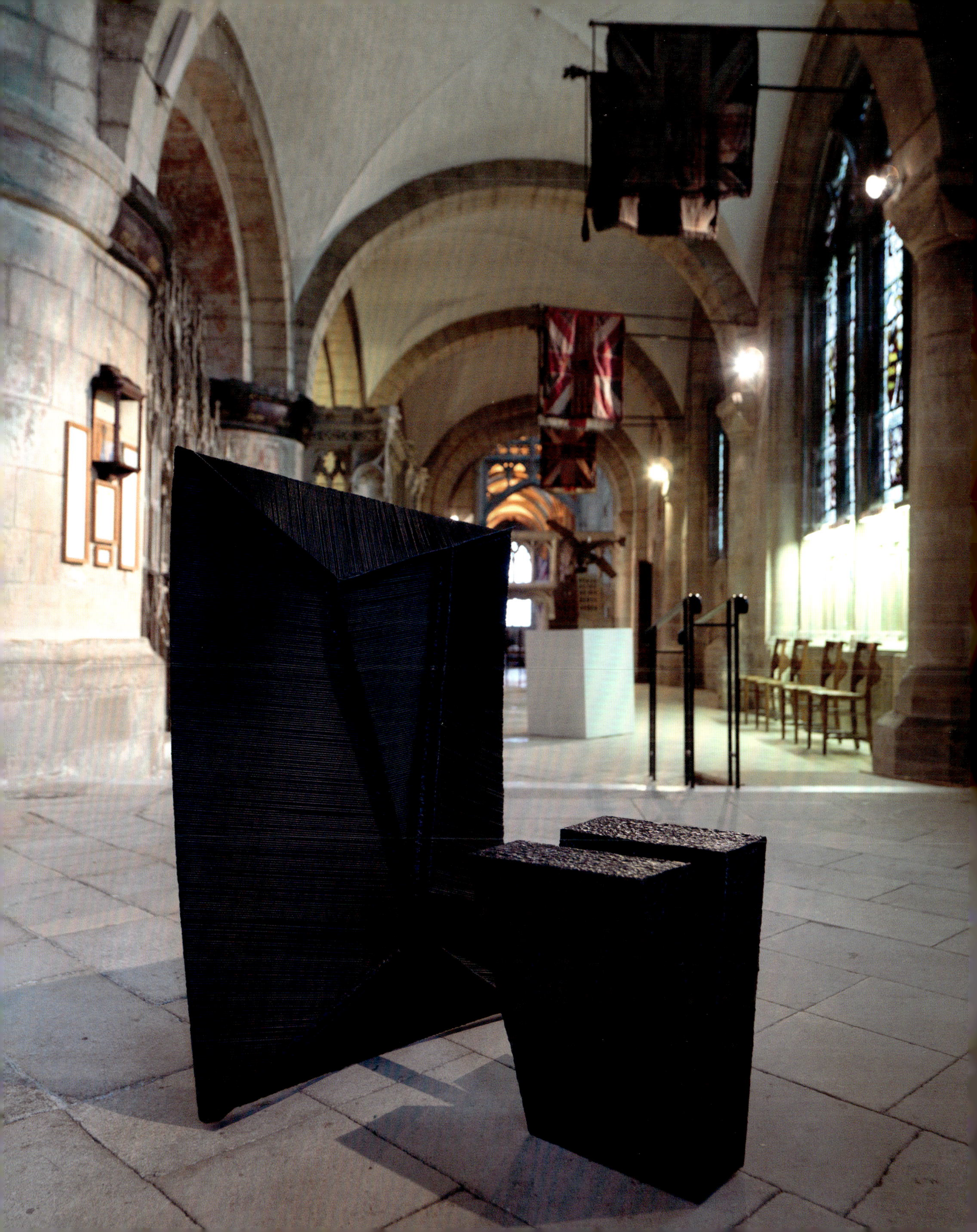

Cantilever Square

John Hoskin

Welded Steel

Unique

245cm high

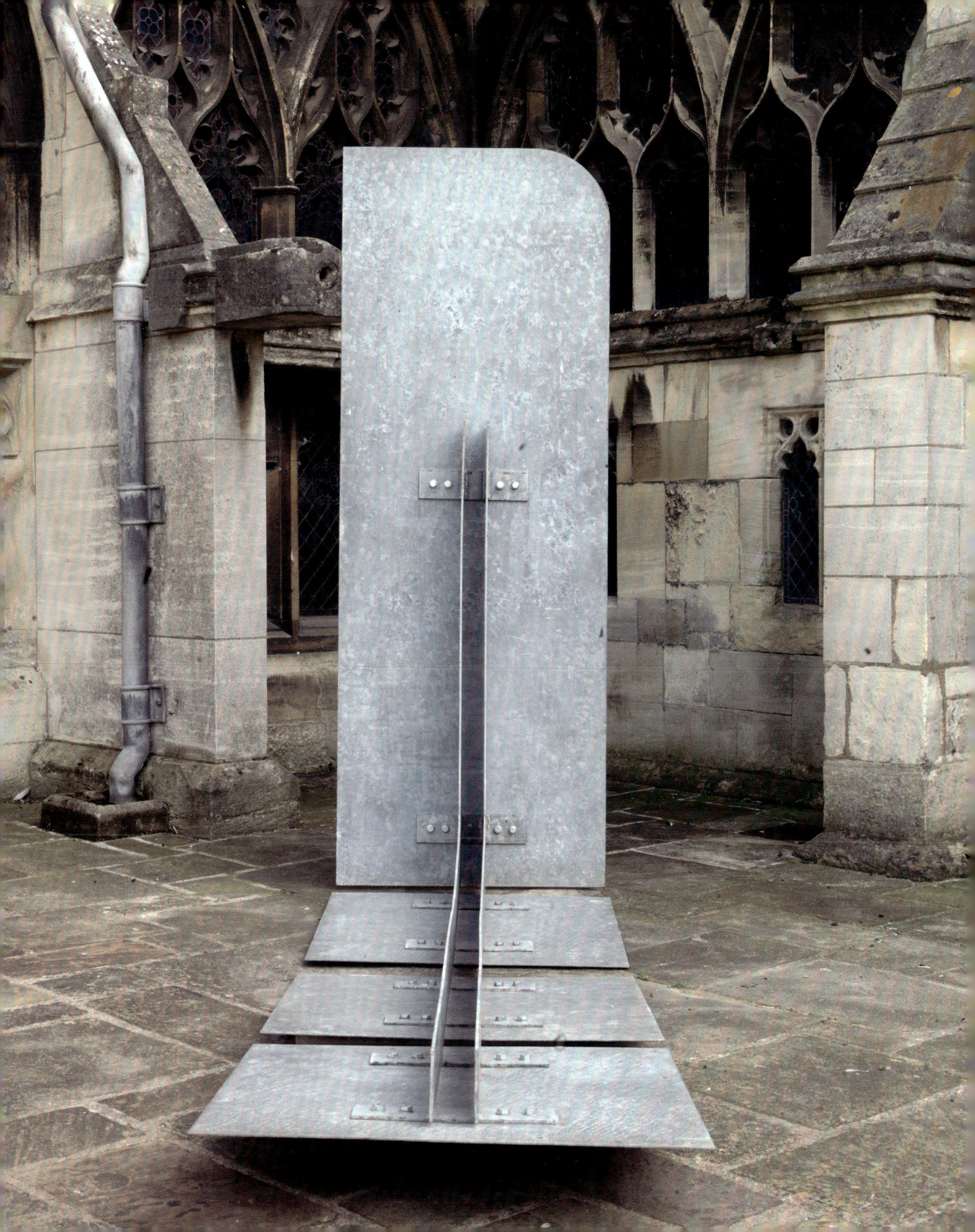

JOHN HUMPHREYS b.1955

Humphreys has always been fascinated by the human figure and the ways in which artists have approached portraiture through the ages. Having worked in the film industry he uses his experience with special effects to create sculpture designed to puzzle and confuse the viewer.

His concern with distorted dimensions forces his audience to think more deeply and to look more carefully at his portraits. Humphreys' sculpture is both surreal and super-real, challenging conventional perceptions of space and hinting at a fourth dimension.

Ipsius Imago a Latere Extensa
John Humphreys
Fibreglass and acrylic paint
Edition of 3
50cm high

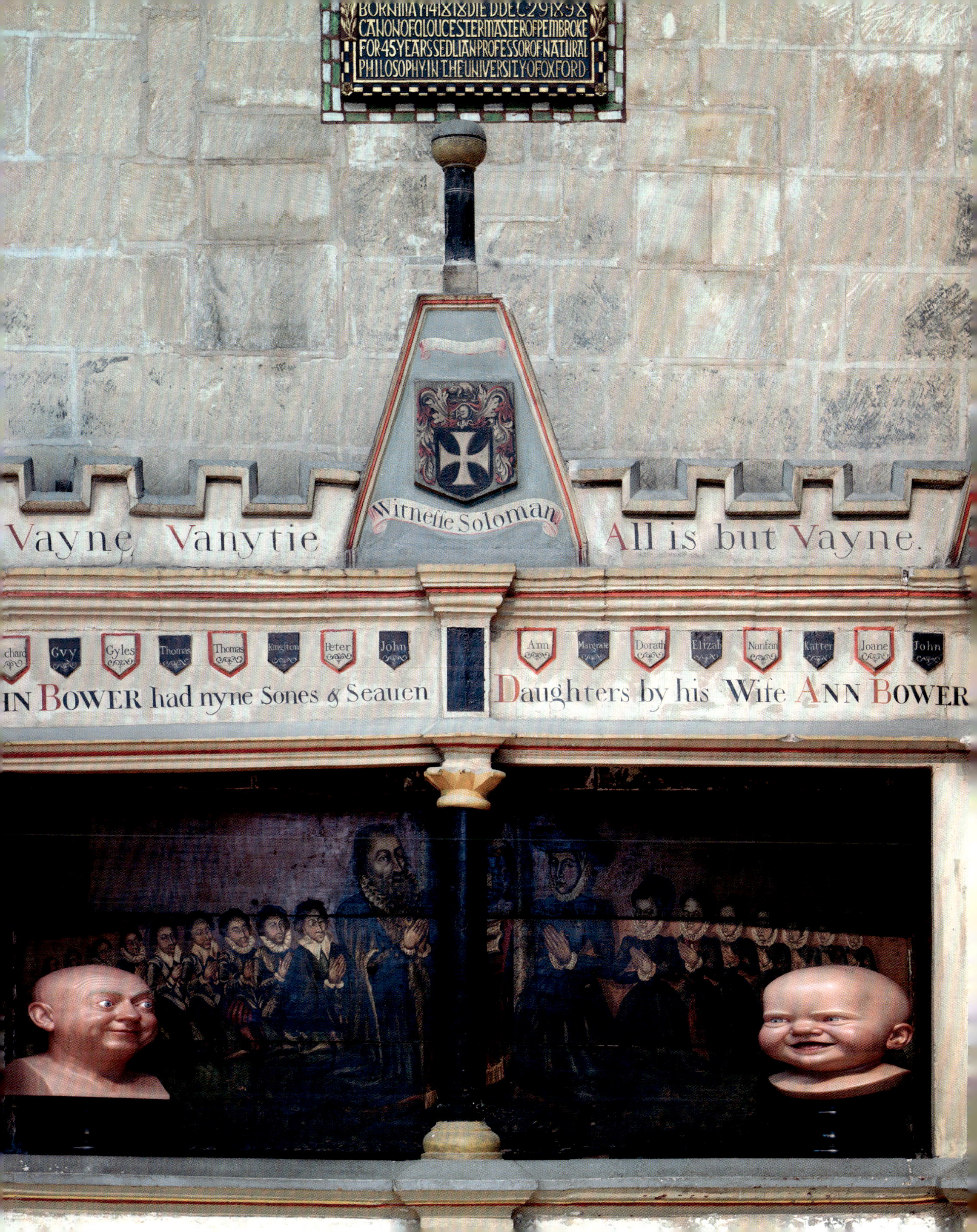
BORN MAY 14 1818 DIED DEC 29 1898
CANON OF GLOUCESTER MASTER OF PEMBROKE
FOR 45 YEARS SEDLIAN PROFESSOR OF NATURAL
PHILOSOPHY IN THE UNIVERSITY OF OXFORD
Witnesse Soloman
Vayne Vanytie
All is but Vayne.
Guy
Gyles
Thomas
Thomas
Kingston
Peter
John
Ann
Margrate
Dorath
Elizab
Nanfan
Katter
Joane
John
IN BOWER had nyne Sones & Seauen
Daughters by his Wife ANN BOWER

Baby Jesus

John Humphreys

Resin

Edition of 3

48cm high

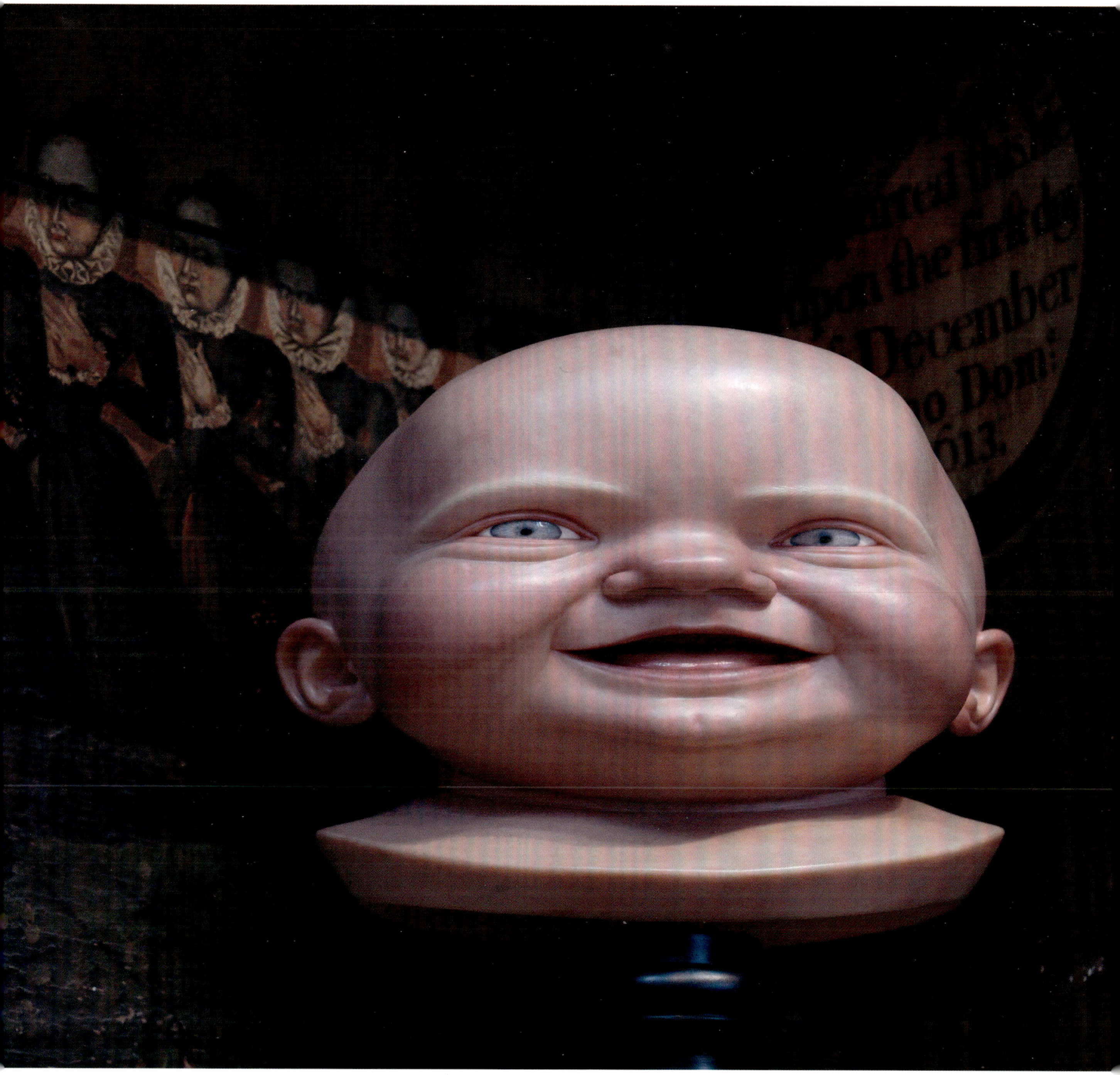
December

STEVE HURST b.1932

'The joy of sculpture is that it is paradoxical, it can mean many different things.

The genesis of this piece was a conversation on Heathrow airport with the Shakespearean actor Bruce Purchase. We arranged to meet for coffee, but his flight was called. From the departure gate he called out "Some other time, dear boy. I'm taking over Gloucester in Berlin". I thought of Berlin when I first went there. I thought of Gloucestershire my neighbour county and the aircraft factory. I thought of childhood, being sent away through the ruins of the Midlands industrial cities, Coventry, Birmingham, Wolverhampton. As a child I witnessed the bombing raid on Derby station. Equally I thought of my first visits to Germany not long after the War, the ruins of Cologne and Hamburg.

Gloucester in Berlin concerns the bombing of civilians no matter what their country or who launches the bombing aircraft. It is a personal attempt to regain the viewpoint of a child.'

Gloucester in Berlin
Steve Hurst
Bronze, steel and wood
Unique
110cm high

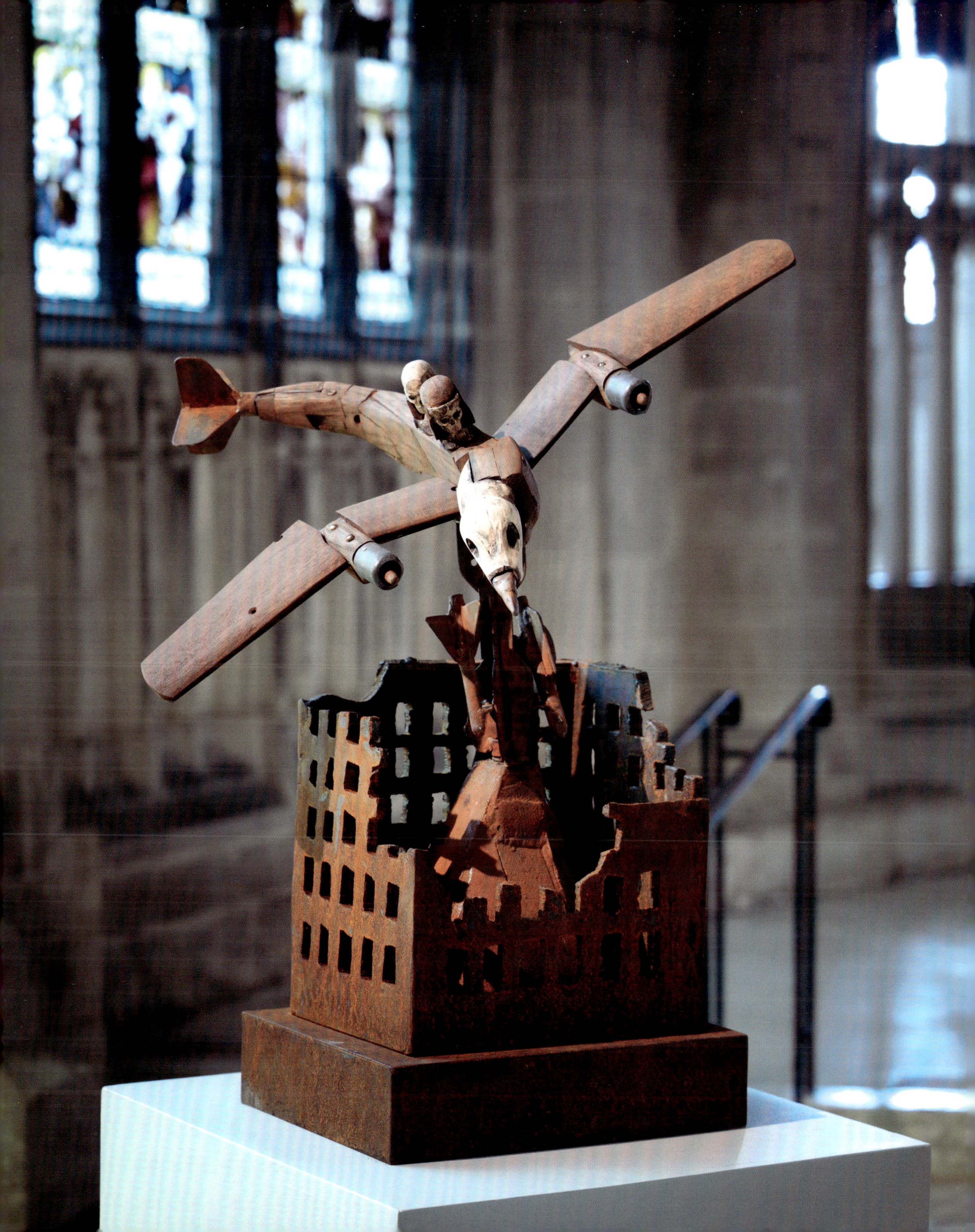

Geometric Organic
Steve Hurst
Bronze
Unique
145cm high

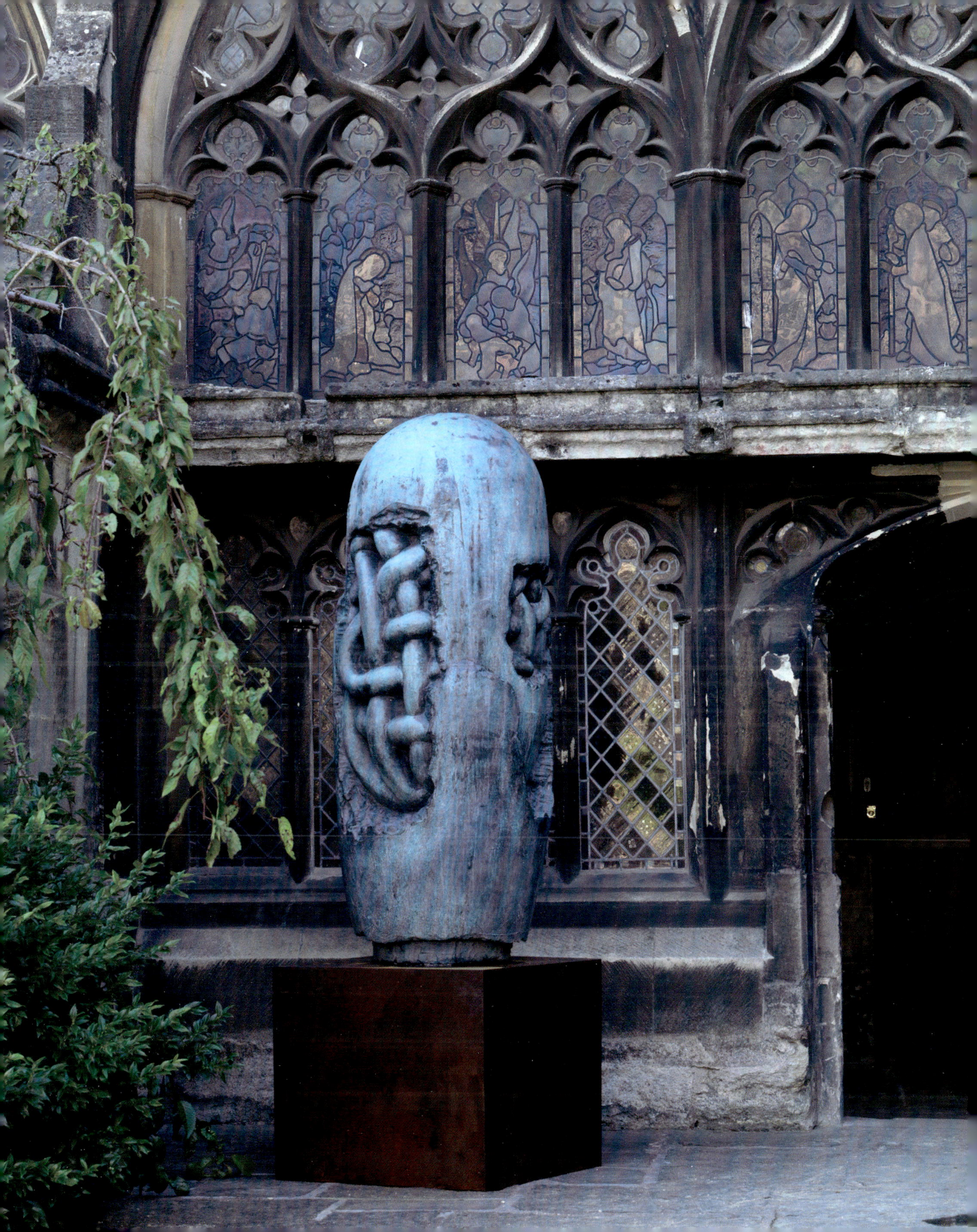

ANDY JOHANSEN b.1982

A skilled craftsman, Johansen works with found objects, forged metal and direct burnouts, drawing inspiration from the human body, organic matter and the tactile qualities of sharp metal and soft textiles.

Heart references the complex system of valves, arteries and veins in the human body and the theatrical, invasive beauty of open heart surgery. After discovering an old and distressed leather football, Johansen was fascinated by its layers of rich texture. Cracked, dirty, torn and frayed, it provided the colour and finish for the final sculpture.

Heart
Andy Johansen
Bronze, copper and stainless steel
Unique
65cm high

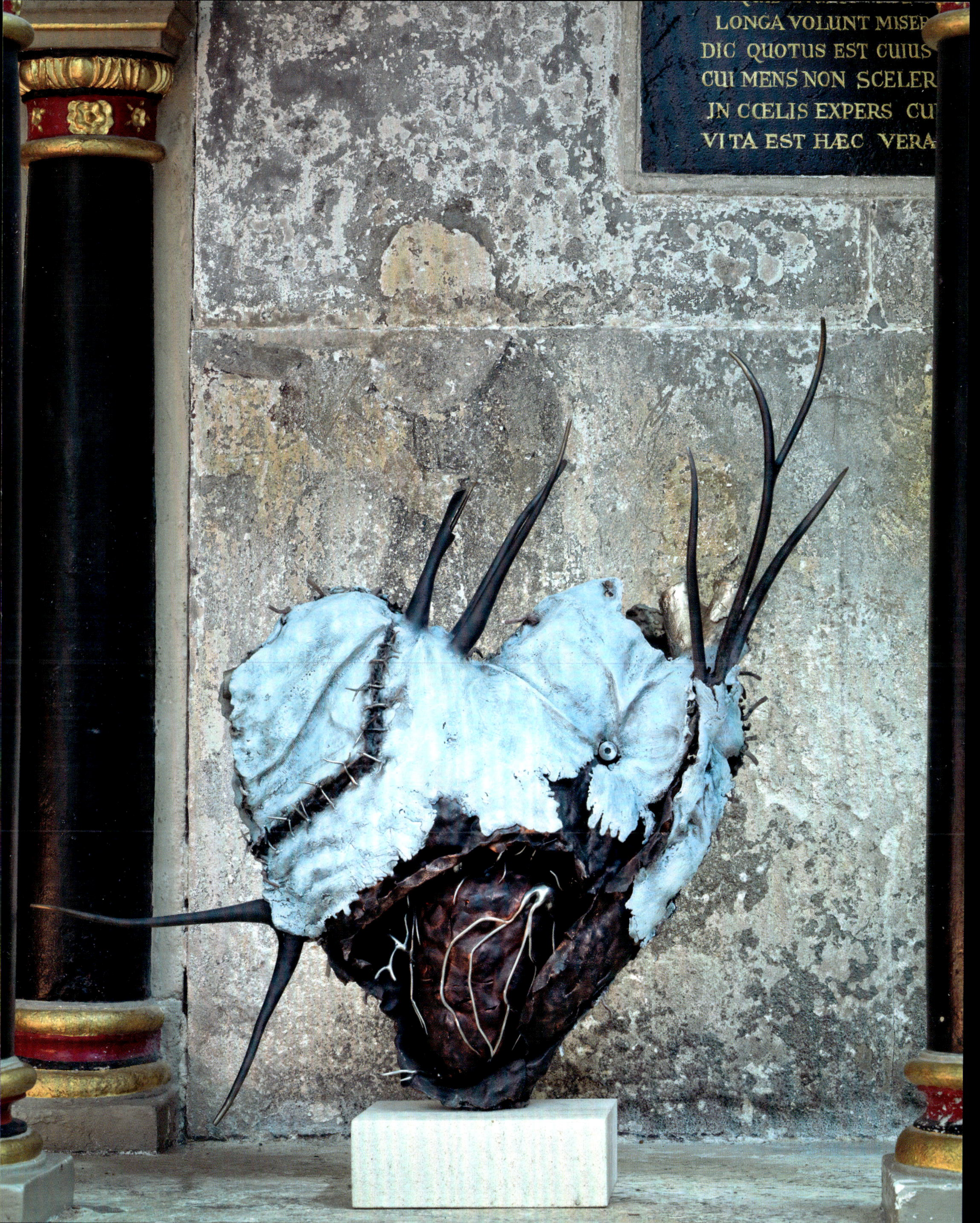
LONGA VOLUNT MISER
DIC QUOTUS EST CUIUS
CUI MENS NON SCELER
IN CŒLIS EXPERS CU
VITA EST HÆC VERA

JONATHAN KENWORTHY FRBS b.1943

'The freedoms of the warrior clans have been dramatically curtailed since my first safaris in 1965. Today the population explosion in East Africa has threatened their lands from all sides. Their rights and customs are questioned by the "New Africa" and they, themselves, are demanding change from within.

And yet, travel down the tracks to Lake Magadi and you will find this latter day David tending his goats and sheep. There he dreams his dream that one day he will live in the warriors' manyatta. His hair will be plaited and his skin will shine with red ochre. Perhaps his will be the spear that kills the marauding lion and he will show his sons the scars. As the heat crackles in the breathless air of long afternoons this is still his kingdom.'

Masai Boy with Goat
Jonathan Kenworthy
Bronze
Edition of 5
90cm high

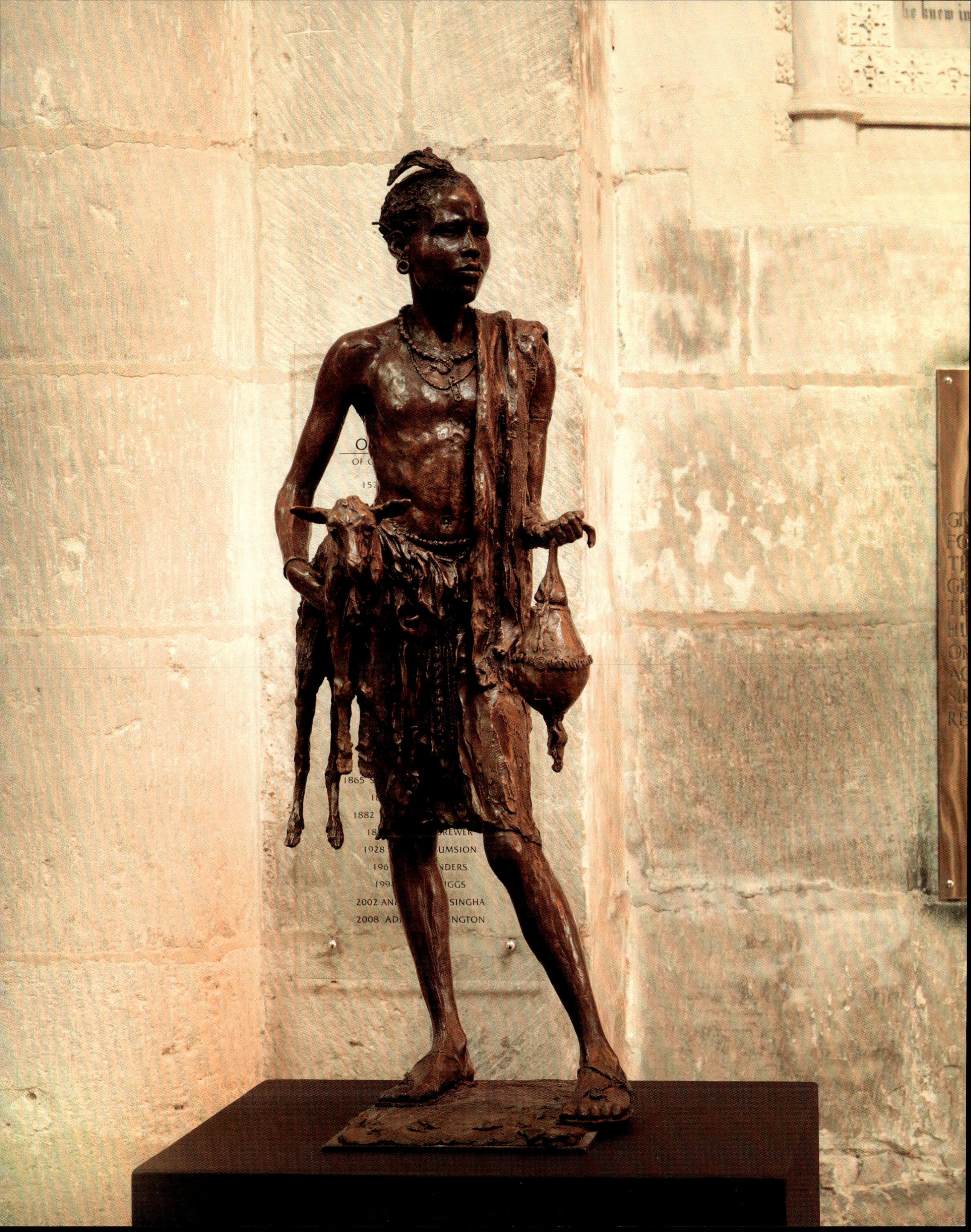

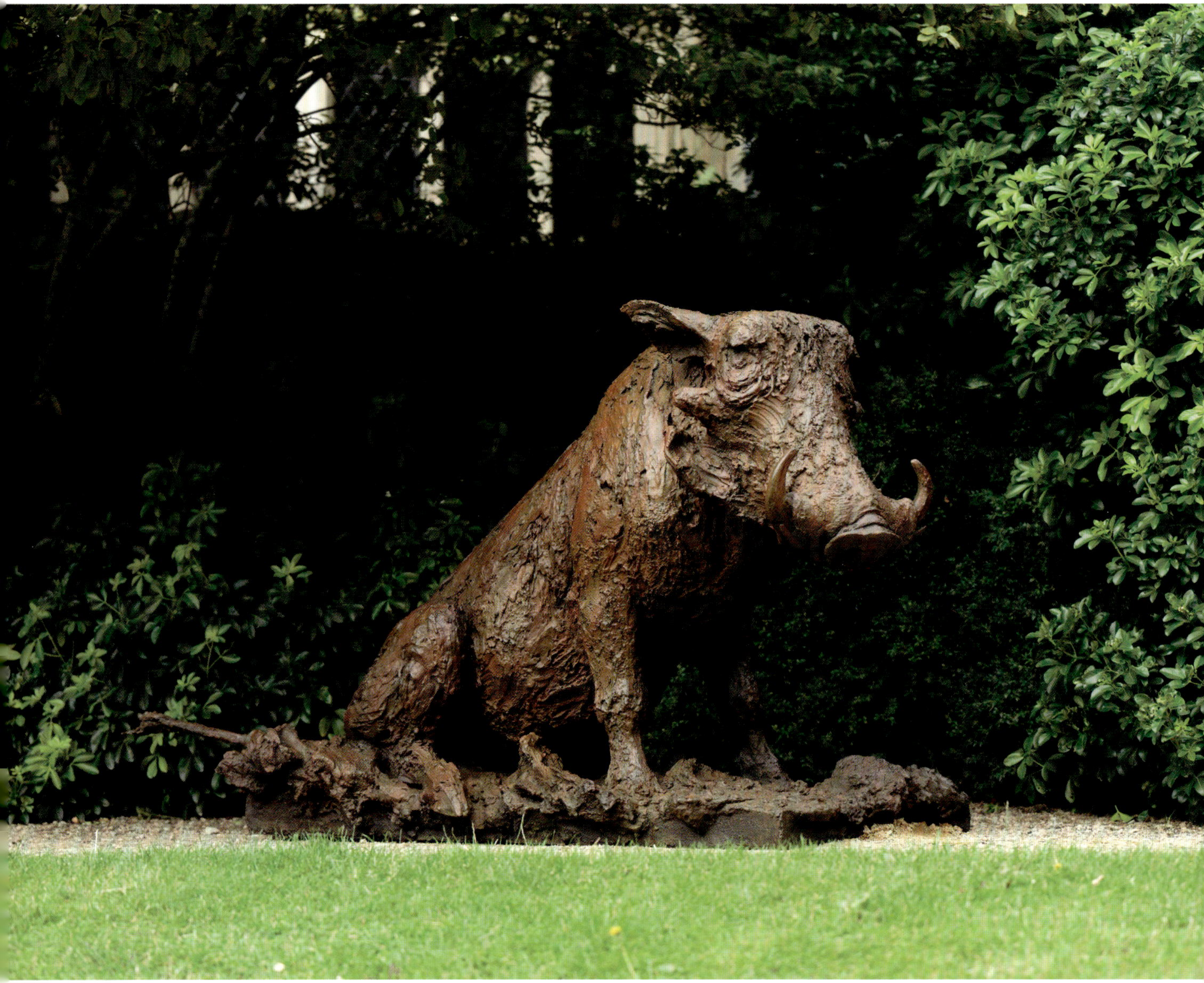

Warthog

Jonathan Kenworthy

Bronze

Edition of 5

122cm high

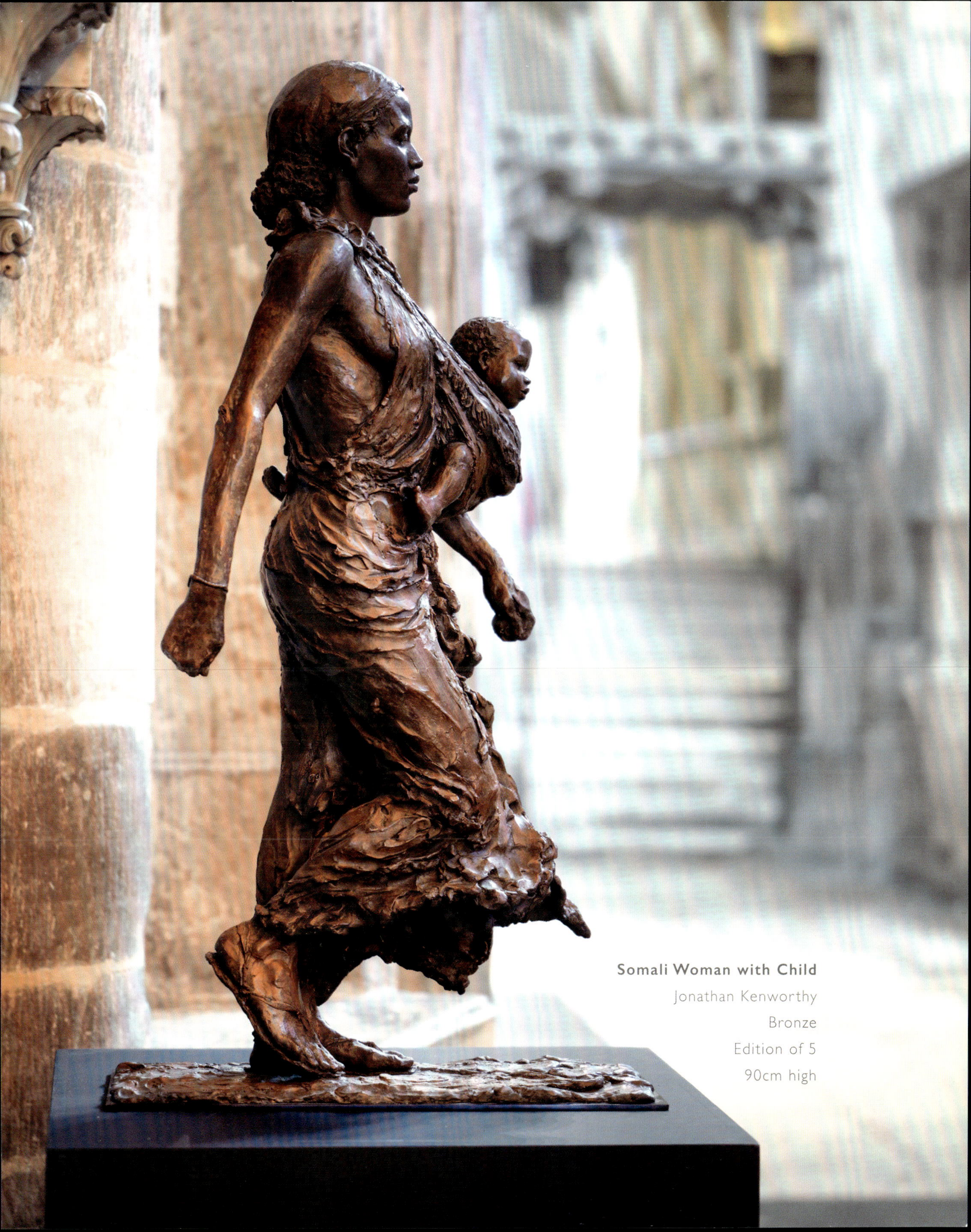

Somali Woman with Child
Jonathan Kenworthy
Bronze
Edition of 5
90cm high

BRYAN KNEALE RA FRBS b.1930

"Astra is a tall vertical sculpture aspiring to the stars that is all about balance. Kneale is constantly making improbable shapes that defy the laws of gravity. (The sound of metal clattering to the floor is a regular occurrence in his studio. He claims to be able to make anything balance – if only for a moment. The problems arise in making the balancing act permanent.) The discs which form Astra's base touch curves at certain points and are delicately balanced, but are also firmly wedged together to support the tower. Kneale has enjoyed himself cutting into the surface of this base with a plasma cutter, piercing it to prevent the forms becoming too solid. He wanted to break up the shapes like a cloud, and give them an informal, accident-like quality."(1)

(1)Andrew Lambirth 'Bryan Kneale: Points of Contact' Exhibition catalogue, Beaux Arts, 2011

Astra
Bryan Kneale
Stainless steel
Unique
254cm high

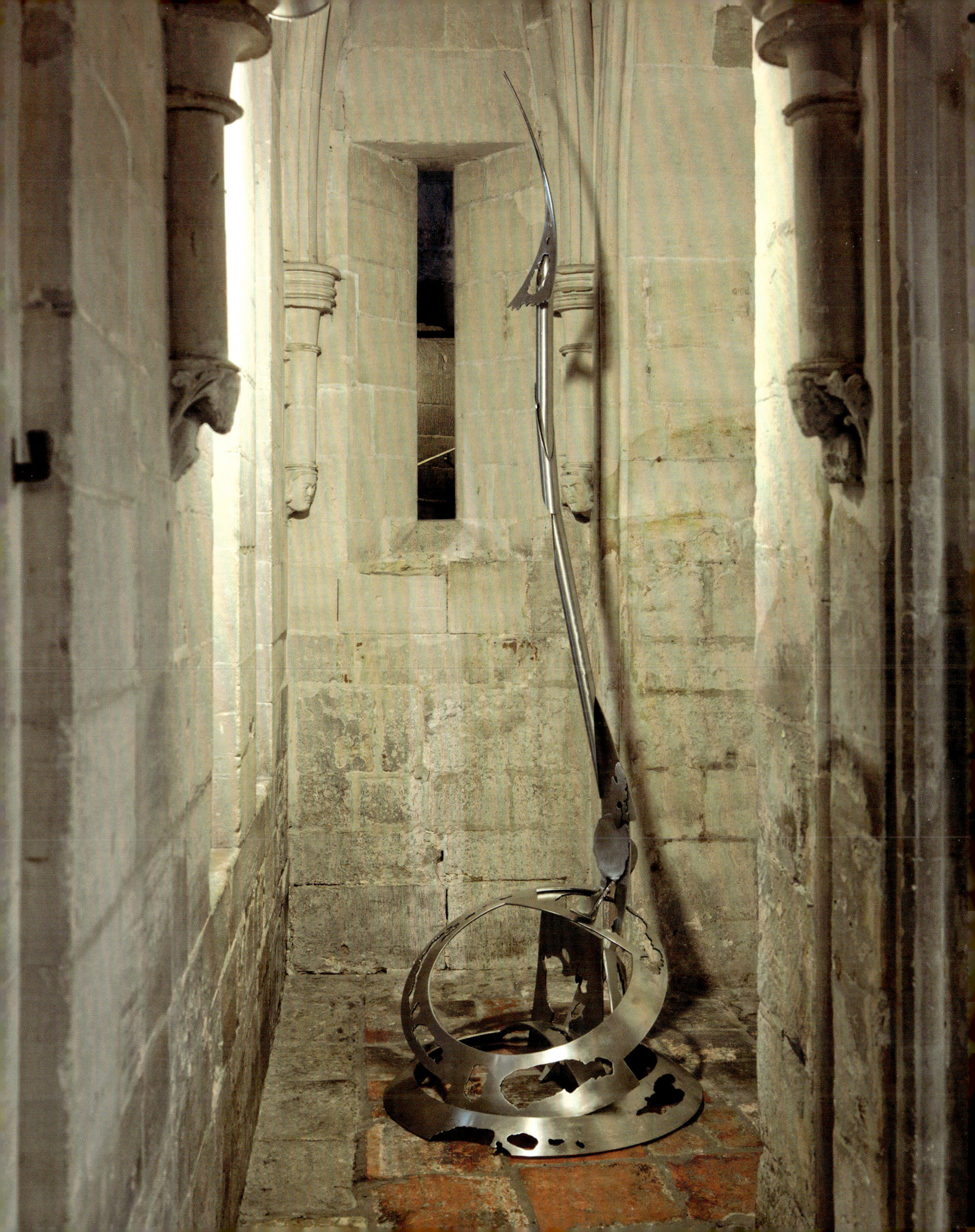

Sky
Bryan Kneale
Stainless Steel
Unique
282cm high

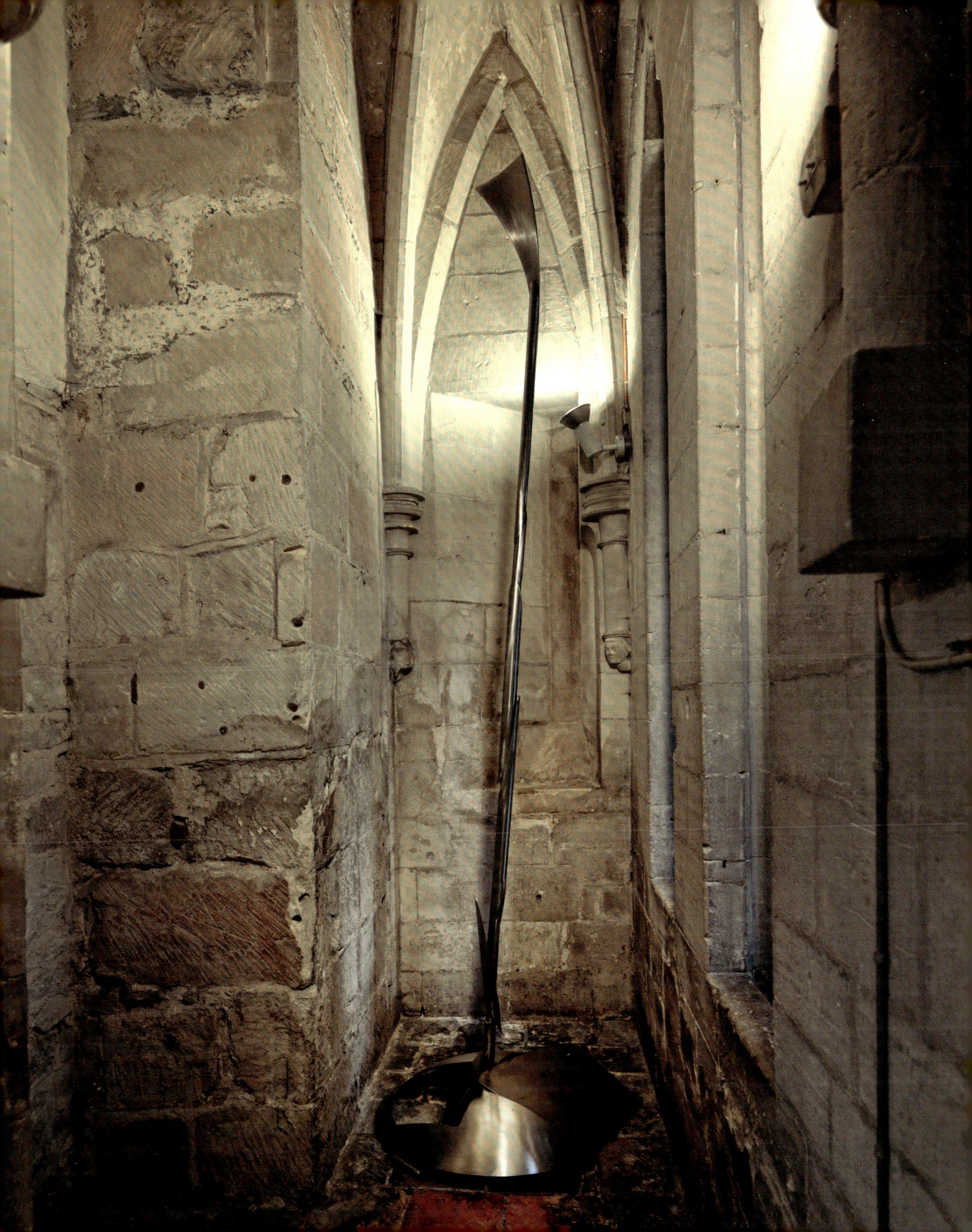

SARAH LUCAS b.1962

In a career spanning almost three decades, Sarah Lucas has continued to confront such 'big themes' as sex, death, abjection, and the slippery notion of Englishness. Spanning sculpture, photography and installation, her work has consistently been characterised by irreverent humour and the use of everyday 'readymade' objects – furniture, food, tabloid newspapers, tights, toilets, cigarettes – to conjure up sexual puns and corporeal fragments.

Lucas's NUDs series, begun in 2009, used stuffed tights – materials familiar throughout her art – to create knotted, fleshy contortions. Erotically suggestive and strangely poignant, the NUDs echoed the biomorphic abstractions of British Modernists such as Moore and Hepworth. Their convoluted forms have been translated into bronze – gleaming objects set atop plinths of stacked stone - which nonetheless carry an essential trace of awkwardness and perversity. These bronze versions were unveiled as part of the exhibition 'Il Palazzo Enciclopedico (The Encyclopedic Palace)', at the 55th International Art Exhibition, Venice. Of this series of bronzes, the academic and critic Alexandra Parigoris has written: "The unashamedly sexual innuendos of the bronze forms retain the sense of the hand that fashioned them. They twist and turn with a gracefulness that the reflections underscore and undercut at the same time. Though still abstract, there are echoes of Matisse's knowing deformations that, early in the last century, heralded in a new way of conveying meaning through the body." [1]

[1] Alexandra Parigoris, 'Sarah Lucas in bronze', in Iwona Blazwick (ed.), Sarah Lucas: SITUATION Absolute Beach Man Rubble, exh. cat. (London: Whitechapel Gallery, 2013), p. 72.

Nduda, 2013

Sarah Lucas

Bronze

Edition of 6

36cm high

Copyright: The Artist, courtesy Sadie Coles HQ, London

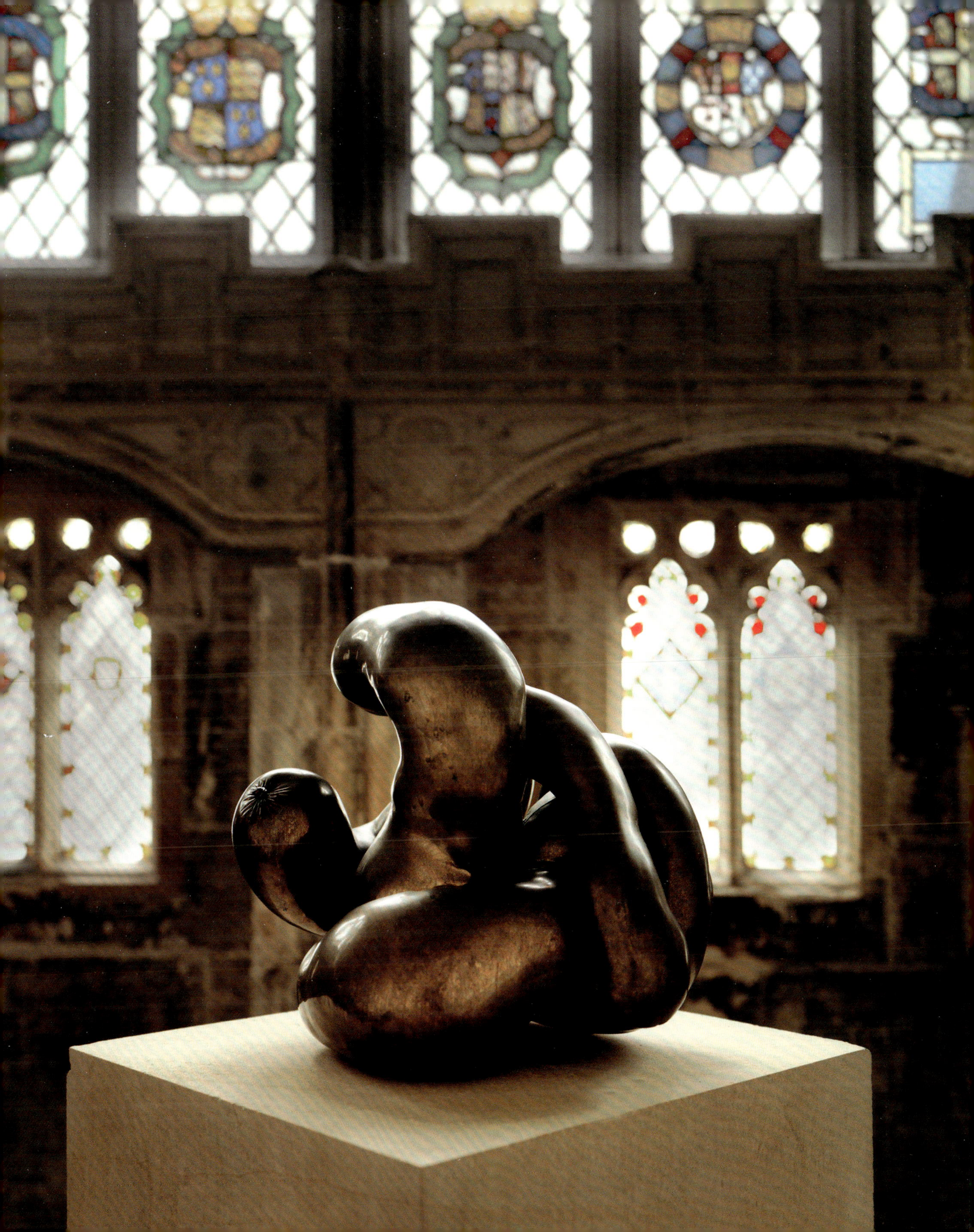

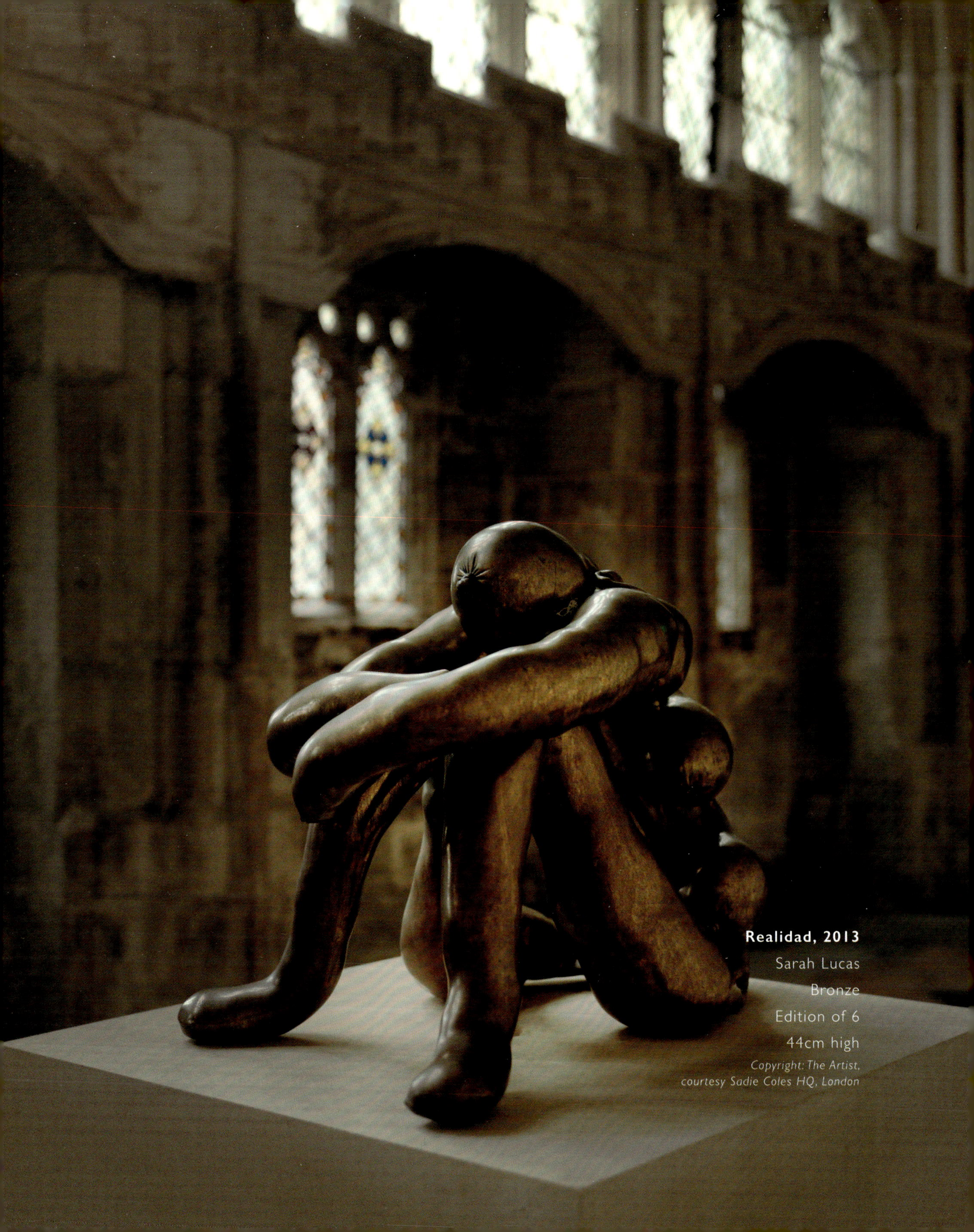

Realidad, 2013
Sarah Lucas
Bronze
Edition of 6
44cm high
Copyright: The Artist, courtesy Sadie Coles HQ, London

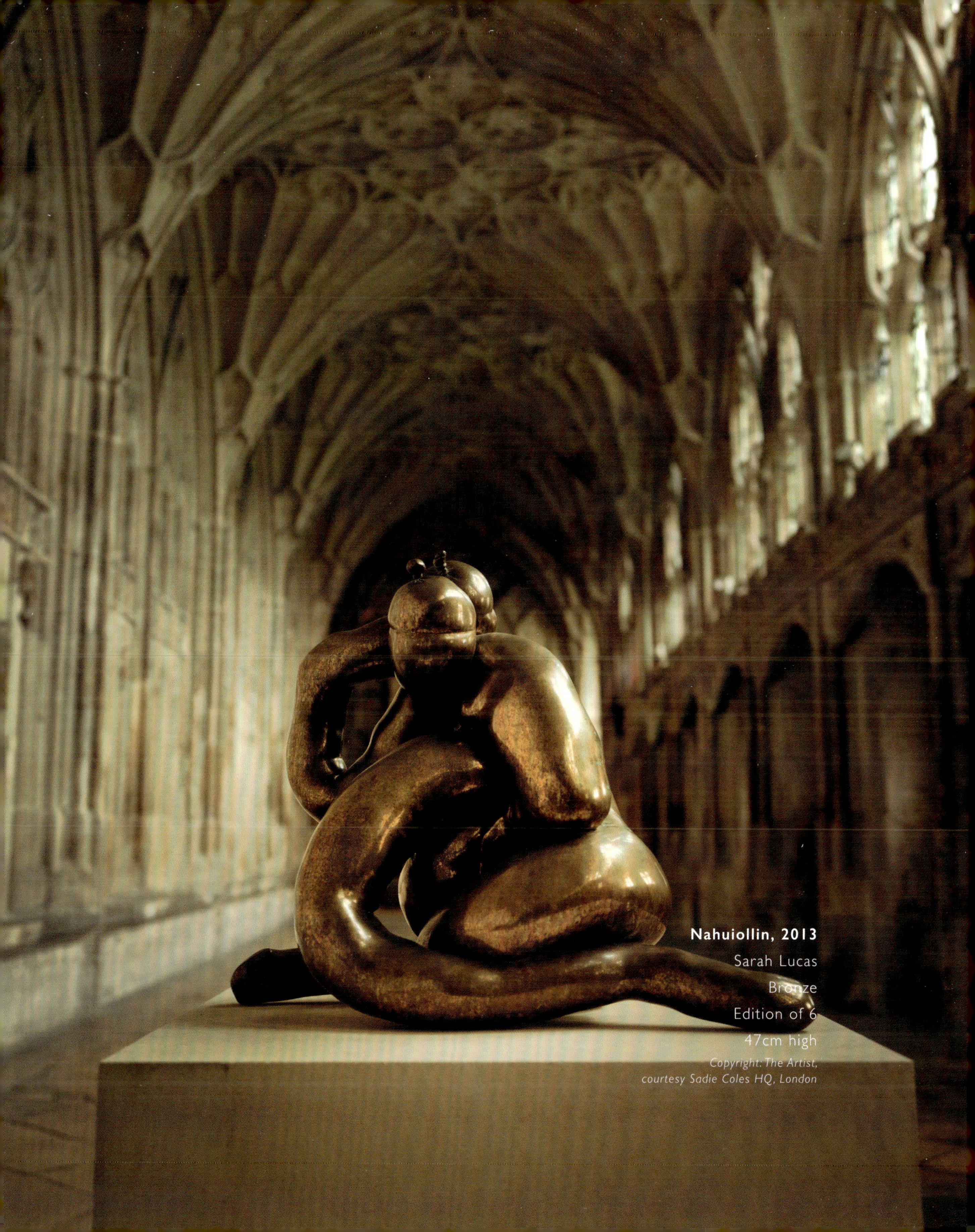

Nahuiollin, 2013
Sarah Lucas
Bronze
Edition of 6
47cm high

Copyright: The Artist, courtesy Sadie Coles HQ, London

CHARLES LUTYENS b.1933

'This uncommissioned Crucifixion, the Outraged Christ is made from discarded hard and soft wood beams and planks, which have been split with an axe and applied to the body of the sculpture by drilling and dowelling. It is bound together with powerful adhesive.

From the beginning, the creation of this work was driven by questions such as: who was this Man, what does 'Son of God' mean, what did He look like, what actually happened on that day and why is it remembered over 2000 years amongst all other crucifixions that have taken place. What about the Resurrection? Was it or not? If it was then surely it already had presence on the Cross.

The figure's left arm is the trunk of a tree with a root-bole in which the hand was found intact. The nails that fasten His hands and feet have gilded heads because they nail flesh to wood. The horizontal beam of the Cross is formed from an old Oxfordshire iron field gate.'

Outraged Christ
Charles Lutyens
Wood
Unique
460cm high

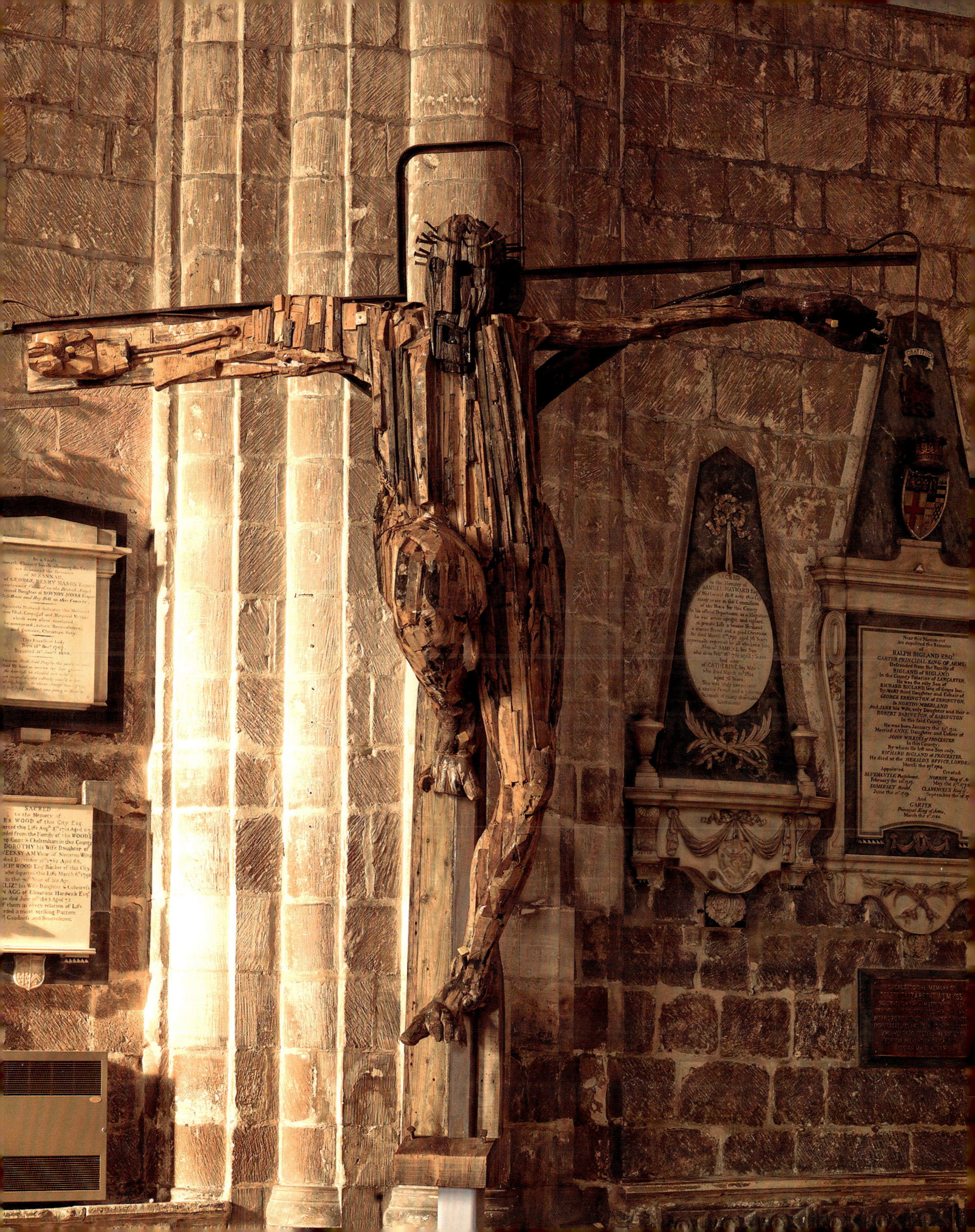

DAVID MACH RA b.1956

'Coat hangers are still a current material for me. They are still able to inspire new ideas. I don't know why I am drawn to them and other materials like them, they are such ordinary, almost nothing things. They are known to us all though and provide common ground to inhabit, for me as a sculptor and for you as a viewer.

I have used such a lot of materials like this; things that exist in their own right without any need of explanation or interference from me; things not seen as material for art; things that let me meet you the viewer, armed with your opinions and your preconceived ideas. Using a tyre or magazine or a coat hanger to make sculpture seems to allow me to inhabit the same territory as you and sometimes is almost perceived as a slap in the face, a provocation. Why am I using something so insultingly ordinary, so mundane when gold and bronze and amazing technology is available?

I like that they may - these sculptures made with these materials - whilst trying to meet the viewer on the common ground I mention, confuse and provoke. It is almost as if they tell stories that you may find hard to believe. They exaggerate. I like that a lot. They are extravagant and excessive. I hope that they entertain and excite you while you decide whether to believe them or not.'

The Thief

David Mach

Coat Hangers and steel

Unique

439cm high

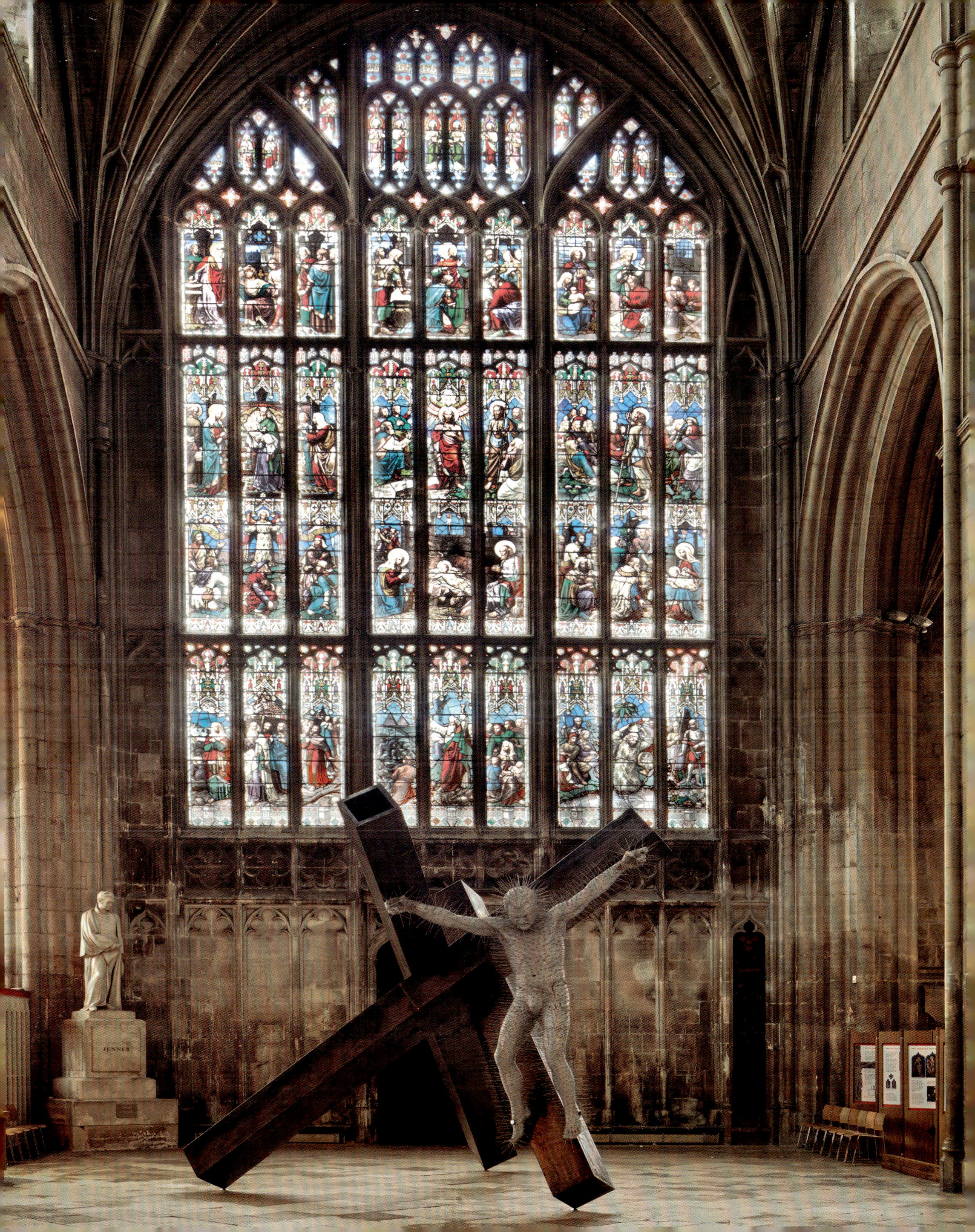
JENNER

Stripped to the Bone

David Mach

Coat Hangers and steel

Edition of 4

80cm high

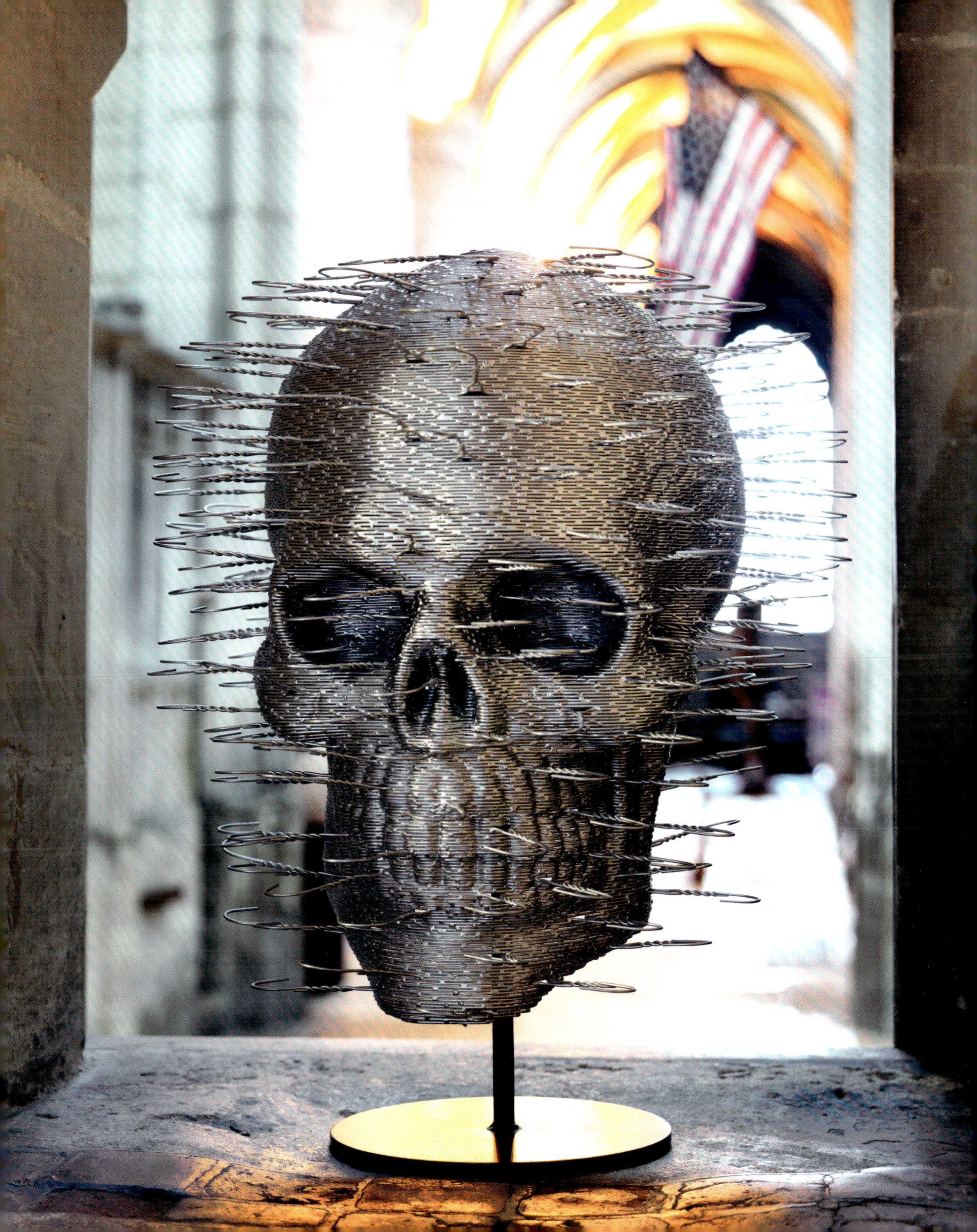

ALISTAIR MACKIE b.1977

'Having swallowed its prey whole, the barn owl's digestive system will extract any nutrients. The indigestible parts are then regurgitated as a compressed pellet. From these the skulls are extracted and pieced together to create a perfect sphere.'

Untitled (Sphere)
Alastair Mackie
Mouse skulls, wood and glass
Edition of 4
35cm high

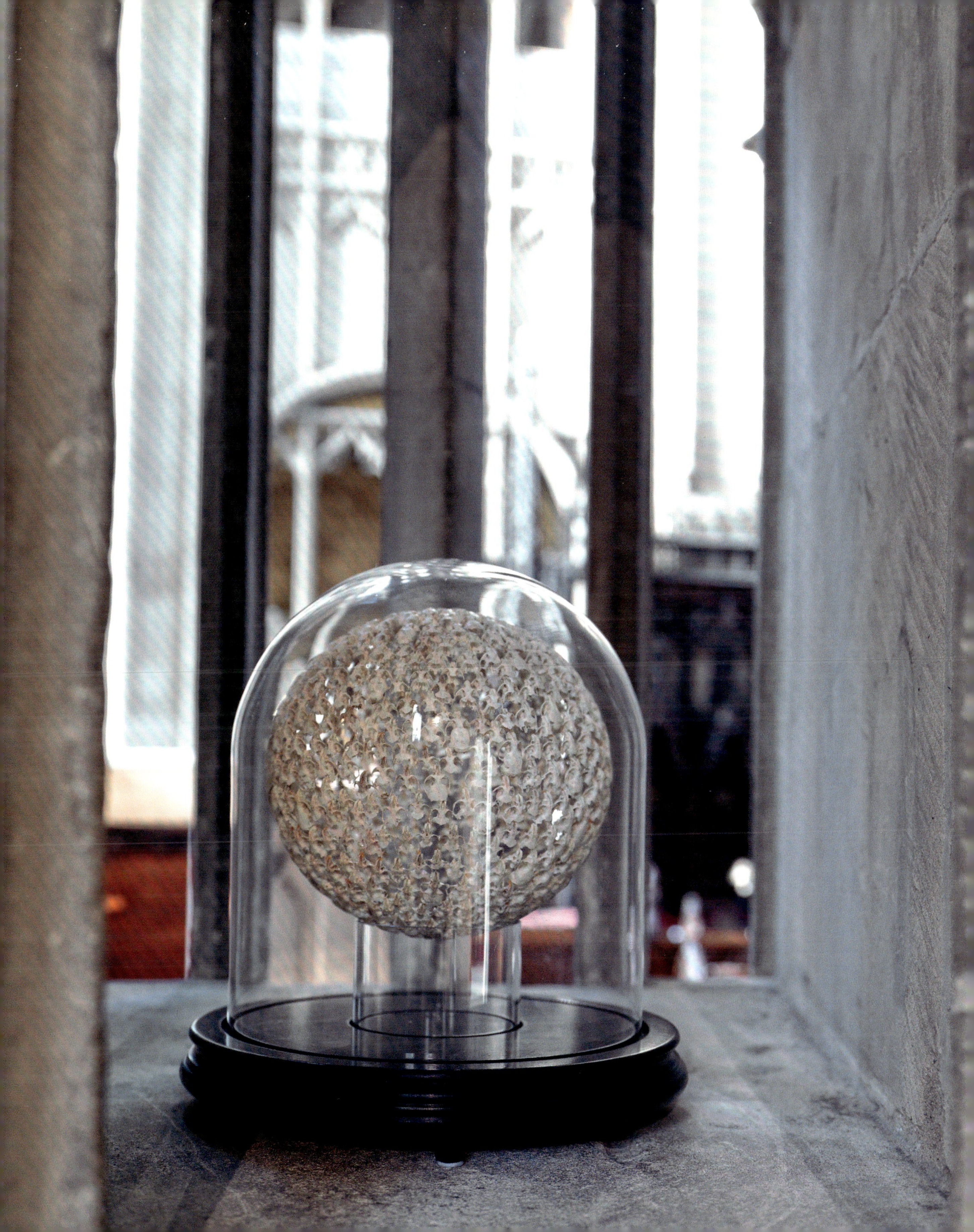

ANITA MANDL FRBS b.1926

'The story of the Dodo's extinction within less than a century of being seen alive by explorers landing on the island of Mauritius has stimulated many writers to describe this extraordinary bird, and many artists have had a shot at drawing or sculpting it. Its name and its history seem not only to have a special appeal to children, as best-known perhaps in Alice in Wonderland but it has also been commonly used as a mascot or logo by innumerable firms to promote the sale of their products.'

Mandl is well-placed as a zoologist and sculptor, her deep knowledge of animal anatomy and behaviour informing her carvings which are skilfully pared down to convey the very nature of a species. Their economy of language, their smooth and lustrous surfaces, together express the essential characteristics of an animal.

Dodo I
Anita Mandl
Bronze
Edition of 6
15cm high

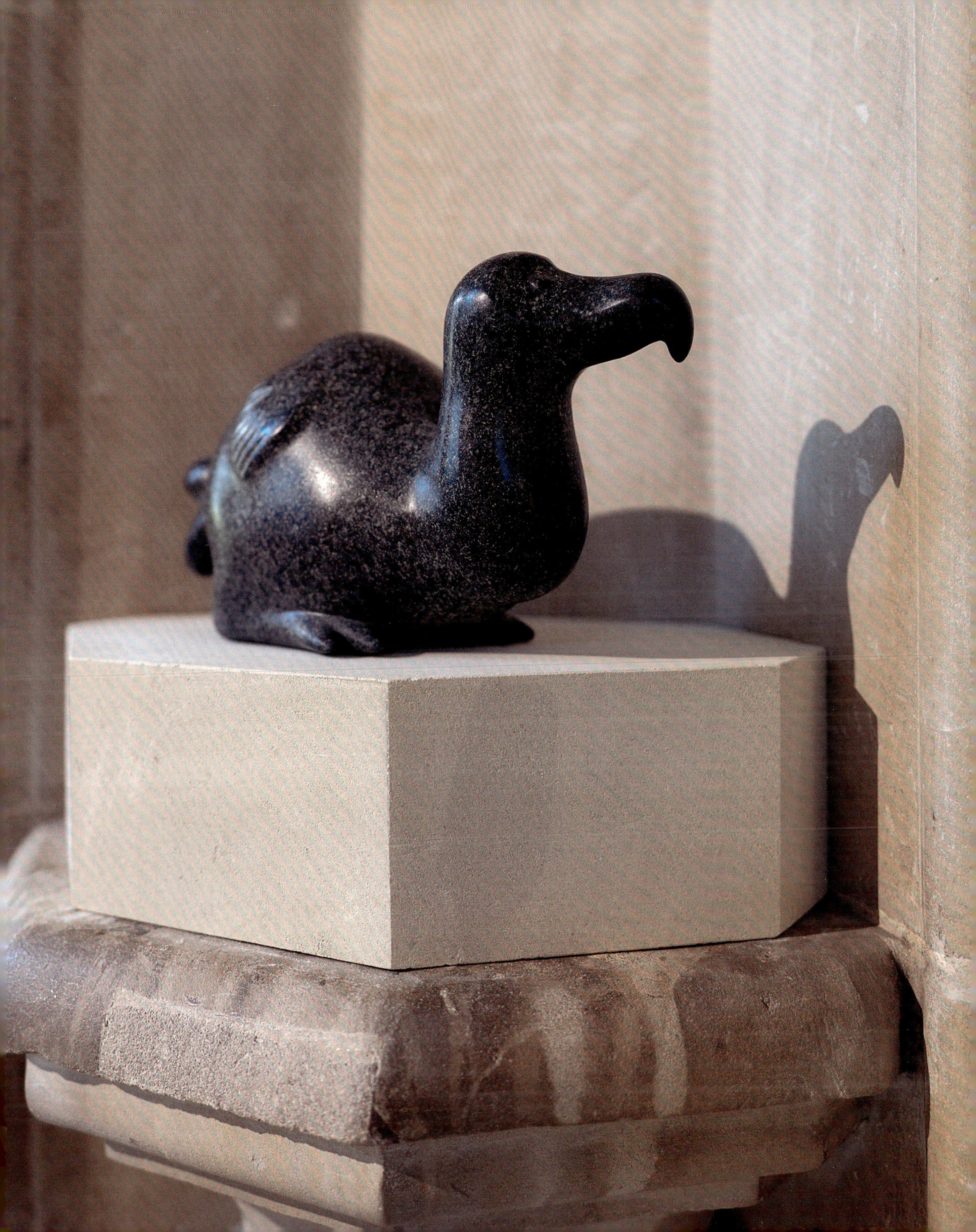

Dodo II

Anita Mandl

Bronze

Edition of 7

22cm high

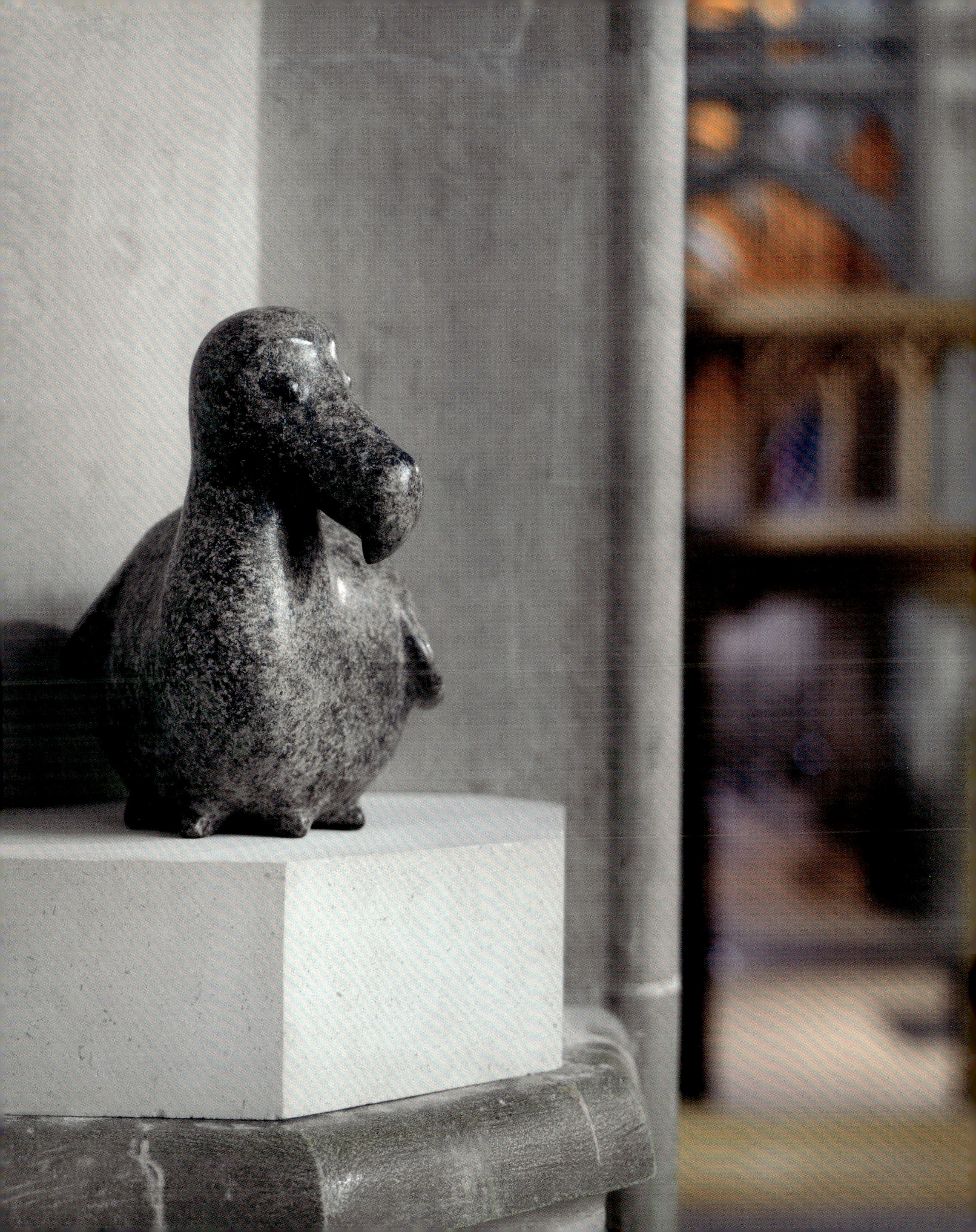

BRIONY MARSHALL ARBS b.1974

2013 saw the 60th anniversary of the discovery of DNA, and Marshall's sculpture is emblematic of the great achievements of modern science. Standing at over two metres tall this DNA molecule is constructed from over 600 human figures joined at the hands and feet, each representing a different atom in a single twist of DNA. Made first in wax and then cast in bronze, the work demonstrates an ambitious aim paired with a rather humbled view of society. The integrity of the structure depends on each figure playing its part and is a powerful representation of the interconnectedness of life.

Marshall's fascination with the scientific understanding of life and matter heavily informs her sculptural practice. She explores the micro world of molecules to discover parallels with the macro world we inhabit as a society, consciously using figurative sculpture for its visceral relevance.

DNA – Helix of Life

Briony Marshall

Bronze

Edition of 3

185cm high

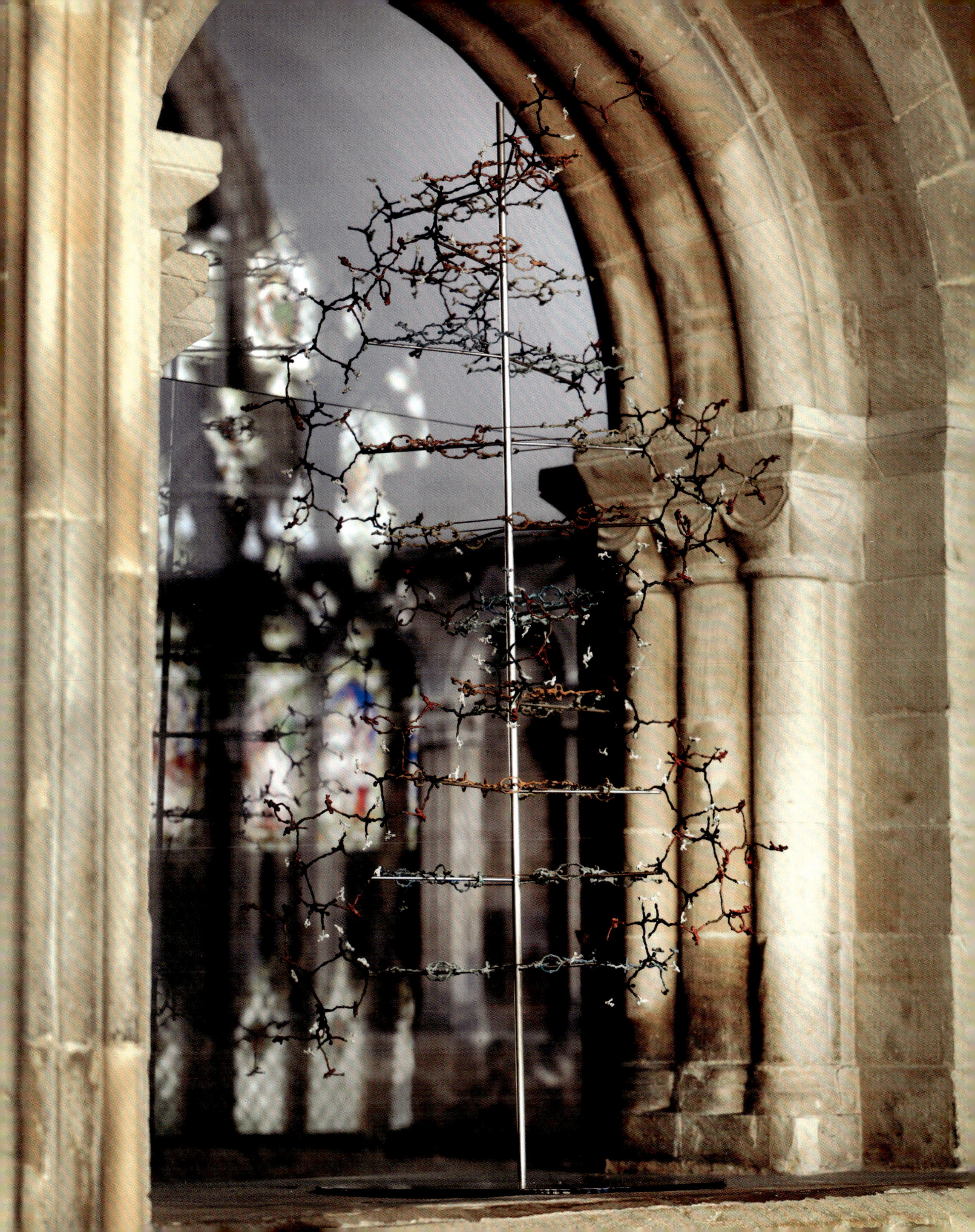

CHARLOTTE MAYER FRBS b.1929

'The Thornflower is an attempt to reconcile in sculptural form two diametrically opposed elements. The thorns, sharp and cruel are cut in stainless steel. The flowers, modelled in wax and cast in bronze are soft and embracing. The sculpture grows from a circular base that speaks of their fundamental unity.

"There is nothing either good or bad but thinking makes it so" said Shakespeare in Hamlet Act 2 Scene 2. It is this 'thinking so' that seems to be at the root of our personal and global pain. Prejudice, racial and religious intolerance, envy, hatred and violence all spring from it. These are the thorns which pierce us. But when we open our heart and see others as ourselves, the flowers begin to bloom, joy enters our life and there is a chance that reconciliation and peace can become an everyday reality.'

The Thornflower
Charlotte Mayer
Bronze and stainless steel
Edition of 12
150cm high

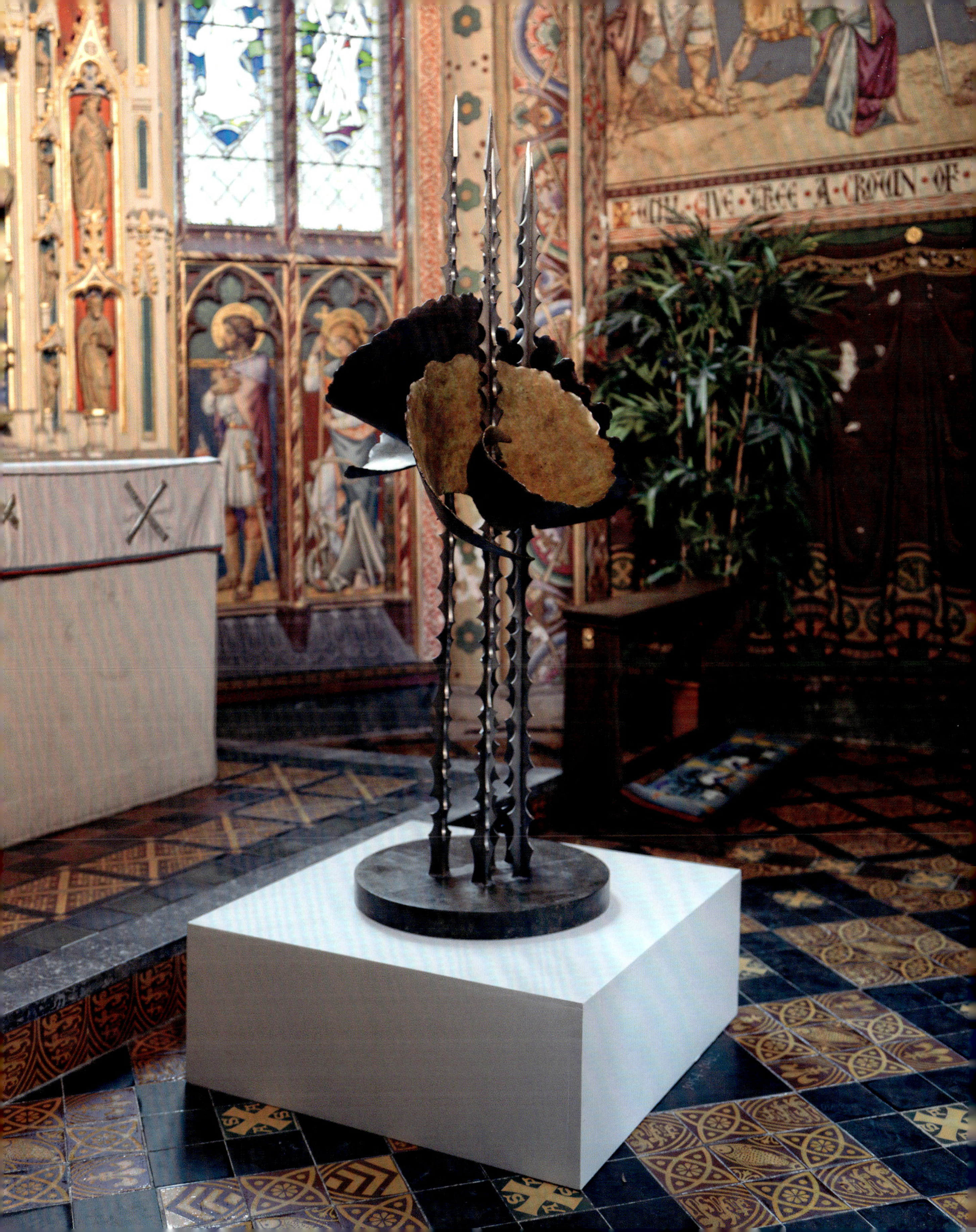
GIVE THEE A CROWN OF

Sea Scarf

Charlotte Mayer

Bronze

Edition of 6

35cm high

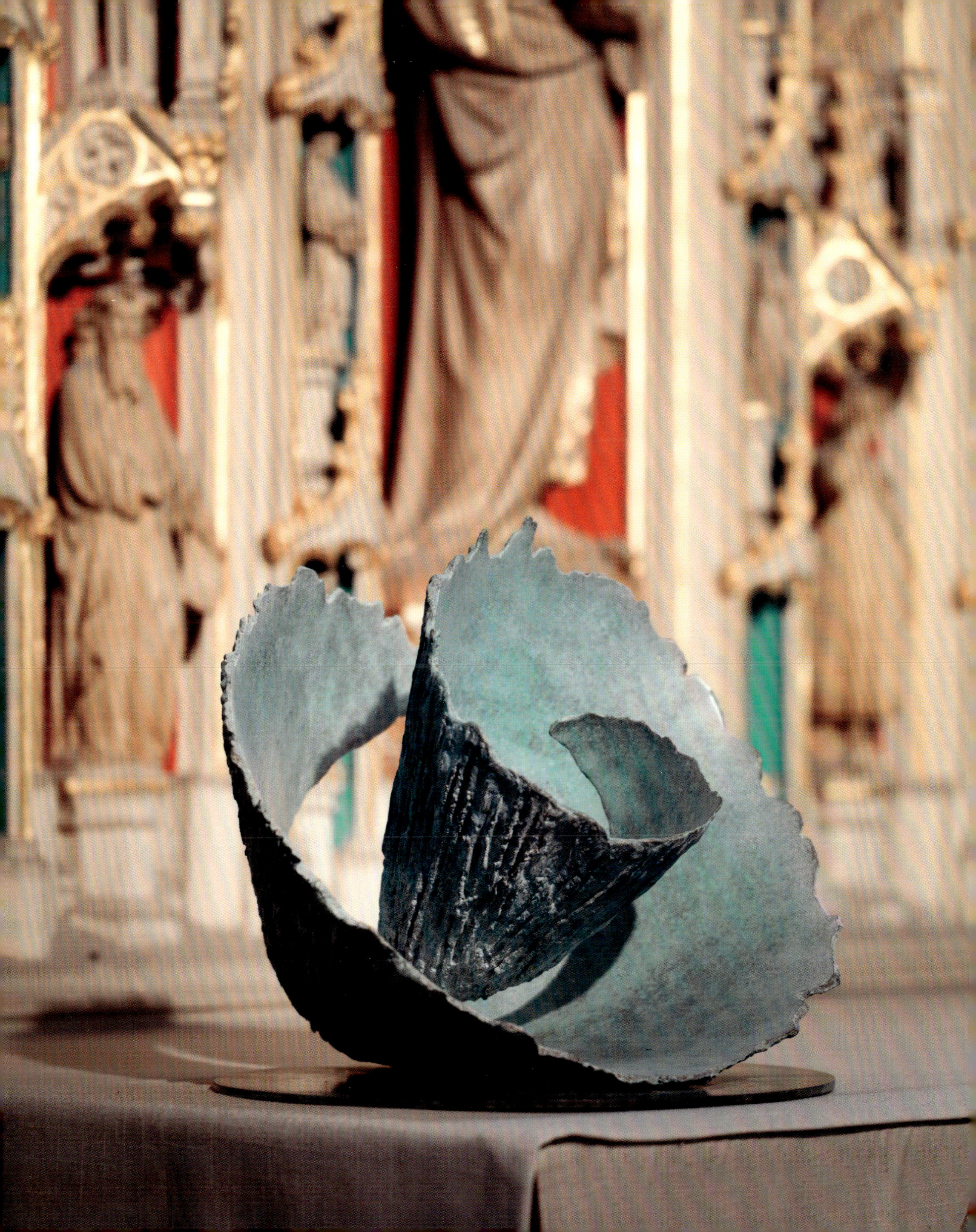

LEONARD McCOMB RA b.1930

'In 1960-64 I began full-time teaching at The West of England College of Art, Bristol.

During that time I was delighted to receive from a friend and a kind supporter, Henry Gifford, Professor of English at the University of Bristol, a present of a matured holly tree trunk from his garden.

At that time I was very interested in the work of Constantin Brancusi as I am still today.

I carved the tree trunk into a co-ordinated rhythm of shapes of various section and proportion inspired by the example of contrast I found in the original holly trunk.

Holly has a close compact internal structure, beautiful to carve to a tight smooth outer surface.

The sculpture and circular base were cast in bronze and polished to a mirror light-reflective surface so they shared a harmony of light and internal energy.'

Tree Form and Circle in Polished Bronze
Leonard McComb
Bronze
Unique
240cm high

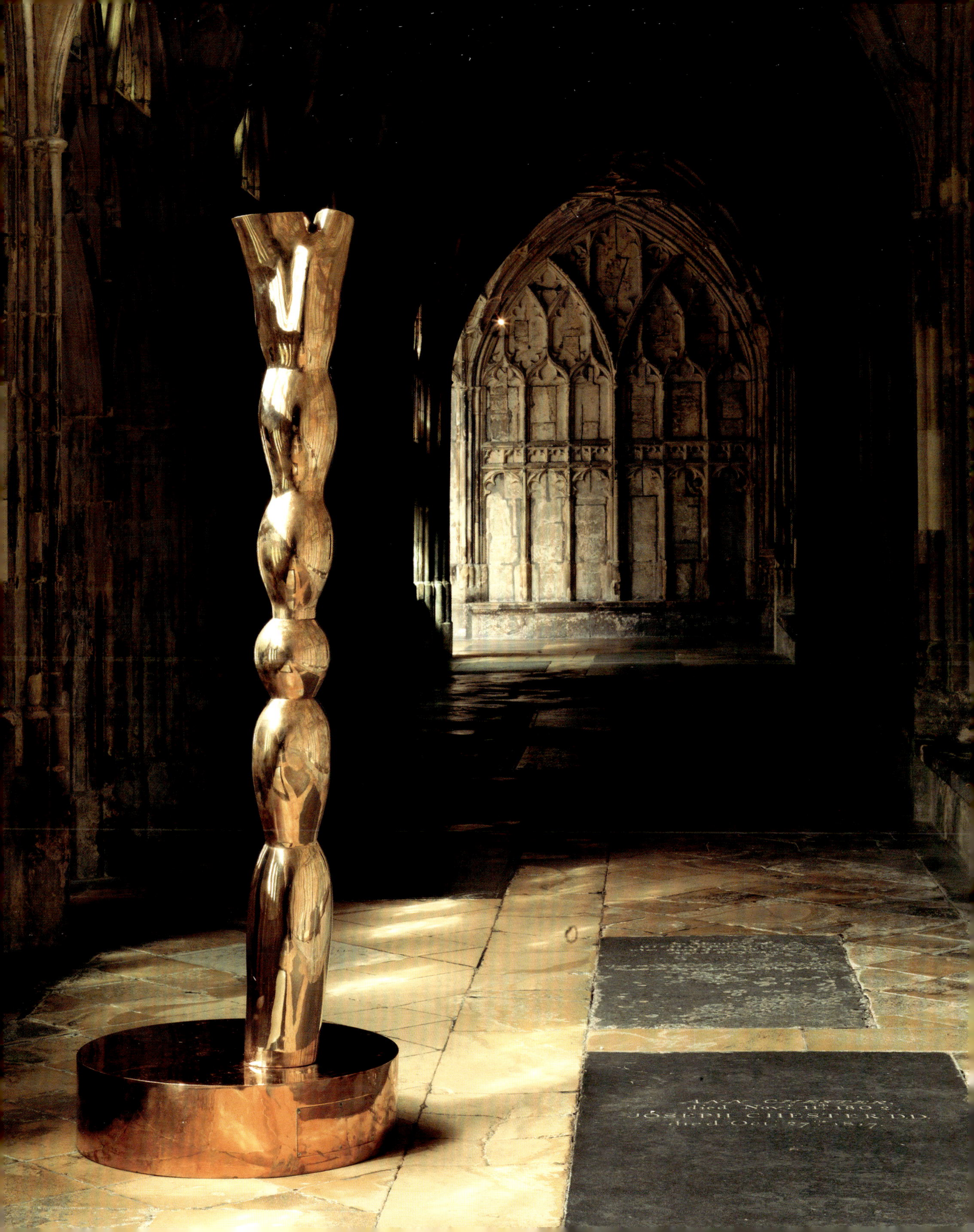
died Nov. 11th 1802
JOSEPH CHESTER D.D.

HENRY MOORE RBS 1898 - 1986

The classic sculpture Reclining Figure - Bone Skirt, is one of Moore's most recognisable and iconic figures. This is the working model for a marble sculpture which was owned by his daughter Mary and was subsequently reworked as a monumental carving in travertine marble. At the time Moore was spending the summers at a villa he had built near the Carrara quarries in Italy.

Moore observed in 1931 "The human figure is what interests me deeply, but I have found principles of form and rhythm from the study of natural objects such as pebbles, rocks, bones, trees, plants ... bones have marvellous structural strength and hard tenseness of form, subtle transition of one shape into the next..."

Moore returned again and again to the reclining figure, initially inspired by the early Mexican Chacmool sculptures he saw at the British Museum in the 1920s. The subject re-occurs throughout his career with infinite variations of form and line; here the use of drapery accentuates the shape and continuous line of the body.

'I want to be quite free of having to find a 'reason' for doing the Reclining Figures, and freer still of having to find a 'meaning' for them. The vital thing for an artist is to have a subject that allows him to try out all kinds of formal ideas – things that he doesn't yet know about for certain but wants to experiment with, as Cézanne did in his 'Bathers' series. In my case the reclining figure provides chances of that sort. The subject-matter is given. It's settled for you, and you know it and like it, so that within it, within the subject that you've done a dozen times before, you are free to invent a completely new form-idea.'(1

(1)Henry Moore quoted in John Russell, Henry Moore, Allen Lane, The Penguin Press, London 1968, p.28

Working Model for Reclining Figure: Bone Skirt

Henry Moore

Bronze

Edition of 9

35cm high

Private Collection c/o Osborne Samuel Gallery

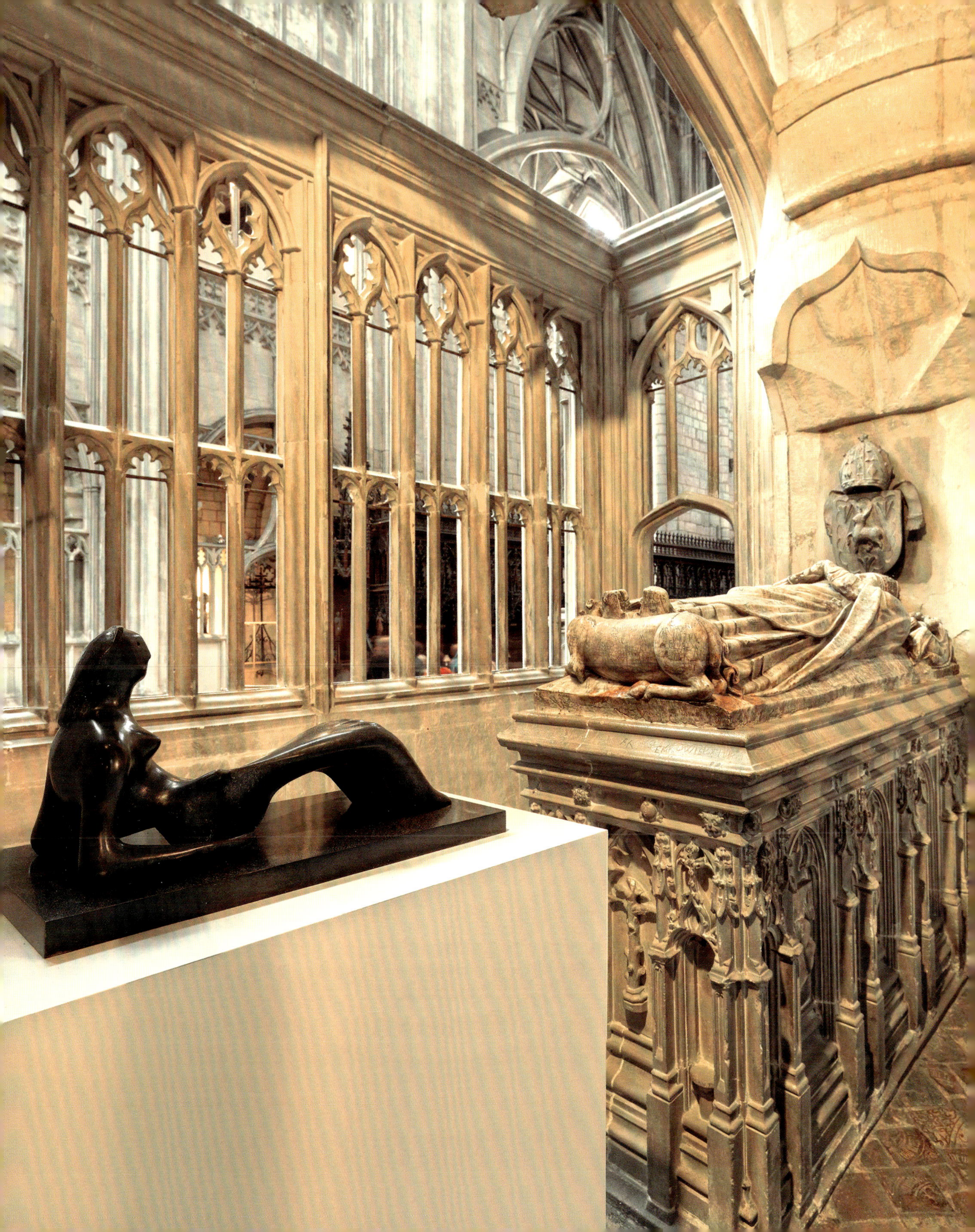

DAVID NASH RA b.1945

'The form for Overlap came from looking at Celtic decoration and

feeling how it reflected the character of Celtic thinking; the weave and flow of different streams of thought and feeling, interlocking, overlapping with nature, family, tradition, weather, streaming of time. The original Overlap is wood, carved from a lime trunk and charred.

Through my career as a wood sculptor, often a form has occurred that I have felt could be translated into bronze, the wood not being a crucial factor of the form as it is in many of my sculptures. Overlap was one of the first pieces that took this step. Others have followed.'

Overlap
David Nash
Bronze
Edition of 3
107cm high

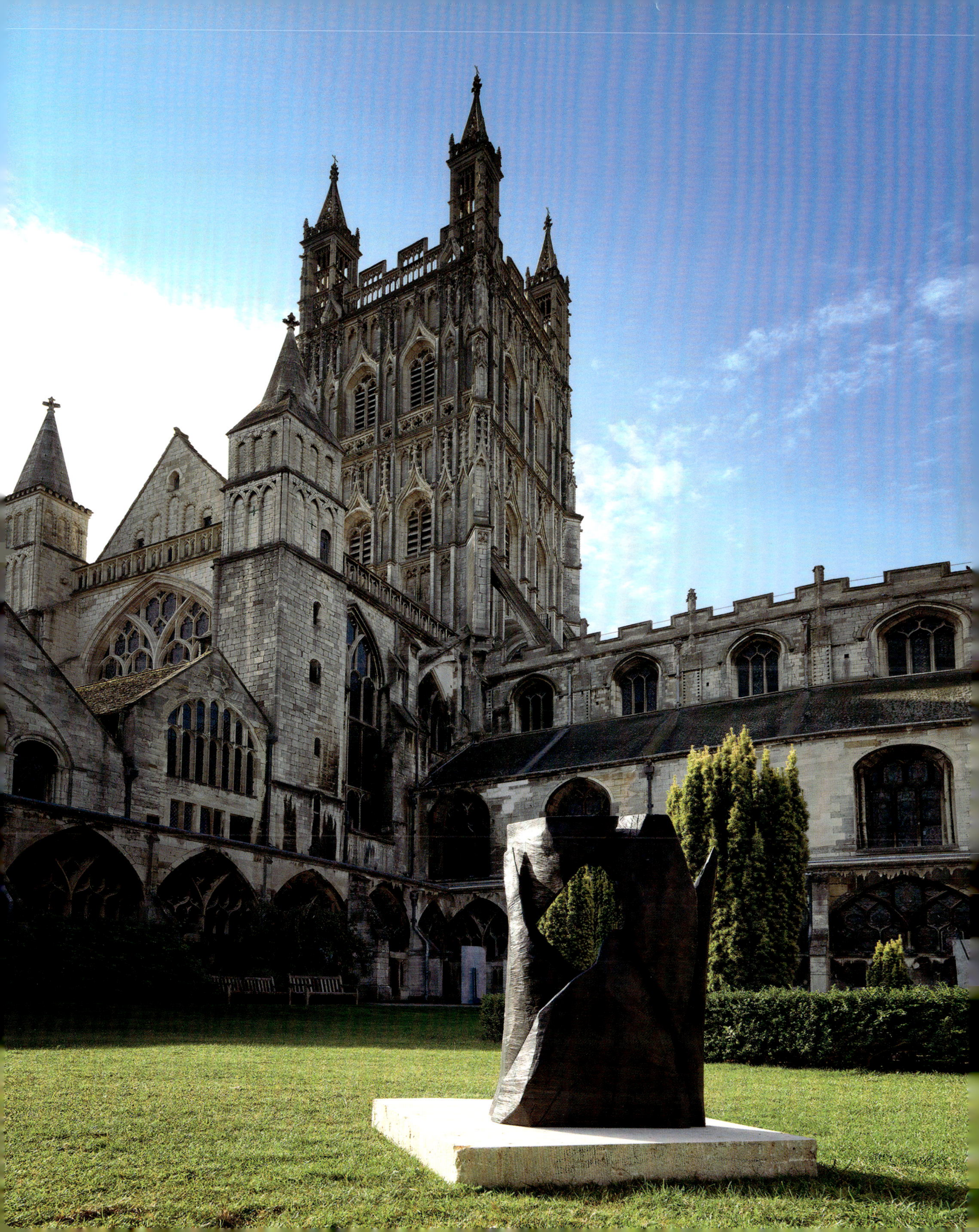

BREON O'CASEY 1928 – 2011

Although O'Casey had been apprenticed to the sculptors Denis Mitchell and Barbara Hepworth early on in his career, it was not until he was in his seventies that he started sculpting:

'I had made several attempts at sculpture in the past...but to no avail. I couldn't seem to think in 3D, but I came to it eventually, through the back door. I had made a number of animal brooches, and these evolved into little silver animals in their own right. Conor Fallon, the Irish sculptor, introduced me to wax as a material, which I found more sympathetic than clay or plaster, and I started to make small wax figures and getting them cast in bronze. And these grew in size.'

His sculptures, unlike his paintings, are almost always based on an animal, bird or person:

'Why this is, I don't know, nor do I care. It's as well to let questions like that alone.'

Large Cockerel
Breon O'Casey
Bronze
Edition of 5
99cm high

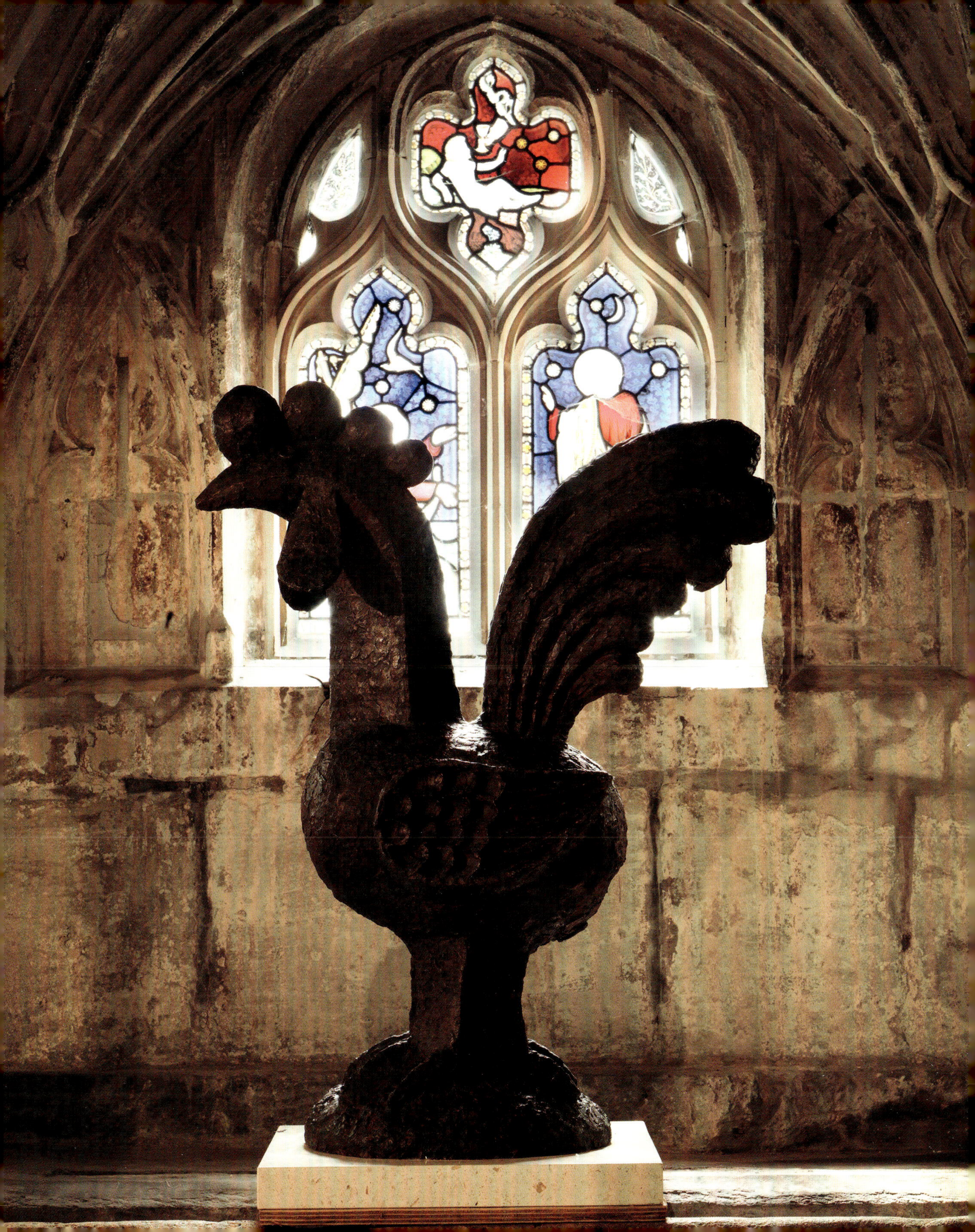

EILIS O'CONNELL RHA b.1953

'Wood, stone, metal, any material that has been subjected to the forces of nature intrigue me. Collecting eroded and attritioned material is part of my creative working process.

Atlantic Oak is a bronze cast of a slab of oak that I found in an old boat-builders yard on the coast of County Mayo.

It was common practice for island boat builders to season oak in sea water for a couple of years. The cellulose in the wood would wash away exposing the hard wood. By mistake, this particular piece of oak was left in the ocean for 33 years so the resulting texture is extremely rare and beautiful.

Despite the years of collecting things, this is the first time that I have not interfered with the found form.

It took 2 years to dry out the wood in my studio and during this time I realised that the only improvement I could make was to keep it vertical and preserve it permanently by casting in bronze.'

Atlantic Oak (detail)
Eilis O'Connell
Bronze and stainless steel
Edition of 3
400cm high

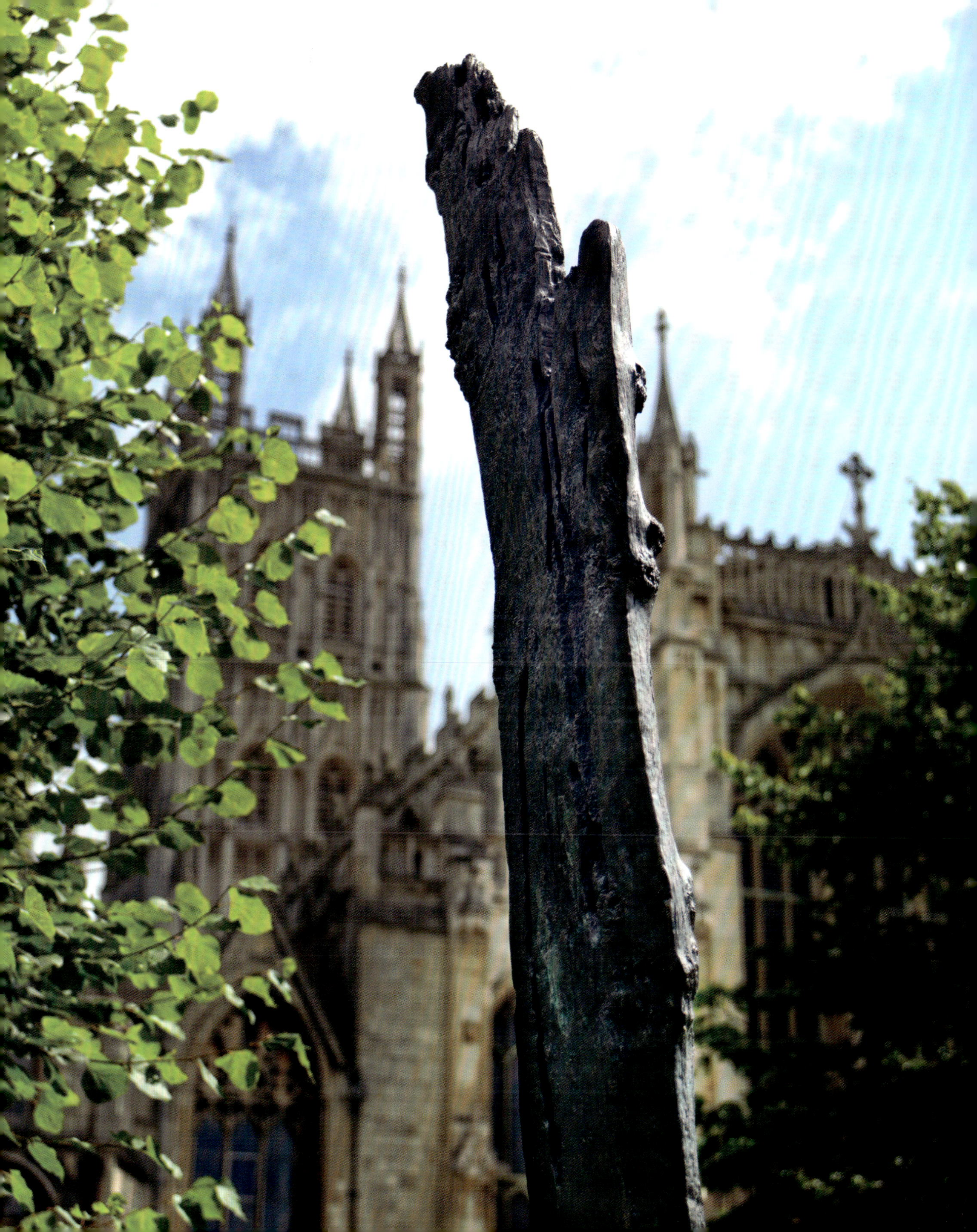

Sheep Skull

Eilis O'Connell

Resin and bone

Unique

28cm high

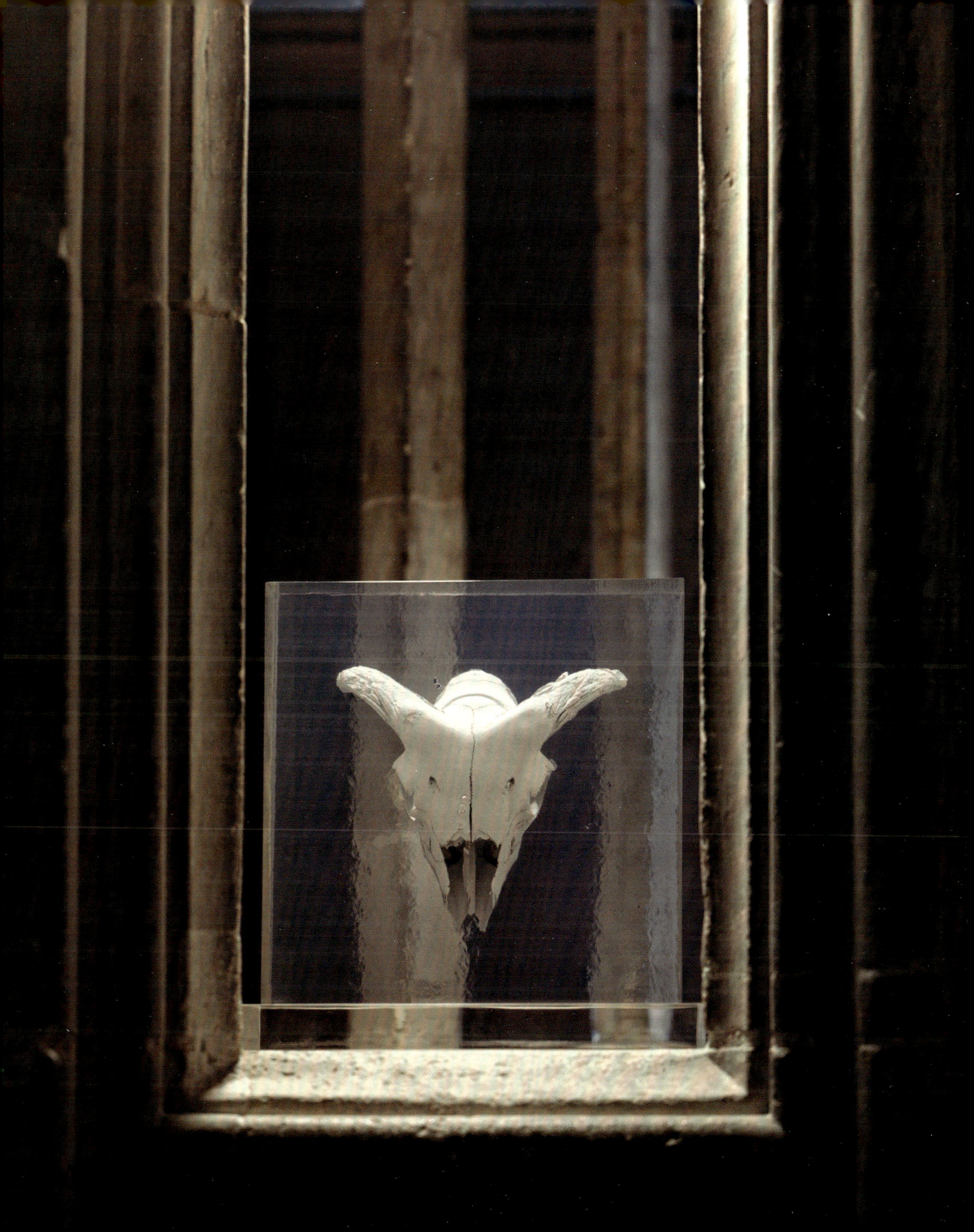

EDUARDO PAOLOZZI RA 1924 - 2005

"Scooped out by the action of the Cyclops' fires,
You can hear the clang of hard blows on the anvils,
The roaring when masses of ore are smelted within
And a throbbing blast of flame from the furnaces.
Here is Vulcan's place......"

Virgil The Aeneid

Vulcan
Eduardo Paolozzi
Plaster
Unique
180cm high

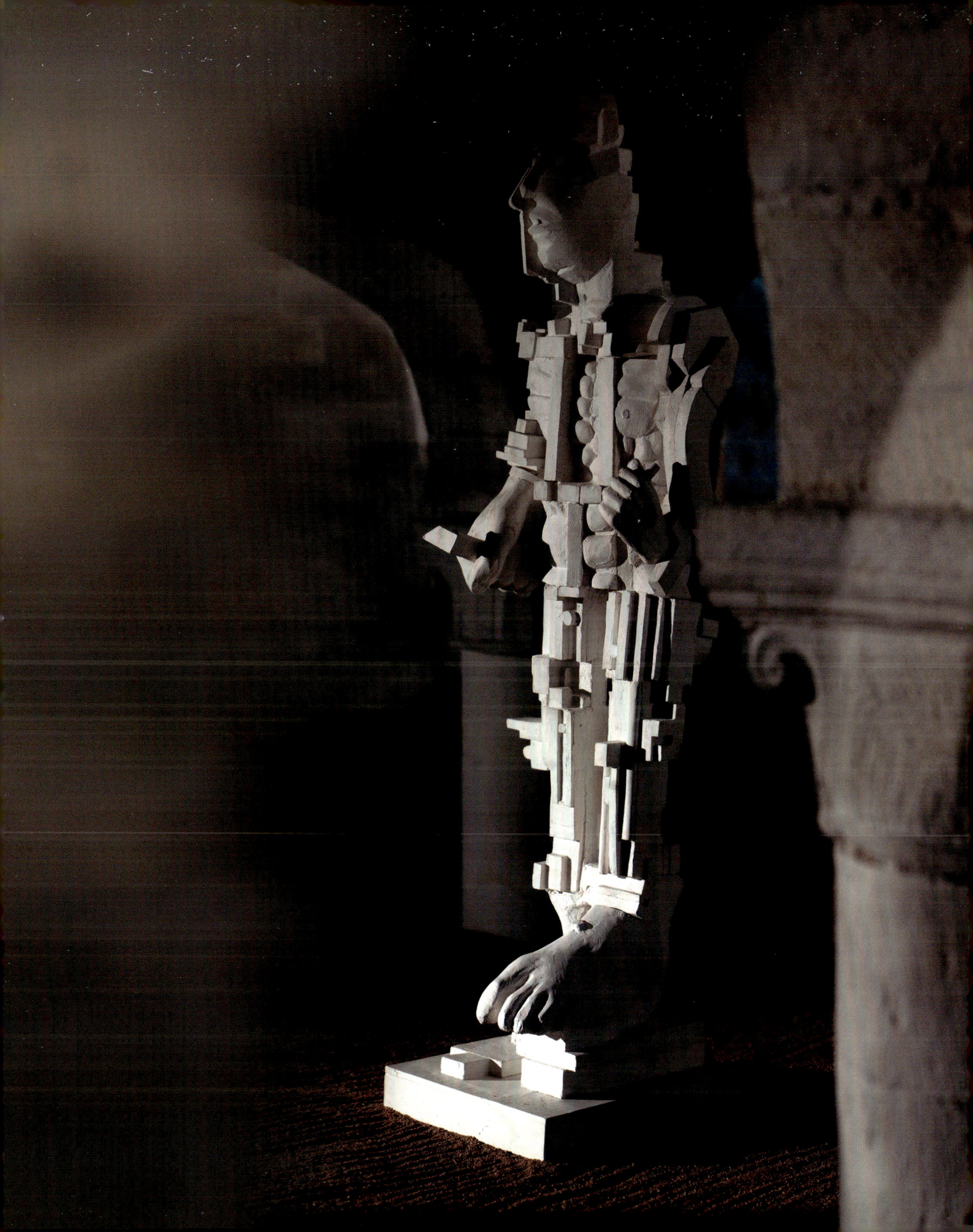

KATE PARSONS b.1955

'East West is based on my cross-cultural experiences of 'material objects' associated with mortality in East Africa (Kenya) and West Africa (Nigeria).

My work is process led, being very much linked to the ritual of the sculptural processes and materials themselves through repetition. The work is a result of a long trajectory of thought and association of my past work involving walls, panels, and floor pieces, with earth being a central feature in the making process and finished concept. The terracotta clay used in past work has had connotations with African earth, and here the rocks are a continuation of this in different form. Themes prominent in my work show reversal and contrast, or binary oppositions, both formally and conceptually.'

East West – Matter of Interpretation
Kate Parsons
Herculite
Unique
Approx. 25cm high

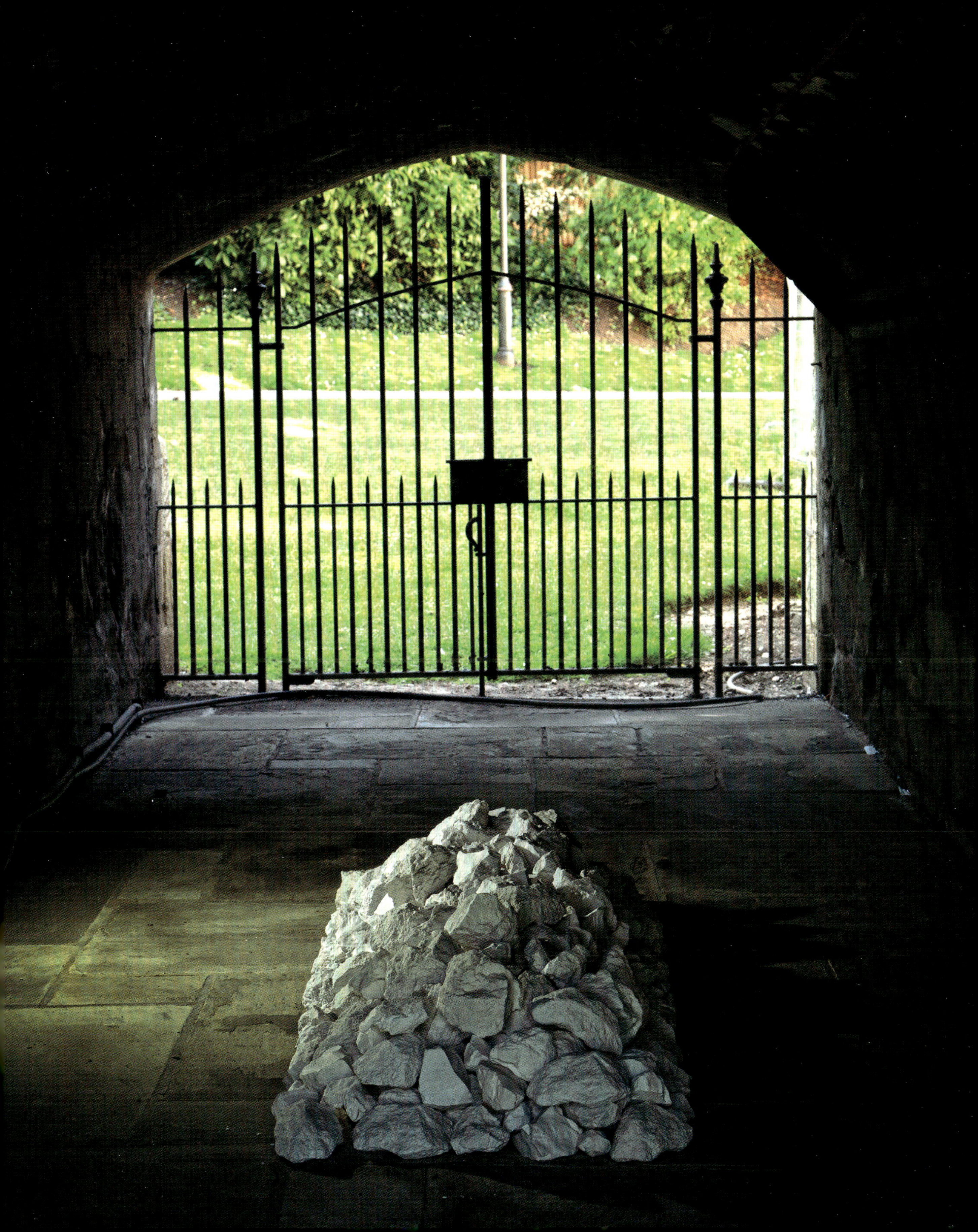

WILLIAM PYE FRBS b.1938

'Vesqua is one of my series of 'Brimming Bowl' water sculptures. Surface tension maintains a flat disc of apparently still water at a level that is right up to the rim of the bronze bowl. A significant flow of water enters the vessel and as this rises turbulence disappears to give an effect of stillness, despite the fact that some 135 litres of water per minute are slipping down the throat of a square internal weir that draws water down to a reservoir below.'

Vesqua
William Pye
Bronze
Unique
110cm high

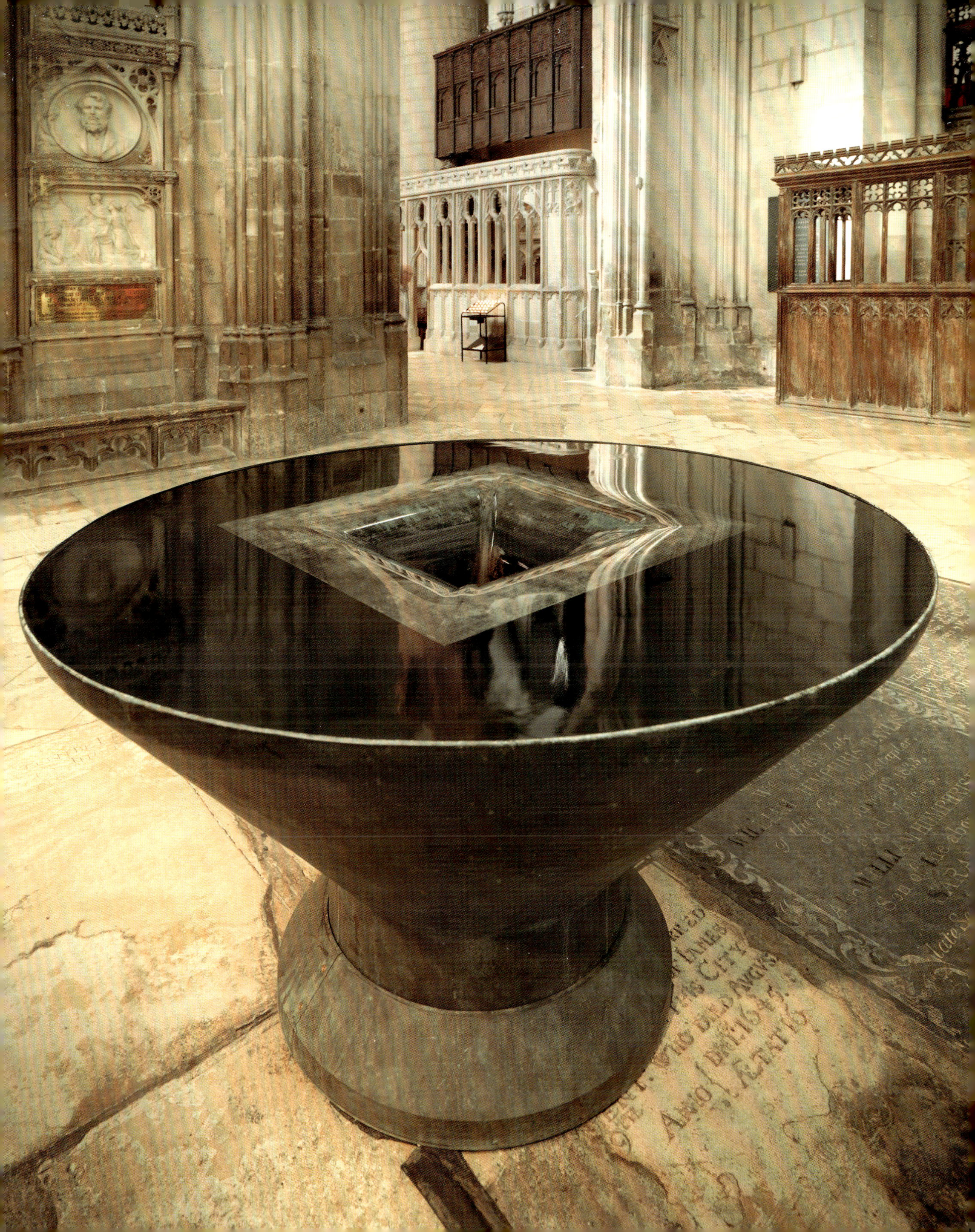

MARC QUINN b.1964

Quinn uses a broad range of materials, both traditional and unconventional. The materiality of the object, both its elemental composition and surface appearance, is at the heart of his work.

In Bread Hand, the form of the finished sculpture is decided by the rising dough and by the heat of the oven; the artist's involvement is minimal and it is the accidental nature of this process which interests him.

'…it seemed like a very expressionist thing with a lot of feeling and meaning in it, but in fact it was a very random thing that had been shaped by gravity, yeast and heat. So it's kind of that interest in how nothing is there and everything is a projection.'

Bread Hand
Marc Quinn
Bread and perspex box
Unique
41cm high

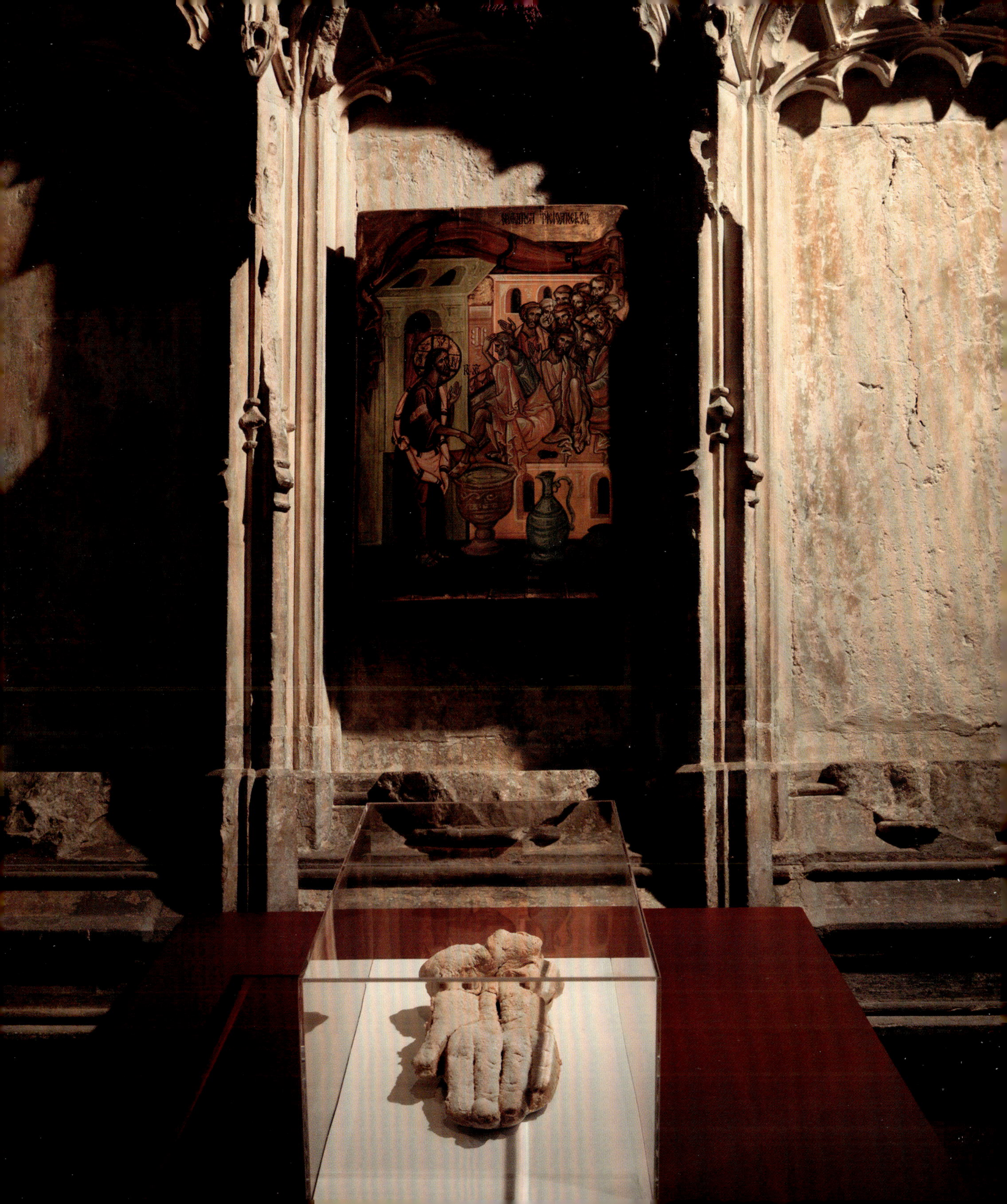

JORDI RAGA b.1990

'Thames is a project that originated in the period I decided to move to London during late 2012. The need was to explore the emotions of an idea that I found on the River Thames as an iconic departure point.

What struck me was the character and force of this dividing artery as viewed from a satellite picture. Later, a line of holes emerged in a mix of geometry and intuition based on the real reference. The result looked for rhythm and balance while testing the limits of the material.

Meditating about the dual value of line -for it divides and unifies- the fascination relies on its capacity to remember a movement while giving an illusion of stillness.'

SEVERN
BEYOND PRINT

Thames is sponsored by Severn

Thames
Jordi Raga
Marble
Unique
180cm high

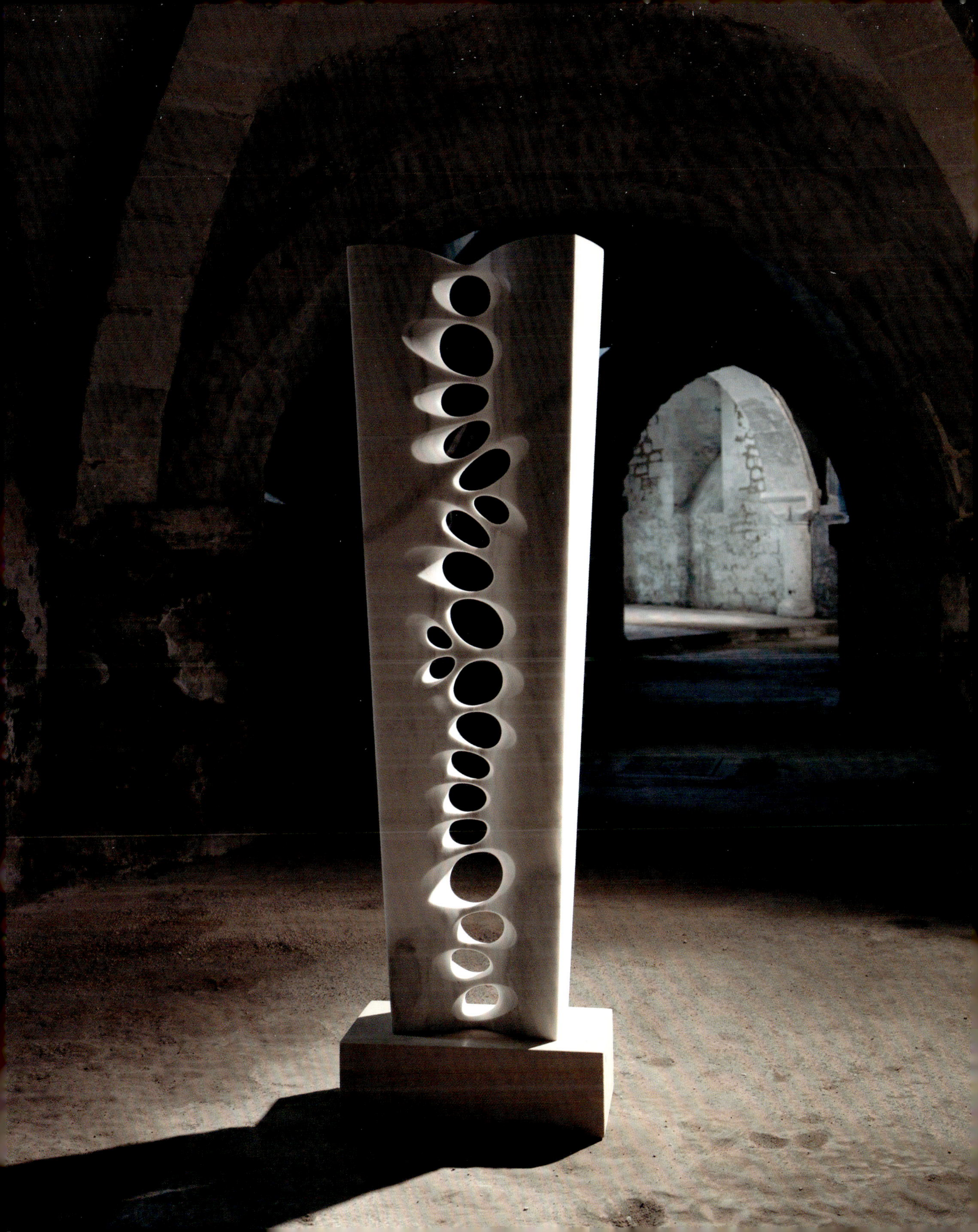

PETER RANDALL-PAGE FRBS b.1954

'Mother Tongue developed from a sketch book drawing of a mouse intestine which evolved into a sculpture exploring our primary and most intimate sense: the 'language' of touch.

Anyone who has a cat will be familiar with finding a mouse's gallbladder on the kitchen floor. It is the only bit they won't eat. One day I had a close look at one and made a few sketches of what turned out to be a rather beautiful form.

Months later I came across these drawings and through a series of maquettes developed the idea for a sculpture.

Mother Tongue is a celebration of our first language, the language of touch which we experience in the womb and at the breast. Perhaps it is wrong to call it a language, it has no grammar or syntax but nevertheless involves a sensual communication which must be at the heart of all tongues.'

Mother Tongue
Peter Randall-Page
Kilkenny Limestone
Unique
115cm high

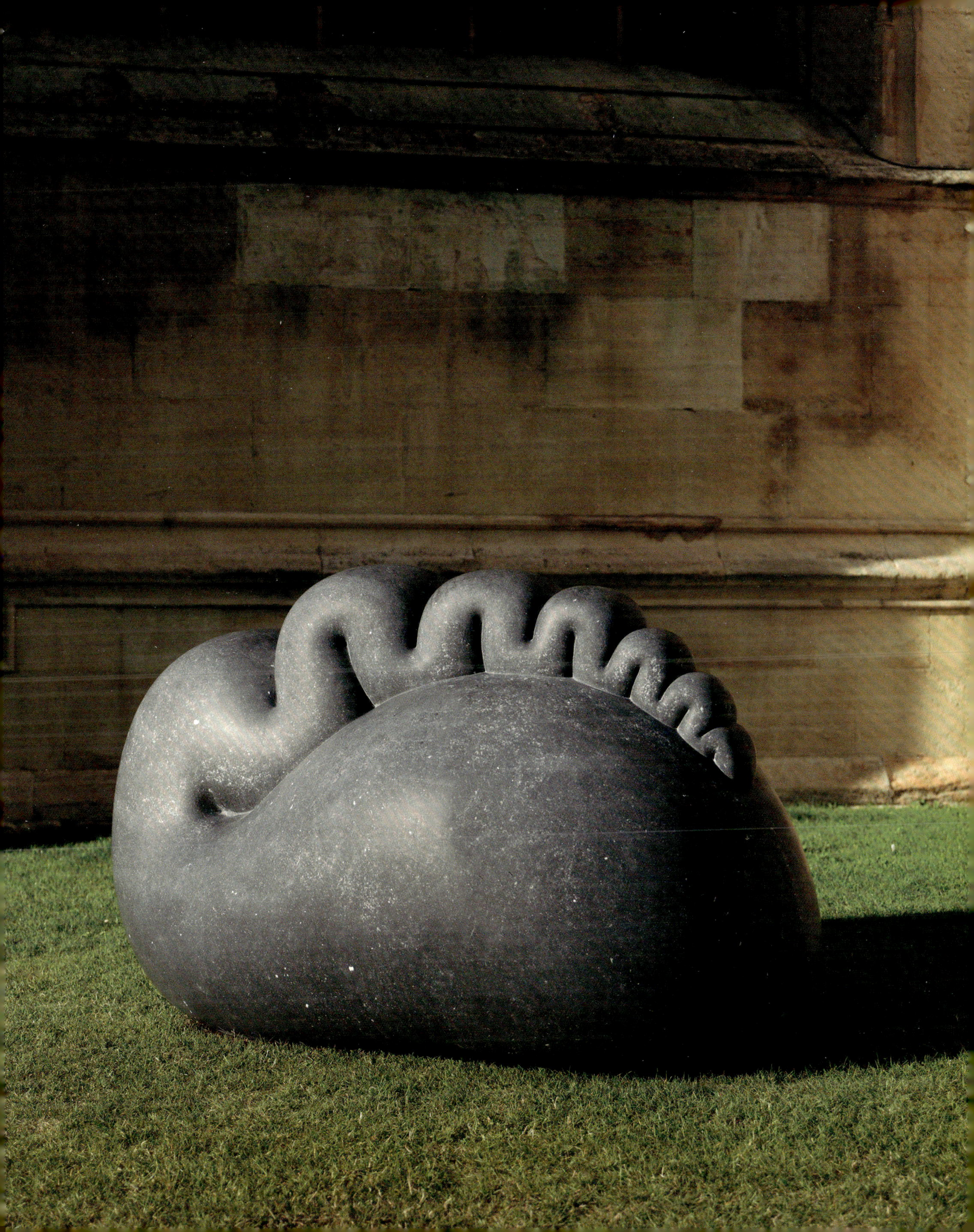

Maquette for Seed

Peter Randall-Page

Bronze

Edition of 12

24cm high

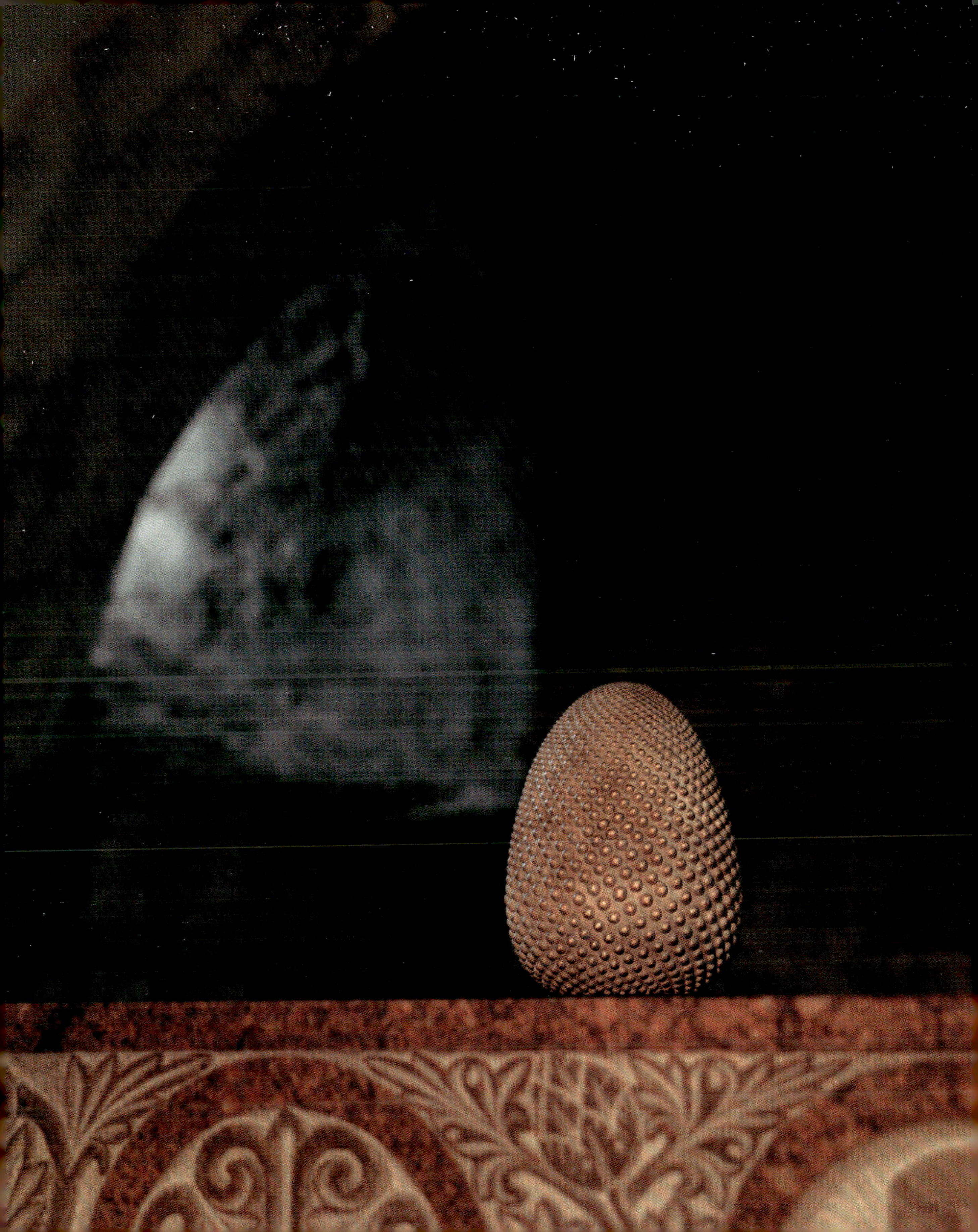

COLIN REID ARBS b.1953

'I went up the scaffold on the outside of Gloucester Cathedral during the restoration and made silicone casts of some of the medieval stonework. It was a wonderful opportunity to get access to stone details high on the Cathedral that are normally inaccessible. The castings were the starting point of Through a Glass Darkly and other works on the same theme. Ancient stone, carved by an unknown craftsman's hands centuries ago and gradually weathering and returning to its natural state is a good starting point. The piece is created by lost wax casting of glass.'

Through a Glass Darkly
Colin Reid
Glass
Unique
54cm high

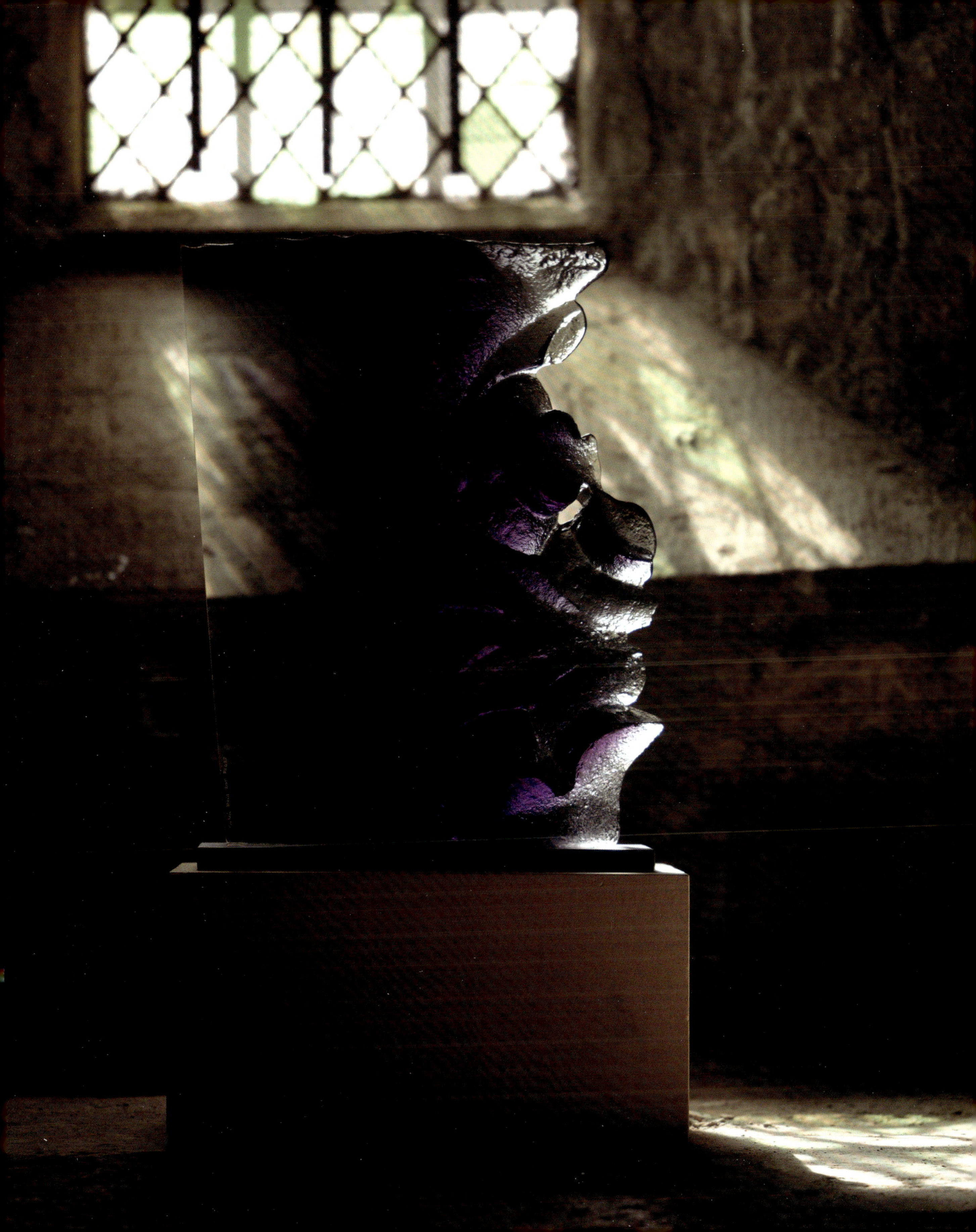

KENNETH ROBERTSON b.1931

'A life-size bronze of a pygmy hippo based on one at Marwell Zoo in Hampshire and created in 2000, this sculpture was commissioned by Peter Prior of Maidenhead.

After seeing a live one in Africa he had thoughts akin to Dr. Seuss in The Lorax that 'unless' we are more careful in our use of resources, places like the Thames Valley will revert to being a swamp with hippos wallowing in it, a situation aided by global warming. Peter thought that the sculpture could combine giving pleasure with reminding us to mend our ways.

The original sculpture was erected where the local children could climb on and enjoy it, which they did enormously. Sadly that first casting was stolen for scrap, which goes to show that even in bronze the species is endangered.'

Unless
Kenneth Robertson
Bronze
Edition of 3
137cm high

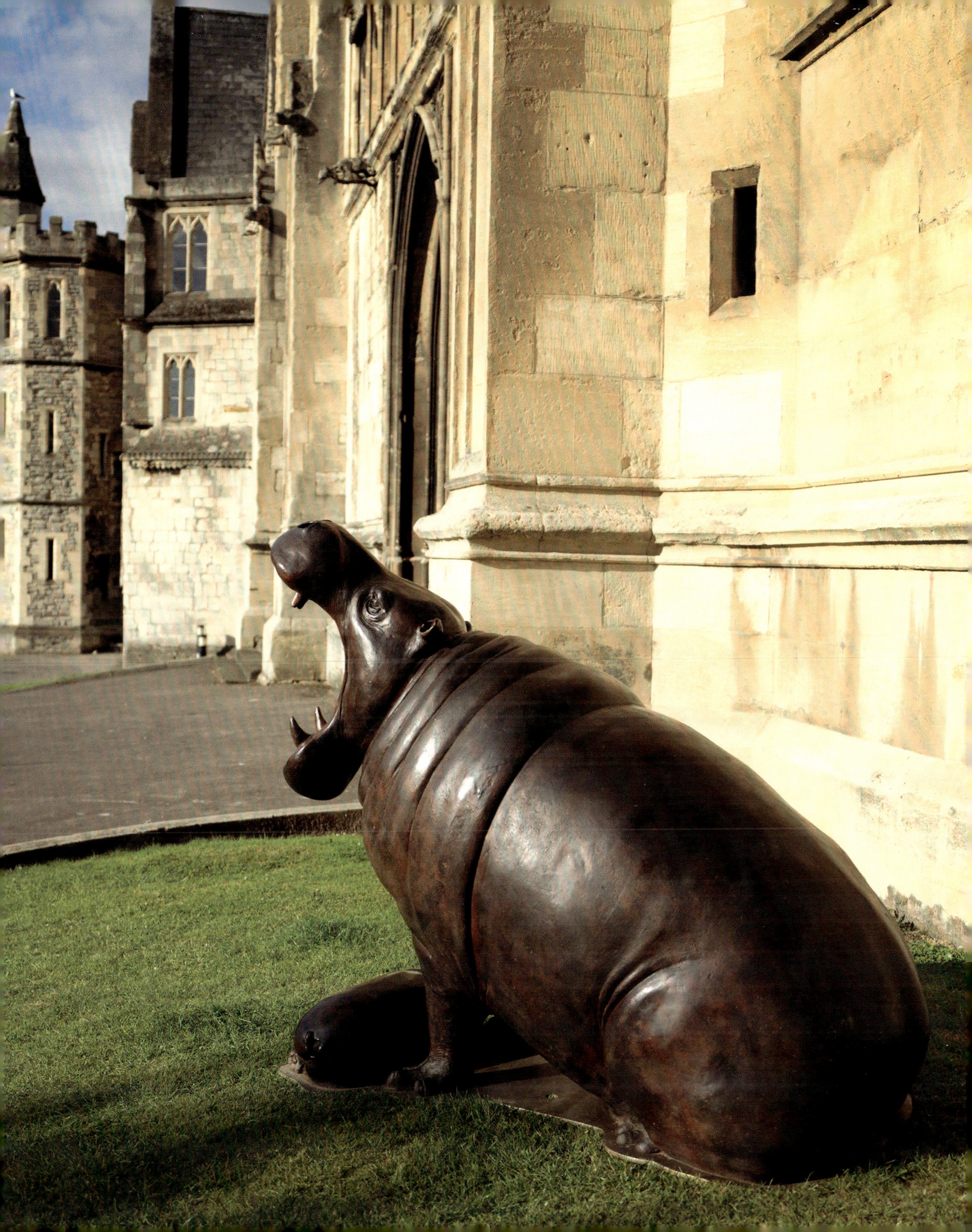

ALMUTH TEBBENHOFF FRBS b.1949

'First I worked with clay and when I outgrew that after 15 years (my kiln was big, but not THAT big) I opted for steel, a material that had fascinated my father before me. This became my main material for the next 20 years until 2006, when I was offered a scholarship to learn to carve marble in northern Italy.

Then followed an intense period of learning another language with both hands and brain. Steel had given me a skeletal structure and the engineering side of my brain loved to solve geometric puzzles, but it didn't give me volume. That I obtained from marble, and the seductive surfaces and beauty of stone.

'Ecstasy' is the result of the last seven years of thinking, working with, breathing, eating and dreaming marble in Pietrasanta. I consider myself extraordinarily lucky to be given these three fantastic materials to express my approach to life, which is voiced so beautifully in a quote from Bodhisattva Padmasambhava: "May your view be as vast as the sky and your actions as fine as barley flour". He probably didn't know marble dust, which works just as well, but it is something to aim for.'

Ecstasy
Almuth Tebbenhoff
Marble
Unique
210cm high

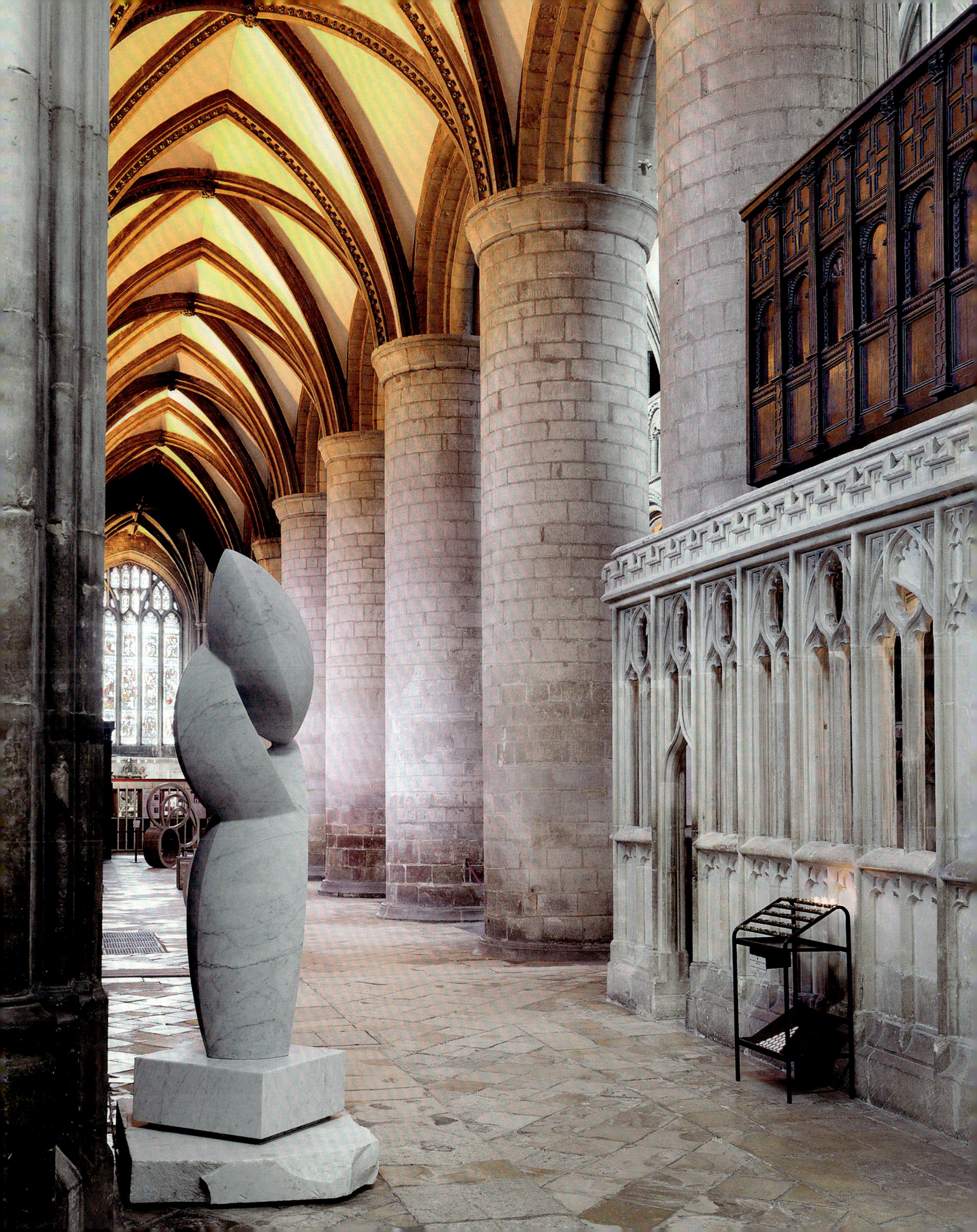

WILLIAM TUCKER RA b.1935

'In the late 1990s, I briefly occupied a studio space, empty except for a lump of plaster about twice the volume of a human head which I had brought with me, a fragment of an abandoned sculpture. It suggested Rodin's Man with the Broken Nose. My plan was simply to make drawings from it but soon I found myself reworking the plaster itself, then modelling new plaster head-like lumps and drawing from them. In the process I discovered that the human head was the most difficult of all subjects for a sculptor who had grown up in abstraction; that modelling and drawing the head involve challenging issues of perception, memory and recognition. In order for the image to be recognized, the head in the drawings faces you, is upright and frontal. The sculptured head is a discrete lump, which can be in any orientation to the ground, and any part of the surface can face you.

Thus the back of the Emperor head rests on the ground, the features face the sky. The sculpture is one of three of these "Imaginary portraits" I developed on a monumental scale.'

Emperor
William Tucker
Bronze
Edition of 5
165cm high

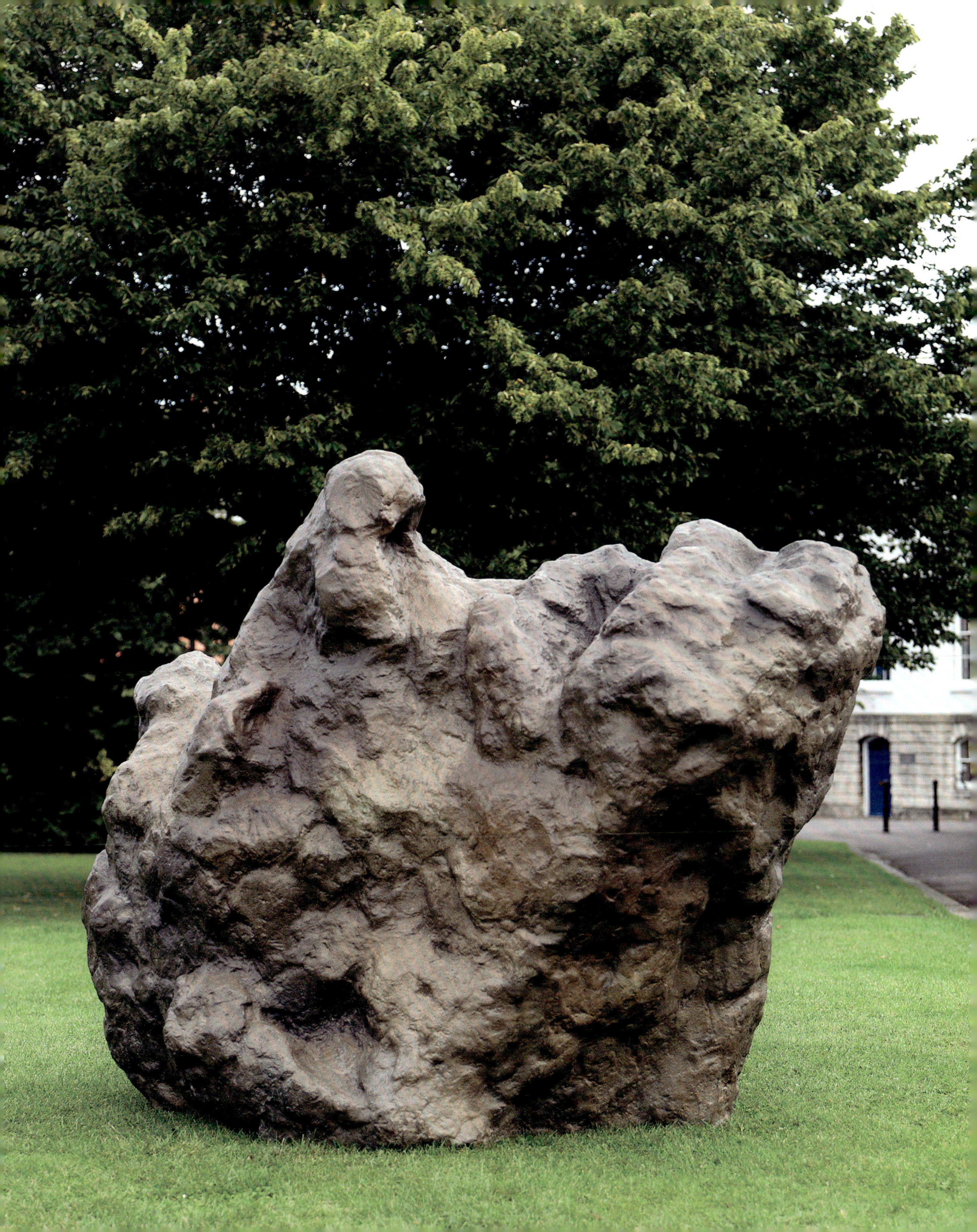

Greek Horse
William Tucker
Bronze
Edition of 6
142cm high

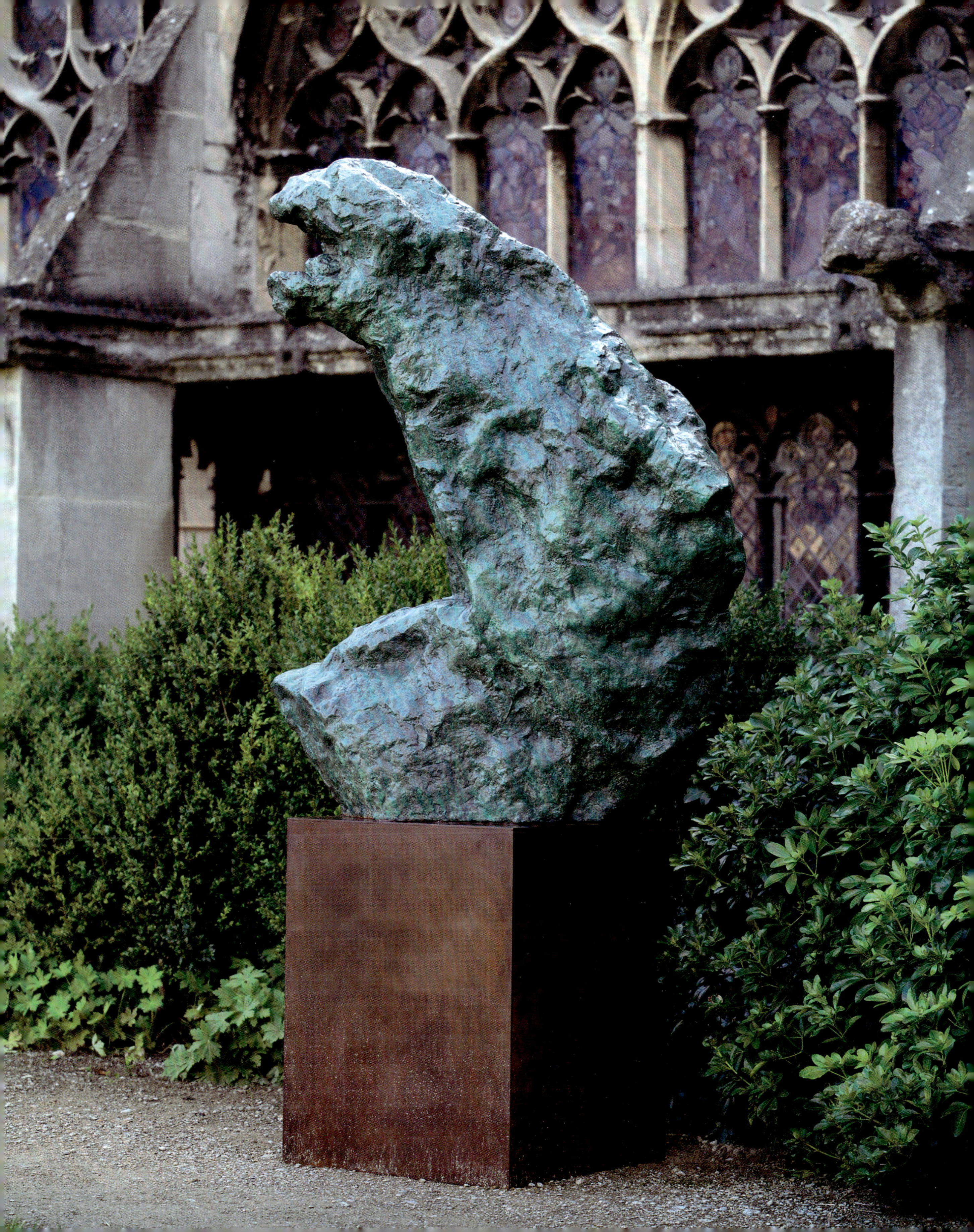

GAVIN TURK b.1967

'At first sight this appears to be the form of a homeless sleeper. Wrapped in a sleeping bag cocoon, its title implies a wonderer living a peripatetic life outside our cultural value systems. But the soft folds of the sleeping bag turn out to be hard metal, a painted bronze cast of this embarrassing cultural phenomenon. With uncompromising stillness the sculpture will never move or wander except at the behest of an art transport hoist. This image, captured forever, allows the viewer to wonder about lives led outside the ordinary; it gives them the power to stare.'

Nomad
Gavin Turk
Bronze
Unique
42cm high
Courtesy Murderme

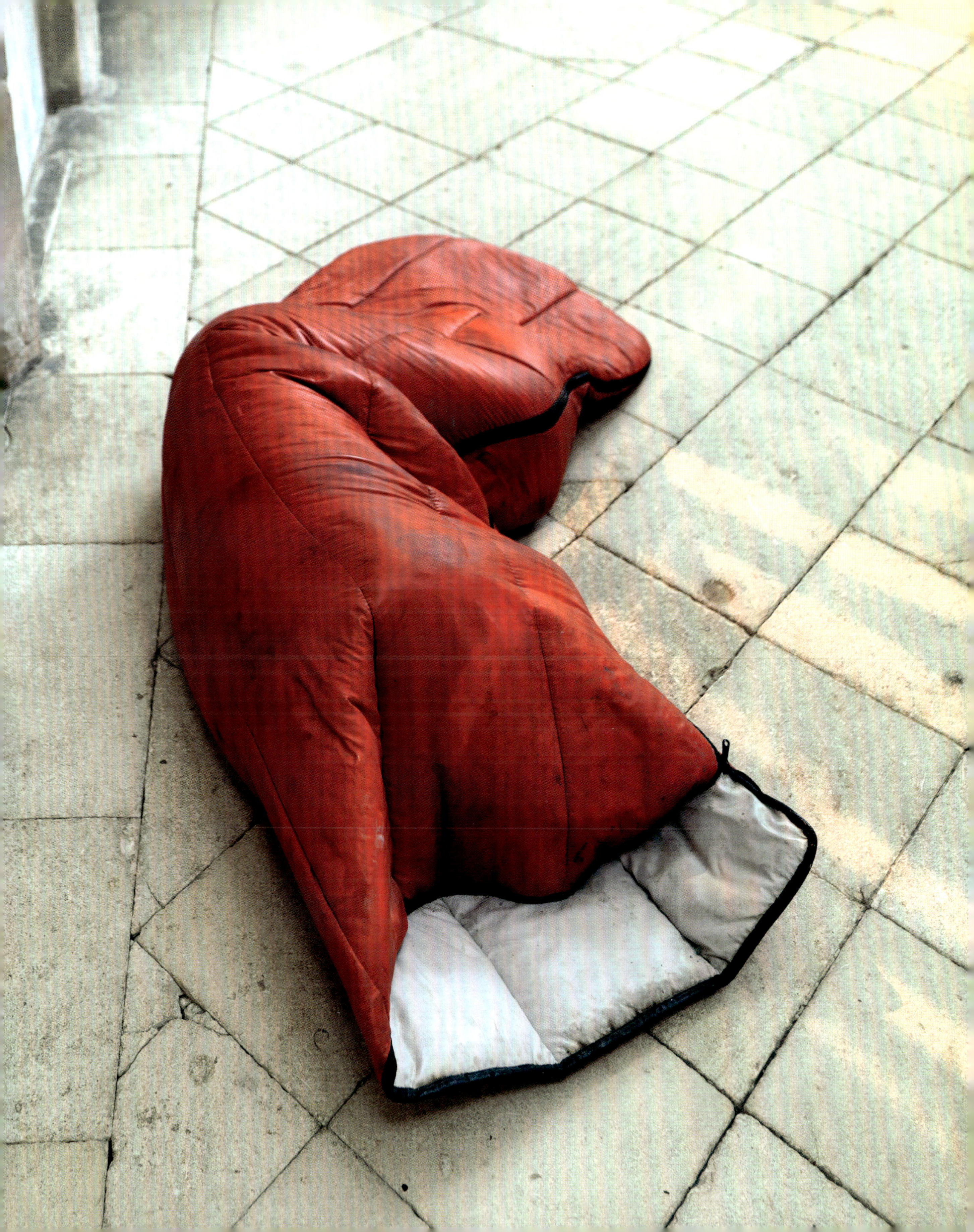

DEBORAH VAN DER BEEK b.1952

Collateral is a monument to the innocent victims of war.

When I heard Donald Rumsfeld use the chilling Orwellian phrase "collateral damage" to gloss over the killing of civilians in Iraq, I knew I had to make a piece in their memory. And not just in theirs, but in all unnecessary war suffering before and since. The mother and few-days-old baby were from a newspaper cutting, killed, I think in Lebanon. I hope it does not diminish their importance to couple them with the giant sculpted skull of a horse - an unbelievable eight million horses died in the First World War, along with many other animals drawn into the fray. The spent rockets and mortar shells were cast from ones brought back from Iraq and Afghanistan; some still had sand on them.

Collateral

Deborah van der Beek

Bronze

Edition of 5

65cm high

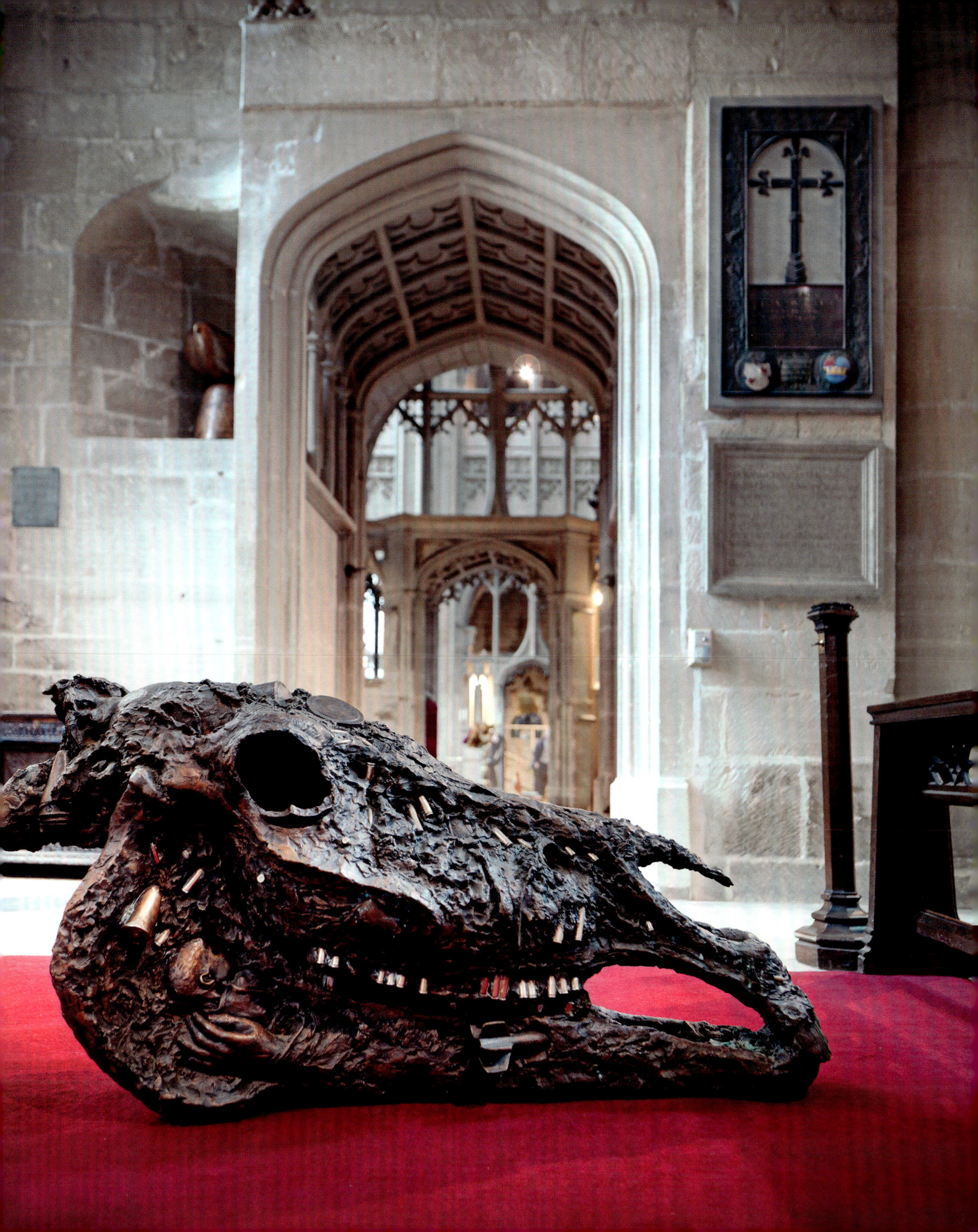

The World Gone Pear-Shaped

Deborah van der Beek

Bronze

Edition of 6

145cm high

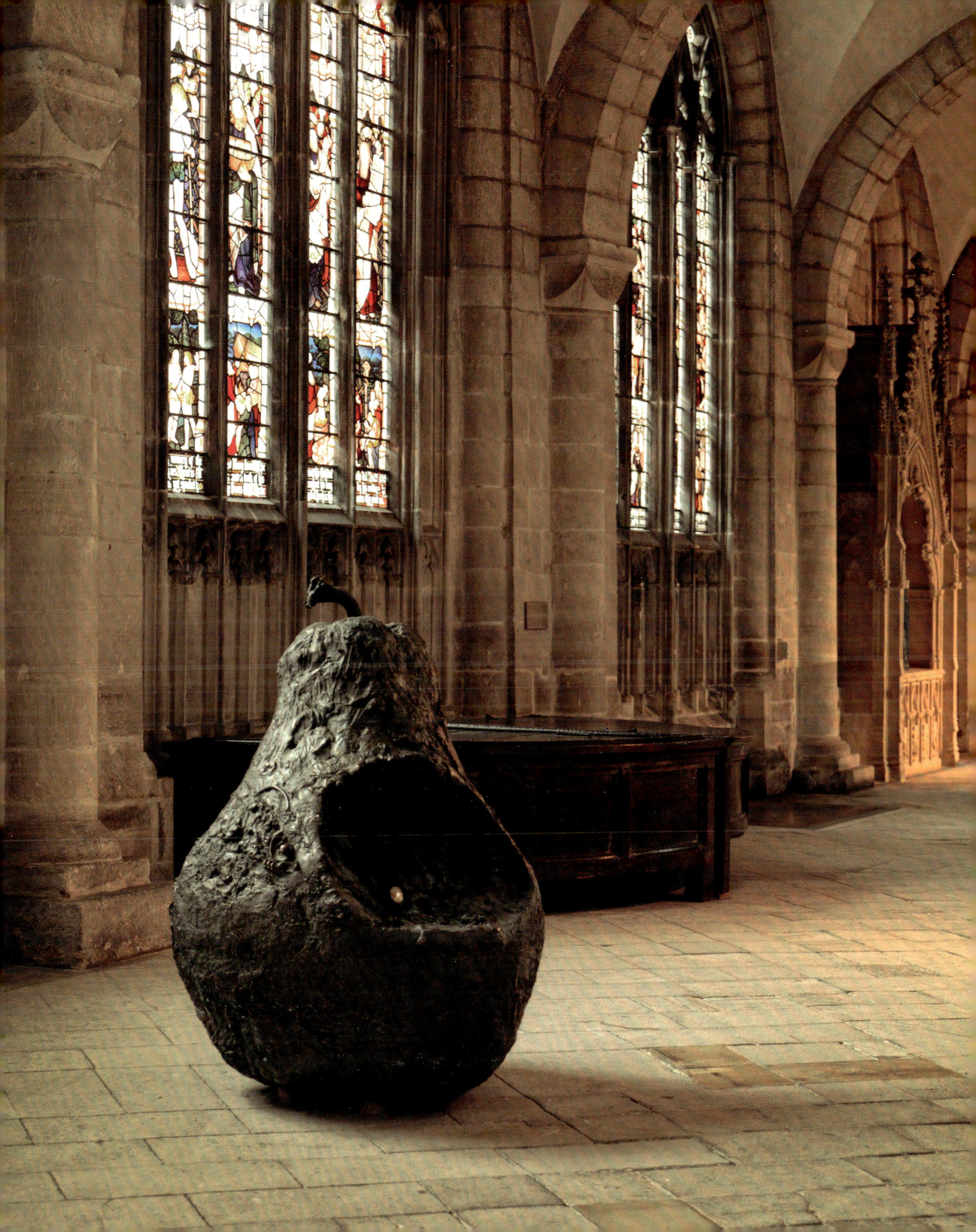

PAUL WAGER b.1949

'Omnibus is the principle sculpture in the Reflections on War series. Unlike conventional war memorials, Omnibus is a neutral statement where I have tried to avoid patriotic sentiment.

Thematic interrelationships of objects are predominant in both Omnibus and in all the Reflections on War pieces. These objects may appear utterly different, however their combination and juxtaposition create a new form where perception between objects, form and related thought is of importance.

My principle theme objective is that of tragedy, loss, reconciliation and the futility of war. Omnibus commemorates this tragic loss and is my contribution toward the centenary year of The Great War 1914 -1918 and in particular to and in memory of those brave uniformed men who made the ultimate sacrifice for their countries.'

"Death is absolute and without memorial" - Wallace Stevens

Omnibus

Paul Wager

Bronze

Edition of 12

261cm high

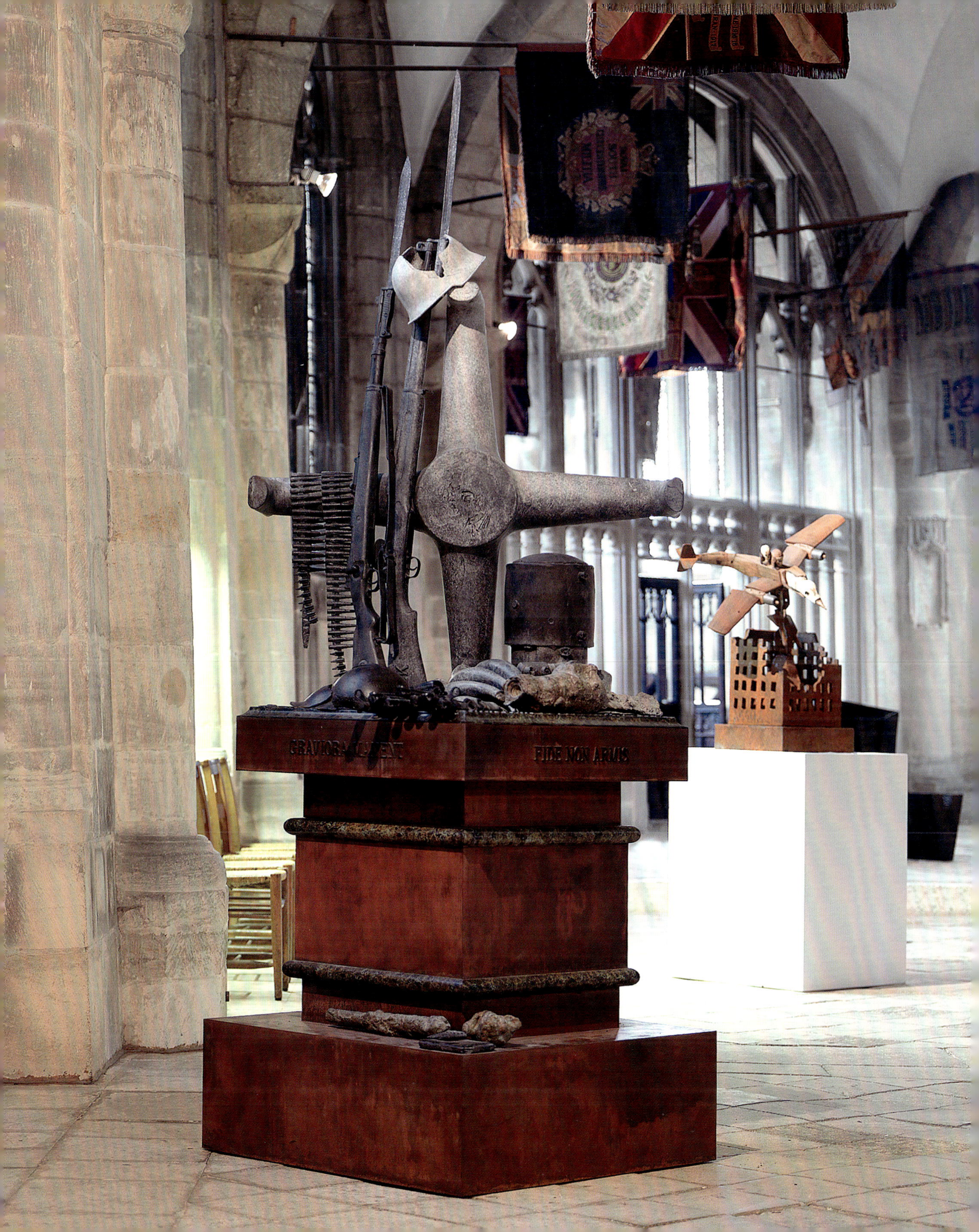
GRAVIORA
FIDE NON ARMIS

JASON WASON b. 1946

'In 1650, the Irish Archbishop James Ussher used his calculations of the life spans of Old Testament patriarchs to determine what he believed to be the exact date of the deluge and even creation. According to Ussher's figures, God sent the Great Flood in 2,501 B.C., and the creation of heaven, earth and all life on it, every animal and every plant, happened exactly 1,503 years earlier. God's first working day was Sunday, Oct. 23 -- in 4,004 B.C. Before then, according to Ussher, there was nothing.

Theories like Ussher's were taken at face value for centuries. Ussher himself was seen as a luminary, and his analyses were appended to the Bible. The creation account itself was already unassailable, although it became increasingly difficult for thinking individuals to reconcile it with nature. When fossils were taken to the church authorities to disprove this 'theory', the naturalists were told that the devil put them there to trick us.

Hence the name of the box: A Devil's Box of Tricks.'

A Devil's Box of Tricks
Jason Wason
Bronze, sand and fossils
Edition of 5
11cm high

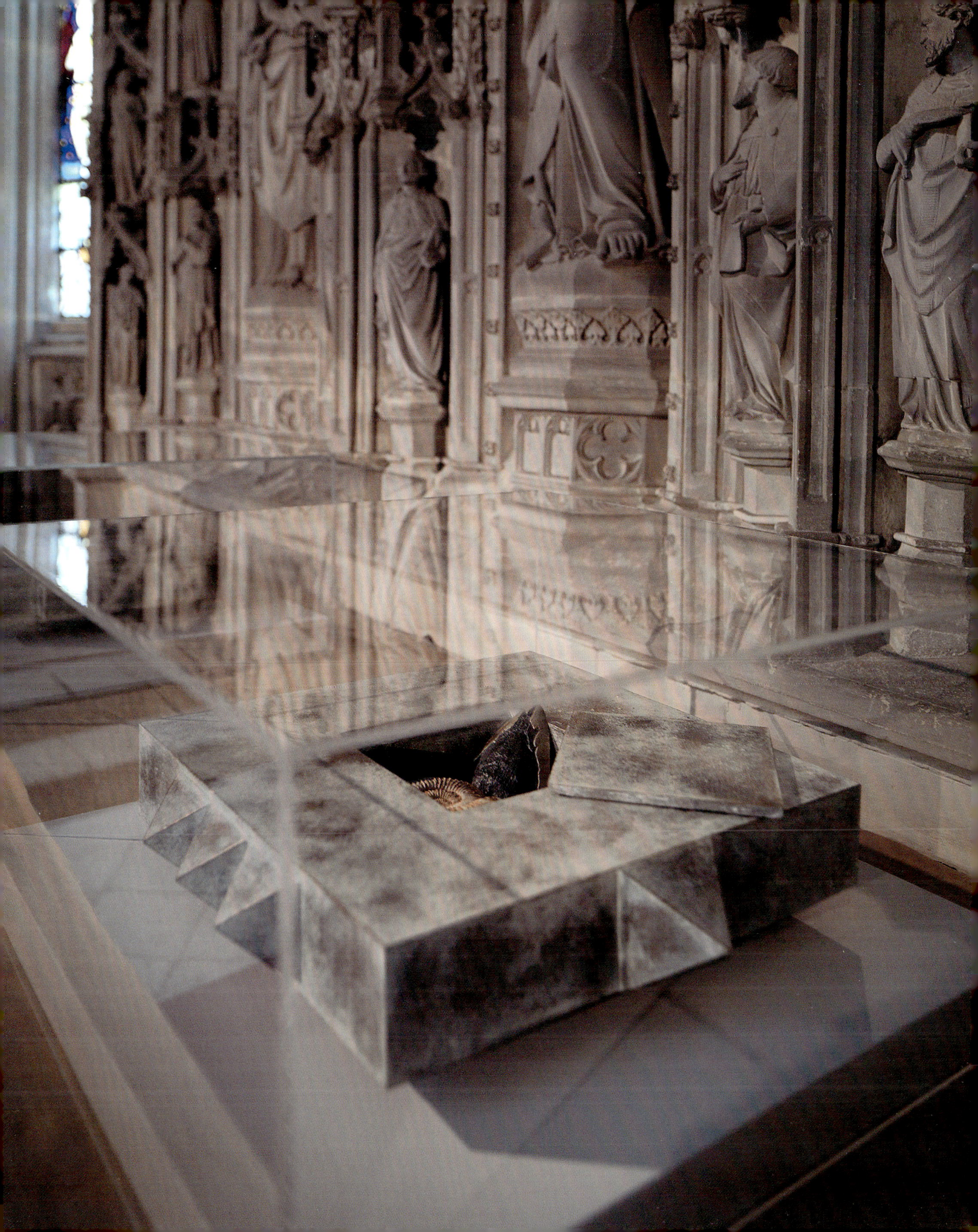

Give Me That Old Time Religion

Jason Wason

Bronze, sand, quartz and iron pyrite

Edition of 5

11cm high

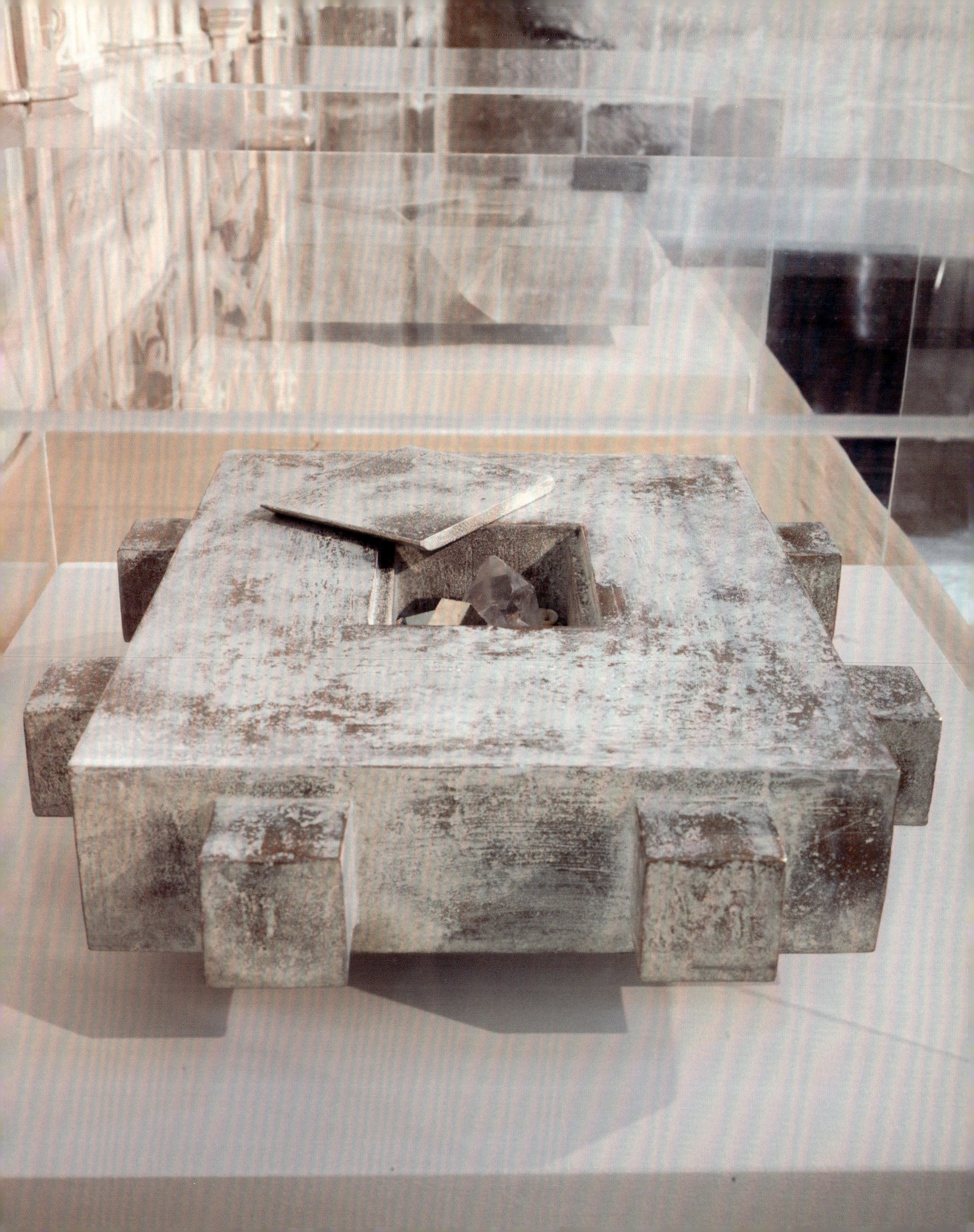

GLYNN WILLIAMS b.1939

'I made a series of sculptures of still lifes on a crate form over a period of about six years; the main protagonists being a bottle, two glasses and a jug atop a wooden crate, these become the "players" in a variety of ongoing dramas. Sometimes the Crate almost disappears and sometimes the objects of the still life are hardly recognisable. All these sculptures beg the assumption that they were once 'complete' but are now reduced/damaged in some way (a bit like museum fragments that speak about a previously perfect life).

Also, I have imported into these sculptures an ongoing interest in shadows and light textures. So Morandi-like etching into the surface to describe shadows and light-fall give the otherwise sombre work a more light-hearted feel. These etched lines carry colour to add to this element.

Still Life on Ancient Stone Crate is carved from a single block of Clipsham Limestone. I have carved it in such a way that it appears to have once been larger when complete but is now distressed to the point of having parts missing/lost. The Clipsham stone is hard and can take fine detail. The forms carved are seriously accurate with the coloured surface etchings bringing the lighter and more playful addition.'

Still Life on Ancient Stone Crate
Glynn Williams
Clipsham Stone and paint
Unique
66cm high

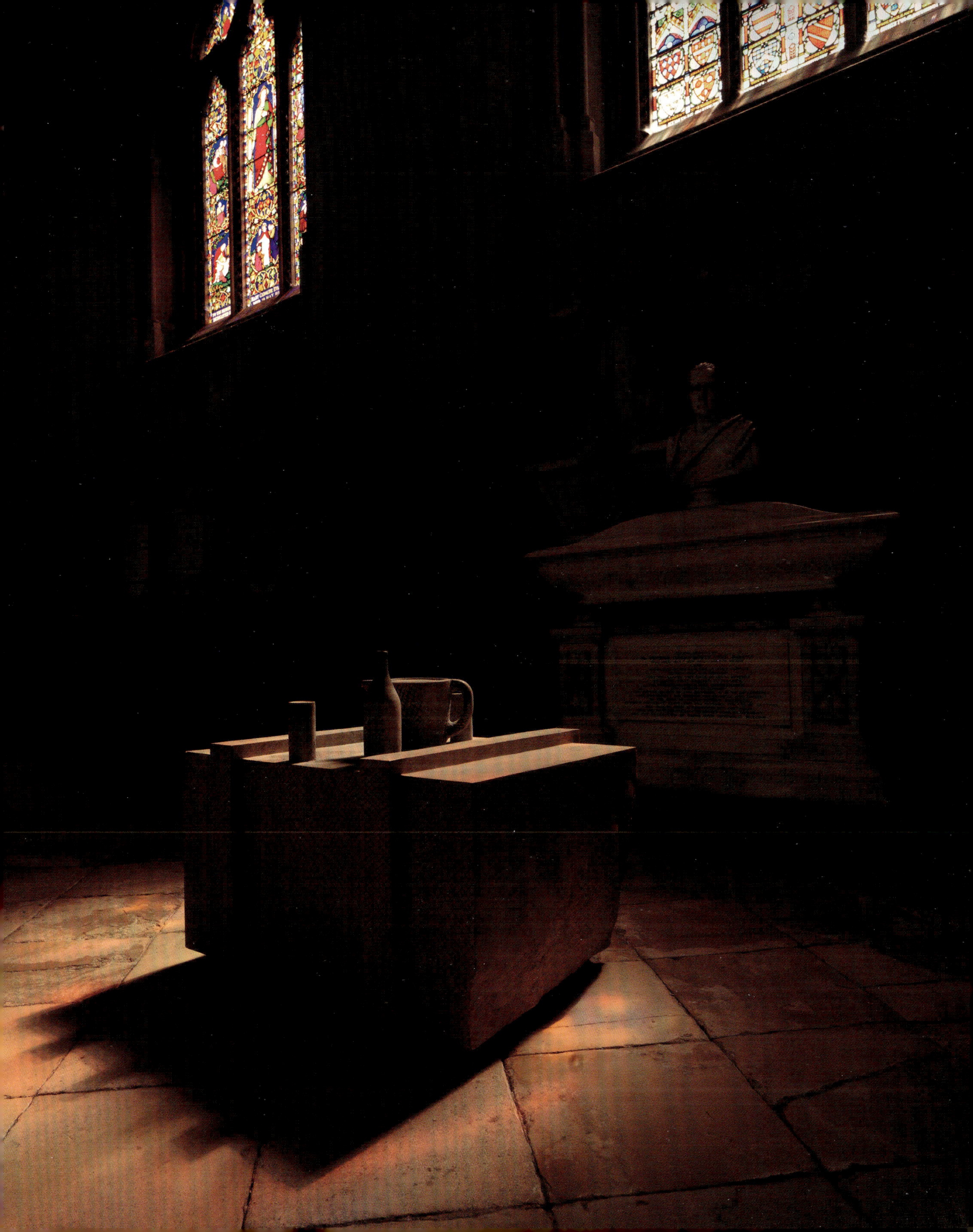

AFTERWORD

'Crucible 2010' was, by any measure of assessment, an incredible success: seventy-six contemporary sculptures, one extraordinary Cathedral and a hundred and thirty-six thousand visitors in two months. The sculptures animated the building with new and exciting life – an enormous melting pot of ideas, images, associations and feelings. The rediscovery of the Cathedral by so many people was in no small way due to the sensitive placement of remarkable sculptures within this historical building: the way in which materials contrasted with one another, the way the context of place provided a new interpretation of the sculpture, or the meeting of contemporary and gothic visions. It was our aim to show a representative cross-section of contemporary sculptural practice and this meant that there was something for everyone. The great danger of exhibiting such diversity is that it has the potential to become a mish-mash of disparate objects. However, in selecting only the best of the many disciplines, an accord of excellence was achieved. Great quality always works with great quality. The Cathedral itself is an amalgam of very many different ages of craftsmanship and yet it works because of the respect and sympathy each age has had for its predecessors.

'Crucible' was not the first exhibition in a Cathedral but it was ground-breaking in its diversity. It is heartening to see that in recent times many Cathedrals and places of worship have embraced contemporary art, making it more accessible to a wider audience. These exhibitions place contemporary sculpture in an historical context and lessen the feeling of intimidation often associated with a gallery setting. Visitors find they can better relate to the work and enjoy the experience even when pieces are less comfortable due to the questions and challenges they pose. Art is not only about beauty and sensuality, it can also be brutal and honest, pricking our conscience and questioning our preconceptions. Taken together the whole experience is uplifting, stimulating and unifying, a powerful endorsement of our species in our time. Homo sapiens artisticus!!!

And so here we are four years on. How will our selection of works for 'Crucible 2' relate to the powerful environment of the Cathedral? How will the sculptures relate to each other, to their medieval precedents and the visitors?

It is with an ethos of respect for

the Cathedral that the sculptures have been selected, a parallel quest for excellence, an appreciation for the artists and craftsmen who built the Cathedral over its long history and a selection of sculptures that collectively articulate something about our contemporary lives. Sculpture has the power to communicate so directly, partly because of its actuality, its existence in our space and partly because it communicates emotionally. Add to this the emotion engendered by the magnificence and beauty of the Cathedral and the exhibition's potency is magnified many times over.

The association between sculpture and Cathedrals has a long history and Gloucester is fortunate to be left with a wealth of medieval sculpture, albeit only a fraction of what it used to contain. Some of those now empty niches and spaces will once again come alive in 'Crucible 2'. One hundred sculptures by sixty-one artists sited throughout the Cathedral and its magnificent Close: expressions of joy and sorrow, of humour and pain, objects that demand questions and others that are quietly reflective. There are grand statements and intimate revelations, exquisite observations and idiosyncratic expressions. The human capacity for sacrifice and forgiveness is endless and such fundamental and powerful emotions continue to preoccupy artists, sometimes to obsession. Inevitably, in this anniversary year, there are memorials to the centenary of World War I, reflecting the Cathedral's role over a hundred years in providing a context and focus for grief and compassion, whilst at the same time never letting us forget.

Rungwe Kingdon
Gallery Pangolin

www.gloucestercathedral.org.uk www.gallery-pangolin.com